# Classic Desserts

BY
THE EDITORS OF TIME-LIFE BOOKS

TIME-LIFE BOOKS/ALEXANDRIA, VIRGINIA

*Cover:* Whole blackberries and a blackberry purée decorate a *flamri* — a molded soufflé pudding made from semolina *(pages 36-37).* To present this fragile pudding in a two-tiered form, the *flamri* was cooked in two separate molds, and one was turned out on top of the other.

Time-Life Books Inc.
is a wholly owned subsidiary of
**TIME INCORPORATED**

*Founder:* Henry R. Luce 1898-1967

*Editor-in-Chief:* Henry Anatole Grunwald
*President:* J. Richard Munro
*Chairman of the Board:* Ralph P. Davidson
*Corporate Editor:* Jason McManus
*Group Vice President, Books:* Joan D. Manley

**TIME-LIFE BOOKS INC.**

*Editor:* George Constable. *Executive Editor:* George Daniels. *Director of Design:* Louis Klein. *Board of Editors:* Dale M. Brown, Thomas A. Lewis, Robert G. Mason, Peter Pocock, Gerry Schremp, Gerald Simons, Rosalind Stubenberg, Kit van Tulleken, Henry Woodhead. *Director of Administration:* David L. Harrison. *Director of Research:* Carolyn L. Sackett. *Director of Photography:* John Conrad Weiser. *Design:* Anne B. Landry (art coordinator); James J. Cox (quality control). *Research:* Phyllis K. Wise (assistant director), Louise D. Forstall. *Copy Room:* Diane Ullius. *Production:* Celia Beattie, Gordon E. Buck

*President:* Reginald K. Brack Jr. *Senior Vice President:* William Henry. *Vice Presidents:* George Artandi, Stephen L. Bair, Robert A. Ellis, Christopher T. Linen, James L. Mercer, Joanne A. Pello, Paul R. Stewart

**THE GOOD COOK**

The original version of this book was created in London for Time-Life International (Nederland) B.V.
*European Editor:* Kit van Tulleken. *Photography Director:* Pamela Marke. *Planning Director:* Alan Lothian. *Chief of Research:* Vanessa Kramer. *Chief Designer:* Graham Davis. *Chief Sub-Editor:* Ilse Gray. *Production Editor:* Ellen Brush

Staff for *Classic Desserts: Series Editor:* Windsor Chorlton. *Series Coordinator:* Liz Timothy. *Anthology Editor:* Liz Clasen. *Staff Writers:* Gillian Boucher, Jay Ferguson, Mary Harron, Norm Kolpas. *Designer:* Rick Bowring. *Researcher:* Alexandra Carlier. *Sub-Editors:* Nicoletta Flessati, Katie Lloyd. *Permissions Researcher:* Mary-Claire Hailey. *Assistant Designer:* Mary Staples. *Design Assistant:* Cherry Doyle. *Quality Control:* Douglas Whitworth. *Editorial Department:* Anetha Besidonne, Pat Boag, Debra Dick, Philip Garner, Margaret Hall, Joanne Holland, Molly Sutherland, Julia West

U.S. Editorial Staff for *Classic Desserts: Editor:* Gerry Schremp. *Designer:* Peg Schreiber. *Chief Researcher:* Juanita T. James. *Picture Editor:* Adrian Allen. *Text Editor:* Ellen Phillips. *Staff Writers:* Carol Dana, Malachy Duffy. *Researchers:* Christine Bowie Dove, Barbara Fleming, Heather Mason Sandifer. *Copy Coordinators:* Allan Fallow, Tonna Gibert, Ricki Tarlow. *Art Assistant:* Cynthia Richardson. *Picture Coordinator:* Alvin Ferrell. *Editorial Assistants:* Audrey P. Keir, Patricia Kim

CHIEF SERIES CONSULTANT

*Richard Olney,* an American, has lived and worked for some three decades in France, where he is highly regarded as an authority on food and wine. Author of *The French Menu Cookbook* and of the award-winning *Simple French Food,* he has also contributed to numerous gastronomic magazines in France and the United States, including the influential journals *Cuisine et Vins de France* and *La Revue du Vin de France.* He is a member of several distinguished gastronomic societies, including L'Académie Internationale du Vin, La Confrérie des Chevaliers du Tastevin and La Commanderie du Bontemps de Médoc et des Graves. Working in London with the series editorial staff, he has been basically responsible for the planning of this volume, and has supervised the final selection of recipes submitted by other consultants. The United States edition of The Good Cook has been revised by the Editors of Time-Life Books to bring it into complete accord with American customs and usage.

CHIEF AMERICAN CONSULTANT
*Carol Cutler* is the author of a number of cookbooks, including the award-winning *The Six-Minute Soufflé and Other Culinary Delights.* During the 12 years she lived in France, she studied at the Cordon Bleu and the École des Trois Gourmandes, and with private chefs. She is a member of the Cercle des Gourmettes, a long-established French food society limited to just 50 members, and is also a charter member of Les Dames d'Escoffier, Washington Chapter.

SPECIAL CONSULTANT
*Jeremiah Tower* is an eminent American restaurateur who lived for many years in Europe, and is a member of La Commanderie du Bontemps de Médoc et des Graves and La Jurade de Saint-Émilion. He has been largely responsible for the step-by-step photographic sequences in this volume, and has worked closely with the other consultants on the anthology selections.

PHOTOGRAPHERS
*Alan Duns* was born in 1943 in the north of England and studied at the Ealing School of Photography. He specializes in food, and has contributed to major British publications.
*Aldo Tutino,* a native of Italy, has worked in Milan, New York City and Washington, D.C. He has received a number of awards for his photographs from the New York Advertising Club.

INTERNATIONAL CONSULTANTS
GREAT BRITAIN: *Jane Grigson* has written a number books about food and has been a cookery correspondent for the London *Observer* since 1968. Alan Davidson, a former member of the British Diplomatic Service, is the author of several cookbooks of the founder of Prospect Books, which specializes in scholarly publications about food and cooke FRANCE: *Michel Lemonnier,* the cofounder and vice president of Les Amitiés Gastronomiques Internationales, is a frequent lecturer on wine and vineyards. GERMANY: *Jochen Kuchenbecker* trained a chef, but has worked for 10 years as a food photographer in several European countries. Anne B kemeier is the co-author of a number of cookbooks THE NETHERLANDS: *Hugh Jans* has published cookbooks and his recipes appear in a number of Dutch magazines. THE UNITED STATES: *Julie Dannenbaum* directed a cooking school in Philadelphia, Pennsylvania, for many years and also conducts cook classes at the Gritti Palace in Venice, Italy, and The Greenbrier in White Sulphur Springs, West Virginia. She is the author of several cookbooks and many magazine articles. *François Dionot,* a graduate of L'École des Hôteliers de Lausanne in Switzerland, has worked as chef, hotel general manager and restaurant manager in France and the United States. He now conducts his own cooking school. *Judith Olney,* author of *Comforting Food* and *Summer Food,* received her culinary training in England and France. In addition to conducting classes cooking, she regularly writes articles for gastronomic magazines. The late *José Wilson* wrote many books on food and interior decoration.

Correspondents: Elisabeth Kraemer (Bonn); Margot Hapgood, Dorothy Bacon (London); Miriam Hsia, Susan Jonas, Lucy T. Voulgaris (New York); Maria Vincenza Aloisi, Josephine du Brusle (Paris); Ann Natanson (Rome Valuable assistance was also provided by: Jeanne Buys (Amsterdam); Hans-Heinrich Wellmann, Gertraud Bello (Hamburg); Judy Aspinall, Lesley Coleman (London); Diane Asselin (Los Angeles); Bona Schmid, Maria Teresa Marenco (Milan); Carolyn T. Chubet, Christina Lieberman (New York); Michèle le Baube (Paris); Mimi Murphy (Rome).

# CONTENTS

# Ending a Meal with Grace and Flavor

ll good food affords pleasure; desserts are devised for pleasure one. At the end of a meal, when appetites are largely satisfied, e dessert restores the palate and hints at sensuous luxury. ven Mrs. Isabella Beeton, a 19th Century English culinary cyclopedist and a woman not much given to effusion, was oved by the subject. In *The Book of Household Management,* e wrote: "If there be any poetry at all in meals, or the process feeding, there is poetry in the dessert."

This declaration is particularly true of the classic desserts at are the subject of this book: custards and creams, soufflés d puddings, omelets and crepes, sherbets and ice creams, fruit llies and such ambitious assemblies as charlotte russe. These eations rely on form as well as content for effect: Even as they mpt the palate, they appeal to the eye with color and shape. me of them are masterpieces of artifice, calling for varied oking techniques—pounding or sieving, beating or churning, olding or freezing. But their ranks also include desserts of istine simplicity, such as a bright-colored fruit purée artfully virled into a mound of snowy whipped cream.

Whatever their degree of complexity, desserts demand close tention to detail, whether in removing the pith from an or- ge peel or in carefully separating eggs for a custard. Happily, e ingredients themselves are seldom elaborate. A few eggs, eam and some fresh fruit are almost all that is required to oduce an exquisite layered Bavarian cream. By using some molina and white wine instead of cream, you can turn the me ingredients into the makings of the soufflé pudding pic- red on the cover.

Sugar, of course, is present in practically any meal-ending sh. Most human beings have an irrepressible appetite for veet things, and desserts exist to indulge it. Indeed, the devel- ment of modern desserts is inseparable from the increasing ailability of sugar. Although sugar was widely used in India the Fourth Century B.C. and gradually spread throughout e Muslim world, it was a rare delicacy elsewhere. In European okery, honey was the main sweetener: The ancient Romans, r example, mixed it with eggs to make *ova mellita,* or honeyed ;gs, the precursor in name and technique of the dessert omelet :monstrated on pages 48-49.

With the Moorish conquest of the Iberian peninsula in the inth Century, Europeans finally became aware of sugar— though the sweetener remained so scarce it was called "white old." Use of the condiment expanded somewhat in the 11th entury, when Crusaders returned from the Holy Land with sugar cane and refined sugar. Those who could afford it sprin- kled sugar on almost everything they ate. By the 15th Century, however, Italian cooks began to follow the more focused Arabic habit of using sugar as a key ingredient of a limited number of dishes. These sweet dishes were eaten by the rich and privileged only: It was not until the Spaniards colonized the Caribbean and began the large-scale cultivation of sugar cane there that the supply of sugar in Europe increased enough to make the condi- ment available to everyone.

Even "white gold" was not the pure, uniformly granulated sucrose we know today. Until the beginning of this century, sugar came in the form of rock-hard loaves. Heavy iron tongs were needed to break up the loaves, after which the sugar had to be pounded in a mortar to make a powder. Refining methods were crude: Cooks who wanted pure sugar first cooked the pow- der to a syrup, and then clarified it by prolonged skimming to remove its impurities.

Although the modern cook is spared such chores by today's refineries, many dessert recipes require the making of sugar syrup—or its browned version, caramel. On page 9 you will find a guide to all of the sugar syrups commonly employed in dessert cookery, and an explanation of the sometimes confusing termin- ology used to describe them.

Egg whites and heavy cream are other dessert essentials that have engendered mysterious descriptions and murky ad- vice. Despite hints to the contrary, producing thick whipped cream or a voluminous, stable foam of egg whites is not a matter of luck, magic or the phases of the moon: On pages 14-15 you will discover how proper equipment and adroit whisking will yield the sort of foam or cream you require. On the same pages, a step- by-step photographic sequence shows you how to recognize the stages through which the beaten whites will pass—and indi- cates the optimum stage for different types of dessert. To make a perfect soufflé, for example, the whites must be soft enough to blend easily with a flavored base; they should be beaten only until they form gently drooping peaks. Meringues need no such blending; to make the meringues firm and almost weightless, the whites must be beaten until they are very stiff.

Any list of fundamental dessert ingredients includes gela- tin, which allows you to set a dessert in an attractive mold, then turn it out for serving. Gelatin can also give added body to mousses or frozen soufflés, but in every instance it must be used with care: too much, and the dessert will be tough and rubbery; too little and the dessert will collapse. Instructions on how to work with ordinary commercial gelatin—whether it is powdered or comes in the less common leaf form—appear on page 16, along with a demonstration of how to prepare an incomparably delicate gelatin from calf's feet.

Other foods intrinsic to dessert cookery, either as integral parts of a dessert or as its eye-pleasing garnish, include chocolate, nuts, fruits and citrus peel. How to handle these ingredients—how to give fruit or peel an attractive, glittering glaze, for example, or how to keep chocolate from burning as you melt it—is explained on pages 10-13.

Immediately following these guides to the use of essential ingredients are chapters dealing with the basic categories of desserts. On these pages are demonstrated techniques that range from the making of a smooth pouring custard to the preparation of fruit purée. The final chapter in this section of the book combines and extends the fundamental techniques to encompass such dramatic constructions as a basket of meringue filled with fruit and ice cream.

The second half of the book is an international anthology of dessert recipes chosen from the best ever published. Some recipes call for precision: It would be unwise to stray too far from the proportions and timings given in a recipe for a fruit jelly or a soufflé, for example. But other recipes—for trifle or ice cream, perhaps—can be adapted endlessly. Working within the guidelines spelled out in the first half of the book, and inspired by the anthology in the second half, an imaginative cook will have no difficulty creating a range of original and delectable desserts.

### Desserts in the menu

Although people have eaten various kinds of sweet dishes since earliest times, the notion of a separate sweet course served at the end of a meal is a relatively modern idea. As late as the 14th

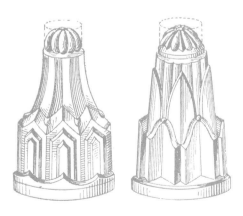

Century, a French banquet might have featured frumenty—a kind of sweet grain porridge—as well as dishes of fruit jellies and fritters, set alongside haunches of venison and platters of lampreys and sturgeon; the guests helped themselves haphazardly to whatever they fancied. The history of some of today's desserts reflects this early lack of clearly differentiated categories of food. Blancmange, for example, a Bavarian cream made with almond milk, gelatin and whipped cream *(pages 26-27),*

was at one time a sweetened concoction composed of pounded chicken breast and sliced almonds.

One reason for the indiscriminate mingling of sweet and savory dishes was undoubtedly ostentation. A table crowded with as many different dishes as it would bear—not to mention the towering sugar models of birds and beasts that sometimes decorated the tables of Italian noblemen—made an impressive display. At the same time, because sweetenings (and the spices that often went with them) were costly, a host who served sweet dishes at every opportunity left his guests in no doubt that he was a man of means.

Even when sugar became widely available, the separation of the dessert from the rest of the meal took time. At first, cooks and their employers alike were reluctant to abandon grandiose table settings. Not until the middle of the 19th Century did the Western world fully accept the idea of presenting foods in the order in which they were to be eaten.

Diners obviously benefited from the new system; at last they were able to eat all of their food while it was at the correct temperature. But cooks benefited too, because their creations could be enjoyed at their best. Cooks also had the pleasant challenge of developing a new and demanding art form: the menu. Dish succeeded well-chosen dish in a carefully calculated sequence that imposed a kind of rhythm, a developing play of crescendo and diminuendo on the diner's palate. And the dessert completed the work.

### Presentation and selection

The art of dessert cookery is the art of temptation, and presentation is therefore a major concern. In the past, this aspect of beguilement sometimes received disproportionate emphasis. The Victorians, for example, favored vast molded and sculpted assemblies decorated with spun sugar and often with gold leaf as well. Regrettably, the very size of these fantastic centerpieces often worked against their appreciation as food: Immense jellies would support their own weight only if they contained so much gelatin that their texture became chewy. Today's trend is toward relative simplicity, but such is the inherent beauty and variety of the cook's materials that the decorative dimension of dessert-making remains important.

The success of a dessert depends not only on the dish itself but also on how it fits into the context of the meal as a whole. Except at feast times, the heartiest of classic desserts—steamed puddings *(pages 40-41)*—generally conclude the most simple meals, with perhaps no more than a meaty soup as the single main course. Conversely, rich, creamy main dishes call for light and refreshing desserts, such as water ices *(pages 54-55).* Or a menu may build up through several dishes of increasing complexity to a lavish—but never ponderous—finale, such as *riz l'impératrice (pages 86-87).*

In any menu, you should try to avoid the repetition of flavors and textures. If you have a main course with a fruit element—duck with orange, for example—you should not include the same fruit in the dessert, and you should never serve more than one rich, egg-bound sauce during a meal. Color is almost as important: A series of creamy-white courses concluded by nilarly colored dessert is likely to be dull, no matter how successful each individual dish may be. Within the bounds of these common-sense restrictions, though, you are free to experiment as much as you please. There are few—if any—hard and fast rules for menu construction.

### ine and desserts

he relationship of desserts to wine, both as an ingredient and an accompaniment, is deeper and more intricate than many ople imagine. The simplest transformation of wine into an tegral part of a dessert consists merely in pouring it over fresh uit. Strawberries and peaches in season, piled into a glass and enched with Champagne, make an ambrosial ending to a

eal. But wine also plays an important part as an ingredient in most every category of dessert considered in this volume, as a ance at the recipe anthology will show. Wine is the central mponent of many jellies (recipes, page 148), for example, as ell as of fluffy custards (recipes, pages 96-98). Wine also frelently appears in many frozen desserts, in puddings such as amri and in fried desserts.

Perhaps because the finer sweet wines are little known in he United States, wine rarely is served with American desserts. In truth, sweet wines can be a supremely pleasurable ccompaniment to the dessert course, as long as serious thought given to achieving a proper match. For the marriage to be a appy one, the wine should be sweeter than the dessert it accomanies; otherwise, the wine may seem thin and acid. To prevent weet wines from becoming cloying, they must be chilled to bout 40° to 50° F. [4° to 10° C.].

Because frozen desserts numb the taste buds, wines should ot, as a rule, be served with ices, ice creams or parfaits (a onderful exception is the Champagne-drenched water ice— self containing Champagne—that appears on pages 54-55). or are wines good accompaniments for very tart desserts based n lemons or limes; the acidity in the fruit alters the taste of the ine in the mouth. Finally, avoid serving wine with desserts ased on chocolate, since that ingredient will overpower the aste of any wine.

Even these strictures leave a wide range of choice in both esserts and wines. Champagne is traditional and festive, but ecause most Champagne is too dry to serve with a sweet confec-

tion, it is no longer favored as a dessert wine. A truly sweet Champagne, however—it will be marked "demi-sec" rather than "brut"—can lend extra sparkle to meringue desserts such as the fruit-filled basket demonstrated on pages 84-85, as well as to crepes suzette (page 47) and Christmas puddings (pages 40-41). A sweet, sparkling wine that may be substituted for Champagne is Italy's Asti Spumanti, whose honeyed, slightly musky flavor recalls the muscat grape from which it is made. This delicious grape grows in hot Mediterranean countries and in California, among other places, and it is also used to make Moscato, a pale, slightly sweet wine. Moscato sets off simple, light desserts such as the fruit-purée-based whips and fools demonstrated on pages 68-69.

The great dessert wines come from cool countries—France, Germany and Hungary—where autumns of mixed sun and mist encourage a fungus-like growth on grapes that are left late on the vine. The fungus—known in France as pourriture noble, or "noble rot"—releases moisture from the grapes, concentrating their sugar, flavor and aroma. When these grapes are carefully picked at just the right moment, they produce wines of unparalleled sweetness and delicacy. These wines are indeed among the noblest of all, and are ideally suited to escort the most luxurious of desserts.

In Germany, these wines, made from the flowery Riesling grape, are rated and labeled according to the care used in gathering the overripened fruit. The sweetest, rarest, most velvety of these wines, produced in small quantities only in the greatest years, are marked "Trockenbeerenauslese," indicating that the grapes were picked one by one from the vines as each shriveled to the perfect point. Beerenauslese wine, only slightly less sweet and rich, is made from shriveled grapes chosen from late-picked bunches in good years. Auslese wines are those made simply from bunches of grapes picked late in the season, with no selection of individual grapes; however, these can be fine sweet wines, well worth drinking at the end of a meal.

In Hungary, sweet wine made from the shriveled grapes is combined with a strong white wine to produce golden Tokay, the premier dessert wine of the 19th Century. Tokay varies in sweetness according to the proportion of sweet wine used, which is indicated on the bottle labels. To accompany rich desserts such as crème brûlée (recipe, page 91), choose the sweetest Tokay, marked "Five-Puttonyos."

Among all such wines, the most renowned are the great French dessert wines produced in the commune of Sauternes in southern Bordeaux and in nearby Barsac. These wines are brilliant and traditional accompaniments to apple desserts such as the filled crepes demonstrated on page 46, but pear desserts and those containing almonds also will be enhanced by a Sauternes or a Barsac. A Bavarian cream or an apple charlotte would also set off a great Sauternes. And one of the most beautiful and complex of all tasting experiences may be that of savoring an almond-milk blancmange (pages 26-27) in conjunction with an old Sauternes; the typically penetrating depth and fruit of such a wine—its sweetness never flat or cloying—interweave perfectly with the delicate flavors of the blancmange. Such an alliance makes a great dessert greater still.

# The Spectrum of Sugar Syrups

Plain granulated sugar often sweetens desserts, of course, but many recipes call instead for a sugar syrup: simple syrup, a liquid solution that blends easily with other ingredients, or candy syrup, which becomes semisolid or solid when cool, and is used to form glazes, garnishes and candy. As the chart opposite shows, both syrups are composed of sugar and water, and both may be made in various densities, depending on their intended use.

For simple syrups, the sugar and water are cooked just long enough to dissolve the sugar into a solution; the density of these syrups is determined by the ratio of sugar to water. To sweeten beaten egg whites, for example, you will need a light syrup fairly low in sugar. A parfait *(page 58),* by contrast, requires a syrup with more sugar and more body.

For candy syrups, the density depends not on the initial sugar-to-water ratio, but on how long the syrup is boiled and how much water evaporates: the less water, the more solid the cooled syrup will be. Candy syrups, usually based on two parts sugar to one of water, may be boiled briefly to serve as a light base for a sauce, or for longer if the syrup is to glaze fruit.

As you cook a candy syrup, the easiest and most accurate way to test its solidity is with a candy thermometer: The temperature of the syrup rises as the water evaporates. If you lack a thermometer, judge the syrup's stiffness by removing a small amount from the pan and observing it as it cools *(box, opposite, below).* At first, the syrup will be liquid enough to fall from the spoon in threads of varying thickness. At higher temperatures, syrup dropped into ice water will form less and less malleable balls *(demonstration, page 61).* At still higher temperatures, it will form increasingly brittle strands. When all the water is gone, the molten sugar will cook to a rich caramel. These reactions and the temperatures that produce them are listed on the chart.

The making of syrup calls for precautions against crystallization, the formation of grains that ruin the syrup's texture. Equipment is important. Use a pan made of a smooth, nonporous metal (surface roughness can cause crystallization) that conducts heat well; the unlined copper pan shown here is ideal. For safety, the pan should be deep, with a volume two to three times that of the syrup. The

pan, spoons and thermometer must scrupulously clean.

Every grain of sugar must dissol during the first, low-heat stage of coo ing; even a single grain could initia crystallization once the mixture boils. I sert the thermometer and stop stirri before the syrup boils: Agitation and ae ation cause cooling, which produces cry tallization. When you test the syru consistency, be careful that no cooli syrup falls back into the pan. If it doe the syrup will crystallize, and you mu discard the mixture and start again.

**Cooking sugar syrup.** This chart shows the amounts of sugar and water used for each type of simple or candy syrup; itaso lists the syrup's approximate cooking time, temperature and appearance when done, and uses. Figures given are for syrup made with 2 cups [½ liter] of sugar; if you use different amounts of sugar, cooking times will vary. For candy syrups, the times are those at which you should start testing density *(box, opposite, below).*

---

## The Technique of Making Syrup

1 **Removing grains.** Combine sugar and warm water in a pan. Let the sugar soak for 10 minutes, then stir over low heat to dissolve it. With a brush dipped in hot water, wash down any grains of sugar that collect on the sides of the pan.

2 **Boiling.** When the sugar has dissolved, stop stirring and increase the heat. Place a candy thermometer in the pan with the bulb fully immersed in the syrup. Boil the syrup rapidly until it reaches the required temperature.

## A Guide to Simple and Candy Syrups

| | Product | Sugar-to-Water Ratio | Approximate Cooking Time | Temperature | Appearance when Tested | Uses |
|---|---|---|---|---|---|---|
| **Simple Syrups** | Light | 1:2 | 2 min. | 200° F. [94° C.] | Clear liquid | Sweetener for beverages and uncooked fruits |
| | Medium | 1:1½ | 3 min. | 200° F. [94° C.] | Clear liquid | Sweetener for creams and uncooked fruits; poaching liquid for dried and sweet fruits |
| | Medium-heavy | 1:1 | 4 min. | 208° F. [98° C.] | Clear liquid | Sweetener for creams, water ices and parfaits; poaching liquid for tart fruits |
| | Heavy | 2:1 | 6 min. | 212° F. [100° C.] | Clear liquid | Sweetener for water ices and parfaits |
| **Candy Syrups** | Small-thread | 2:1 | 6 min. | 217-220° F. [103-105° C.] | Fine, short thread | Sweetener for ice creams, ice-cream sauces and icings |
| | Large-thread | 2:1 | 11 min. | 220-234° F. [105-110° C.] | Coarse, long thread | Sweetener for ice creams, ice-cream sauces, icings and puddings |
| | Soft-ball | 2:1 | 14 min. | 234-240° F. [112-116° C.] | Rapidly flattening ball | Sweetener for ice-cream sauces, icings and puddings; base for candy |
| | Firm-ball | 2:1 | 15 min. | 244-248° F. [118-120° C.] | Malleable ball | Sweetener for ice-cream sauces; base for candy |
| | Hard-ball | 2:1 | 17 min. | 250-266° F. [121-130° C.] | Rigid ball | Base for candy |
| | Soft-crack | 2:1 | 19 min. | 270-290° F. [132-143° C.] | Pliable strands | Base for candy |
| | Hard-crack | 2:1 | 20 min. | 300-310° F. [149-154° C.] | Brittle strands | Base for candy, praline and decorative spun threads; glaze for fruits |
| | Caramel | 2:1 | 21 min. | 320-350° F. [160-177° C.] | Thick, golden brown to amber liquid | Base for candy and decorative spun threads; glaze for fruits; liner for molds; flavoring |

## Testing a Syrup's Progress

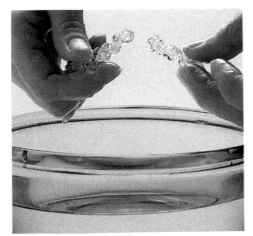

**The small-thread stage.** After five seconds of boiling, move the pan off the heat, and dribble a spoonful of syrup into a bowl. If the syrup falls in a fine, short, elastic thread *(above)*, it has reached the small-thread stage.

**The hard-crack stage.** Let the syrup boil three to four more minutes, take the pan off the heat and drop syrup from a spoon into ice water. Lift out the solidified strand and bend it. If it snaps, it has reached the hard-crack stage.

**The caramel stage.** After five minutes of boiling, the syrup will begin to color. Pour a spoonful of syrup onto a white plate; if the caramel is a deep amber *(above)*, place the pan in cold water to arrest the cooking.

# A Panoply of Edible Embellishments

When they are given decorations of contrasting colors and textures, desserts become even more tempting. Some such embellishments require little or no preparation—flower petals or chopped nuts, for instance. Others, such as those shown here, call for a bit more work but endow desserts with a special flair.

Threads of caramel are a prime example. Spun from a spoon and allowed to harden, they lend an amber glitter to frozen desserts *(right)*. Do not put them on warm desserts; heat softens caramel.

Similarly, you can pour melted chocolate onto a flat surface, let it harden, then scrape it up into delicate scrolls *(opposite, bottom)* that provide a pleasing contrast on a creamy frozen dessert.

More complex and colorful decorations are made by immersing fruits or fruit slices in heavy sugar syrup *(below)* to coat them with a shiny casing. Or you can poach fine strips of citrus peel in a light sugar syrup, then roll them in sugar to give the peel *(opposite, top)* a crunchy crust. Like glazed-fruit garnishes, the sugared peels are appropriate additions to both fruit purées and puddings.

## Forming Golden Wisps of Caramel

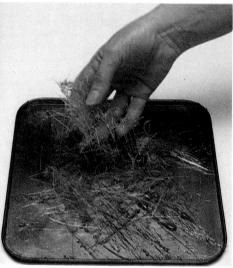

**Making caramel wisps.** Prepare caramel *(pages 8-9)*. Use a spoon to dribble the caramel in a thin stream onto a tray lightly coated with flavorless vegetable oil. Move the spoon over the tray to make a delicate crisscross tracery *(left)*. Allow the caramel to cool and harden. Lift it gently from the tray with your fingers *(right)* or a small spatula and store in an airtight container.

## Coating Fruit with a Shimmering Glaze

**Glazing fruit.** Wash the fruit and let it dry. When it is dry, dip the fruit — strawberries, grapes and gooseberries are used here — into a hard-crack syrup *(page 9)*. To dip stemmed fruit such as grapes, hold the fruit by the stems or loop the stems of a small bunch through the tines of a fork. Impale other whole fruit or fruit slices one at a time on a skewer. Dip the fruit in the syrup, then hold it over the pan until excess syrup has drained. Cool the dipped fruit on a rack.

## Preparing Crusty Citrus Strips

1 **Preparing citrus peel.** Wash the fruit (here, an orange and a lemon), dry it and, with a vegetable peeler, remove the peel, taking care not to include any of the bitter, white pith. Slice the peel into ⅛-inch [3-mm.] strips.

2 **Cooking the peel.** Drop the strips of peel into a simmering light sugar syrup (*page 9*) and poach them for about five minutes. Lift the strips a few at a time from the syrup, using a two-pronged fork to keep them from sticking together. Lay the strips on a plate to cool.

3 **Coating the strips.** Roll the cooled strips of peel a few at a time in a plate filled with sugar to coat each one completely. Spread the strips on a sheet of wax paper to dry for at least 15 minutes. Store them in a tightly covered container in the refrigerator; they will keep for several months.

## Creating Chocolate Scrolls

1 **Pouring the chocolate.** Put semisweet baking chocolate into a heavy saucepan or the top of a double boiler and stand the pan over barely simmering water. As soon as the chocolate melts, pour it onto a flat, hard surface—a marble slab, as shown, or a baking sheet.

2 **Spreading the chocolate.** With a narrow-bladed spatula, quickly spread out the chocolate to the thickness of a playing card. Make the surface of the chocolate as smooth as possible.

3 **Forming the scrolls.** Working away from yourself, gently push a sharp knife along the work surface, holding it with both hands and keeping the blade at a 45-degree angle to the surface. The chocolate should roll up into scrolls; if it hardens too much and starts to powder, warm the knife in hot water.

# Nuts: A Rich Resource

Used as flavorings for creams and ice creams, fillings for crepes, and decorations or toppings for almost any dessert from meringues to soufflés, nuts are indispensable. Fresh-shelled almonds, hazelnuts, pecans, pistachios and walnuts may be used whole, or they may be toasted in the oven, ground up, or caramelized—all relatively simple preparations, as demonstrated here.

Shelling nuts is usually a simple task that requires only an efficient nutcracker. Inside their shells, many nuts are further enclosed by thin, papery skins that are often bitter and usually are removed. To loosen their skins, blanch almonds and pistachios in boiling water (below). To remove the clinging skins of hazelnuts and Brazil nuts, dry them out by toasting them for 10 minutes in a 325° F. [160° C.] oven. After toasting or blanching the nuts, peel off the skins with your fingers (smooth nuts such as almonds slide readily out of their skins), or roll them briskly in a towel, a method that is especially effective with small, rounded

nuts such as pistachios (box, opposite, top left). After peeling blanched nuts, dry them briefly in the oven.

Thick-shelled chestnuts require special handling, as demonstrated on pages 70-71. And before opening a coconut, you must drain the milky liquid inside by piercing the nut with a skewer through all three of the soft indentations, or eyes, in its husk. After all of the liquid has been poured out, use the back of a large cleaver to break the coconut—a sharp tap about one third of the way from the end opposite the eyes will crack it open along a weak seam. Use a knife to slice the white flesh away from the shell, then grate or chop the flesh.

Small nuts also may be chopped, as shown here (box, opposite, top right). Or they may be used whole as a garnish: Dip them in heavy syrup (page 9) to give them a glittering finish. To sliver a nut such as an almond, pry the two halves of the nut apart, place each half flat side down and cut it lengthwise into five or six pieces. You can give chopped or slivered nuts extra flavor and color by toasting

them in a 350° F. [180° C.] oven for one t two minutes. If nuts are to serve as a fla voring or filling, grind them into a fin dust, using either a mortar and pestl (below, right) or, to save time, a foo processor. Grinding the nuts will releas their aromatic oils, which blend we with many ingredients.

When you want a delicate nut flavo without the nuts' coarse texture, as for custard ice cream (page 58) or a Bavaria cream (page 26), make a nut milk: Infus pounded almonds or grated coconut i milk or water (opposite, bottom right).

Almonds—with or without skins, an sometimes lightly toasted—are the basi of praline (opposite, bottom left), a versa tile flavoring that is made by cooking th almonds with caramelized sugar (page 8-9) and letting the mixture harden int a brittle slab. The smoky-tasting pralin can be broken up coarsely for toppings, o ground to a powder and used to flavo soufflés and ice creams. It will keep for a long as three months if stored in a tightl covered container.

## Peeling Blanched Nuts by Hand

1 **Softening the skins.** Pour shelled nuts—almonds are used here—into a pan of boiling water. After a minute or so, remove a nut. If the skin slips off easily, the nuts are ready. Drain them.

2 **Removing the skins.** With your fingers, slip the loosened skins off the nuts. Drop peeled almonds in a bowl of cold water to keep them white. To dry the nuts so that they keep longer, spread them on a baking sheet and place them in a preheated 325° F. [160° C.] oven for about five minutes.

## Crushing Nuts in a Mortar

**Pounding nuts.** Put peeled nuts— almonds, in this case—in a mortar. To prevent the nuts from spilling over as you work, do not fill the mortar to more than a third of its depth. Using a pestle, pound and grind the nuts until they are reduced to the consistency specified in your recipe.

## A Quick Method for Peeling Round Nuts

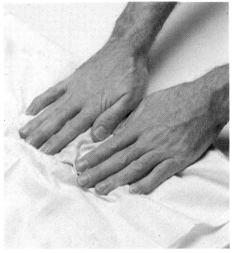

1 **Loosening the hulls.** Lay a clean towel on a work surface. Fold the towel around blanched or toasted nuts — here, parboiled pistachios. Rub your hands lightly back and forth over the towel so that the nuts roll inside it.

2 **Peeling the nuts.** After a minute or two of rolling, unwrap the nuts. Most of them will have shed their skins. If any skins cling, remove them by hand; repeated rolling will damage the nuts.

## Chopping Nuts

**Rocking the knife blade.** Put a pile of peeled nuts — hazelnuts, in this case — on a chopping board. Position a large knife above the pile, resting the fingers of your free hand on its tip. Using the tip as a pivot, move the blade in a rocking motion; chop slowly at first so the nuts do not jump off the board.

## Preparing Praline

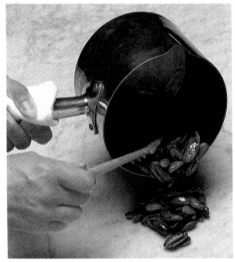

1 **Caramelizing the almonds.** Put equal volumes of peeled almonds and sugar in a heavy pan. Cook over very low heat, stirring constantly. When the sugar turns pale amber, tip the mixture onto an oiled marble slab (above) or baking sheet. Spread out the praline.

2 **Crushing the praline.** Let the praline cool for about 10 minutes until it forms a hard, solid mass. Then put it in a plastic bag and, using a rolling pin, crush the praline until it reaches the desired degree of fineness.

## Making a Nut Milk

**Straining the milk.** Pour hot milk or water over pounded almonds or, as here, grated coconut. Let the nut meat infuse in the milk for one hour, then strain the milk through a muslin- or cheesecloth-lined sieve. Squeeze the nut meat in the fabric to wring out all of its juices; add them to the milk.

# Egg Whites: A Multipurpose Foundation

Scores of desserts depend on beaten raw egg whites for texture and volume. Beating traps air bubbles in the whites, expanding the volume of the whites and progressively stiffening them.

How much the whites should be beaten depends on how you intend to use them. Whites beaten to soft peaks *(Step 3, below)* support most soufflés and mousses *(pages 32-35)*, but for meringues *(pages 28-29)* the whites must reach the firm-peak stage *(Step 4, below)*.

Such desserts stand or fall on the volume and stability of the beaten whites. These qualities depend on the temperature of the eggs and how you separate them, your choice of equipment and its cleanliness and how you do the beating.

Your first task is separating white from yolk *(Step 1, below)*, which may be done well in advance. If, for example, you make a dessert with yolks alone—custard, for example *(pages 20-25)*—you may store the whites, tightly covered, in the refrigerator for four to five days, or in the freezer for up to three months. Al-

ways separate eggs with great care; the slightest trace of fat will keep the whites from mounting fully—and yolks are rich in fat. If a yolk leaks into the white, you may be able to remove the yolk with a piece of eggshell. Crack each egg over a small bowl before adding the white to the mixing bowl, so that a mishap affects only one egg. Let the egg whites come to room temperature before you beat them: Chilled whites do not mount as well.

The best bowls for beating egg whites are made of unlined copper; a reaction between the metal and the whites creates a stable foam. (Another reaction, however, will discolor the whites if you leave them in the bowl for more than 15 minutes.) If you lack a copper bowl, use a glass, ceramic or stainless-steel one; aluminum bowls discolor the whites. Egg whites beaten in noncopper bowls can be stabilized with cream of tartar—¼ teaspoon [1 ml.] per four egg whites—added when the whites are foamy *(Step 2, below)*. In any case, use a large bowl—the whites will expand to as much as seven times their original volume. And use a

hemispherical bowl: A flat-bottomed o[ ] will impede beating.

For beating whites, no utensil is mo[ ] effective than a balloon whisk, who[ ] wire loops quickly force air into the eg[ ] Rotary beaters or portable electric mi[ ] ers do not pass through the whole body [ ] the whites, and standing electric mixe[ ] aerate whites so fast they may overbe[ ] them, producing a dry, inelastic mass.

All equipment for beating egg whit[ ] should be clean and free of grease. Co[ ] per bowls require special care, since ta[ ] nish can interfere with the reaction th[ ] strengthens the whites. Rub the inside [ ] a copper bowl with a solution of 2 te[ ] spoons [10 ml.] of salt and 1 tablespo[ ] [15 ml.] of vinegar or lemon juice; rin[ ] the bowl with hot water and dry it we[ ] Other bowls—and all whisks—must [ ] washed in hot soapy water, rinsed in w[ ] ter mixed with lemon juice, then dried[ ]

Whisk the egg whites continuously u[ ] til they are ready; a pause may ma[ ] them subside or separate into liquid a[ ] lumps—a process known as graining.

## Whisking to the Desired Peak

  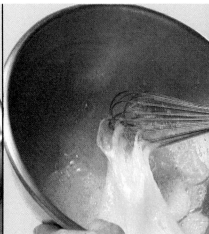

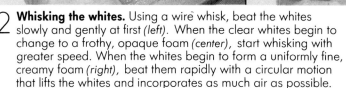

1 **Separating eggs.** Crack each shell on a small bowl; upend the egg and pull off the top of the shell, leaving the yolk in the bottom. Let the white drip into the bowl *(above)*. Pass the yolk back and forth between the halves until all the white has dripped into the bowl. Transfer the white to a larger bowl.

2 **Whisking the whites.** Using a wire whisk, beat the whites slowly and gently at first *(left)*. When the clear whites begin to change to a frothy, opaque foam *(center)*, start whisking with greater speed. When the whites begin to form a uniformly fine, creamy foam *(right)*, beat them rapidly with a circular motion that lifts the whites and incorporates as much air as possible.

## A Cold Trick for Whipping Cream

Heavy cream is stiffened just as egg whites are: by beating air into it. What makes the cream thick is its butterfat, which clusters around the air bubbles as you whip the cream. Whipping cream may contain anywhere from 30 to 40 per cent butterfat; the fatter cream, found in specialty markets, makes the thickest whipped cream.

Cold will partly solidify the butterfat and help cream thicken, so chill the cream and the bowl and whisk used for beating, and beat the cream over ice.

Beaten this way, 1 cup [¼ liter] of heavy cream will double in volume and thicken to the soft-peak stage *(Step 1)* in as little as two minutes. It is now ready to be sweetened and flavored (if sugar is added earlier, it will impede the thickening process), and then may be used in desserts such as *riz à l'impératrice (page 87)*. Further whisking produces the stiff peaks *(Step 2)* called for in many recipes. Do not beat the cream beyond this stage: It will turn into butter.

1 **Starting to beat.** Pour chilled heavy cream into a chilled bowl set in ice. Whisk the cream slowly; when it foams, whisk quickly, lifting the cream in a circular motion. When faint marks appear on the cream's surface *(above)*, the cream is lightly whipped.

2 **Beating cream stiff.** Continue whisking at a slower pace, lifting the whisk frequently to check the cream's consistency. Beat until the cream lifted on the whisk clings in a stiff peak.

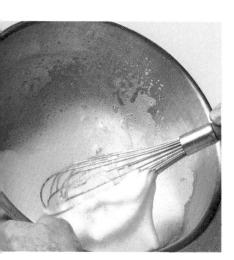

3 **Testing for soft peaks.** As soon as the whites offer a definite resistance to beating, lift up some of the mixture with the whisk. If the whites form a soft, slightly drooping peak *(above)*, they are firm enough for soufflés and mousses.

4 **Testing for firm peaks.** For the degree of stiffness required for meringues, beat the egg whites for a few seconds more, then test them again. When the whites stand up in stiff, pointed peaks, you may begin to whisk in sugar to make meringue *(page 28)*.

# Gelatin: A Transfiguring Element

Gelatin is the fundamental stiffening agent in many cold, molded desserts. It supports translucent wine or fruit-juice jellies, and helps set Bavarian creams *(pages 26-27)* and such elaborate desserts as *riz à l'impératrice (pages 86-87)*.

The purest gelatin, with the most delicate flavor and richest body, is a homemade product extracted from calf's feet *(right; recipe, page 164)*.

Preparing such gelatin for a dessert is a daylong process. The calf's feet first must be soaked for several hours, then simmered for an even longer period to draw out the gelatin. Next the liquid must be allowed to cool so that fat can be removed with ease. To neutralize any trace of meatiness, the jelly is then reheated, sweetened, and lightly flavored with spices and citrus peels and juice. Finally, the jelly must be clarified—simmered with beaten egg whites and eggshells, and strained through a cloth. Minute solid particles in the jelly adhere to the cooked egg whites and shells, which in turn are trapped by the cloth.

Calf's-foot jelly is particularly worth making for desserts in which gelatin is a principal ingredient—such as the fruit jelly on pages 72-73. And it can be stored in a refrigerator for up to five days or frozen safely for two to three months.

However, commercial gelatins—made primarily from the skin and bones of pigs—are quite adequate for desserts that require only a small amount of gelatin because of the presence of other stiffening agents. For example, the consistency of Bavarian cream *(pages 26-27)* is determined as much by its rich supporting mixture of cooked egg yolks and whipped cream as it is by gelatin.

Of the commercial varieties, powdered gelatin is the easier to use; leaf gelatin requires a preliminary soaking of up to 30 minutes. Brands of gelatin differ slightly in setting strength. If the manufacturers indicate how much to use, follow their instructions; if not, use about 1 tablespoon [15 ml.] of powdered gelatin—or four sheets of leaf gelatin—to set about 2 cups [½ liter] of liquid to a consistency that can support its own weight.

1 **Splitting the calf's feet.** If your butcher has not soaked the feet, immerse them in cold water for several hours to remove blood, then rinse them. Cut each foot in half at the end of its long bone *(above)* and split the front of the foot in two. To keep each foot white while you work, place it in a bowl of cold water.

2 **Removing scum.** Put the calf's feet in a pan and cover them with fresh, cold water. Parboil the feet for eight to 10 minutes; drain and rinse them. Put them in a clean pan and add cold water to cover them by 1 inch [2½ cm.]. Simmer gently, with the lid just ajar, for at least seven hours. Skim off scum occasionally.

## Dealing with Leaf and Powdered Gelatin

**Dissolving leaf gelatin.** Place the sheets of gelatin in a bowl of cold water and let them soak. When the leaves are supple—after 10 to 30 minutes, depending on the commercial brand used—remove the softened gelatin and put it in a small, heavy pan with a little water. Set the pan over low heat, stirring until the gelatin dissolves and the liquid in the pan is clear.

**Dissolving powdered gelatin.** For each 1 tablespoon [15 ml.] of gelatin, put ¼ cup [50 ml.] of cold water into a small bowl and pour the powder into it. Allow the mixture to stand for about two minutes; the gelatin will soften and begin to swell. Stand the bowl in a pan of hot water over low heat for about three minutes, stirring until the gelatin has completely dissolved.

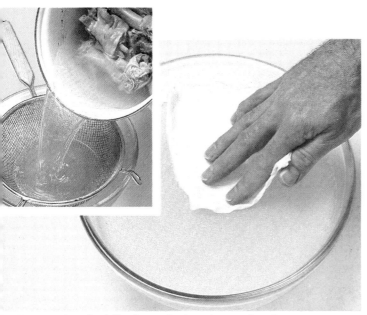

3 **Degreasing the jelly.** Strain the liquid into a bowl *(inset),* discard the calf's feet and put the liquid in the refrigerator overnight to set. Remove the jelly from the refrigerator and scrape off any fat with a spoon. If any small globules of fat remain, mop them up with a towel wrung out in hot water.

4 **Clarifying the jelly.** In a pot, heat the jelly gently until it melts. Add the flavorings: orange and lemon juice and grated peel, spices and sugar *(left).* In a bowl, beat egg whites with white wine until soft peaks form *(page 15).* Add the whites, together with the crushed eggshells, to the jelly. Whisk over medium heat until a thick froth forms *(right).* Stop whisking and let the jelly boil. Reduce the heat and maintain the barest simmer for 15 minutes.

5 **Straining the jelly.** Set a jelly bag in its stand over a bowl; inexpensive bags and stands are available at kitchen-equipment shops. Ladle the liquid jelly into the bag *(left)* and let it drip into the bowl. If necessary, repeat until the liquid in the bowl is clear. Chill the liquid until the jelly sets *(below).*

# 1

# Custards, Creams and Meringues
## The Adaptable Egg

In his encomium to the egg, the 19th Century Scottish philosopher and gastronome Eneas Sweetland Dallas wrote that there is "nothing in the way of food more simple than the egg, and nothing so quick and marvelous in its manifold uses and transformations." Among these transformations are custards, creams and meringues. As unalike as these desserts seem, all are based on eggs, and all may be easily varied just by altering the ingredients combined with the eggs or the cooking methods used.

The most versatile of these desserts is pouring custard, its English origin honored in its French name, *crème anglaise*. To make it, egg yolks, sugar, flavorings and cream or milk are stirred together over gentle heat. The mixture thickens into a smooth, rich custard that may be used as a sauce, topped with sugar and broiled to make *crème brûlée (opposite; recipe, page 91)* or employed in molded and frozen desserts. If, however, the egg yolks and sugar are whisked with wine, the result is the foamy custard *(page 21)* known in French as *sabayon,* in Italian as *zabaglione*.

Pouring and wine custards are essentially thick liquids; firmer desserts require a stiffening agent. The simplest stiffener is egg whites. Added in small quantities, as in baked custard cream *(pages 22-23),* the whites set the custard lightly during cooking; more whites produce a custard stiff enough to be turned out of a mold *(pages 24-25)*. Because these desserts must firm up, they are not stirred during cooking; instead, the pots or molds are immersed in heat-diffusing hot water. The water must be kept at a moderate temperature—about 185° F. [85° C.]—that will set the mixture but prevent it from overheating and separating.

A creamy molded dessert that requires no cooking after it is assembled can be made by using gelatin rather than egg whites. The lightest of these desserts, blancmange *(pages 26-27),* uses cream and gelatin but no eggs; its name emphasizes that it was once the delicate "white food" for invalids. Combining a pouring custard with gelatin and cream yields that most spectacular of desserts, Bavarian cream *(pages 26-27)*.

Meringues *(pages 28-29)*—made from egg whites, sugar and flavoring—offer a similar range of effects. Slowly baked, the beaten whites become crisp shells; gently poached, they emerge soft and fluffy, fit to float on pouring custard in the presentation known as *oeufs à la neige* in France and floating island in the United States.

m taps with a spoon crack the
ramel glaze of a burnt cream, or *crème
lée,* making it easy to include some
ze with each portion of custard. To
ep the custard cold and firm while
topping melted under the broiler, the
sh was set in a pan of ice cubes.

# Pouring Custard: Both Sauce and Ingredient

Gentleness is the watchword when making the delicate desserts called stirred custards. Based on egg yolks, sugar and liquid, such custards must be kept in constant motion as they are slowly heated, causing the protein of the yolks to coagulate evenly, without lumping.

When the liquid ingredient is milk or cream, this careful preparation will produce the creamy emulsion called a pouring custard *(demonstration, right; recipe, page 165)*. It may serve as a dessert on its own, or it may form the base for other desserts. Stiffened with gelatin, it is the foundation of Bavarian cream *(recipe, page 101);* mixed with cream and frozen, it produces the silkiest of ice creams *(recipe, page 166)*.

When you choose wine as the liquid ingredient, the result is a foamy emulsion in which the egg yolks triple in volume *(box, opposite)*. In Italy, Marsala is the most popular liquid *(recipe, page 165)*. But other fortified wines such as sherry or Madeira can be substituted, as can almost any white wine, sweet or dry.

For both creamy and foamy emulsions, the ratio of egg yolks to liquid is high. The pouring custard here uses three egg yolks for each 1¼ cups [300 ml.] of milk; the wine custard uses six yolks for the same measure of wine. Sugar is beaten thoroughly into the yolks to flavor them and to help keep them smooth during the cooking period.

Gentle heat is the most vital of all defenses against congealing yolks. A heavy pan allows a pouring-custard mixture to be cooked safely over low, direct heat, as here (the temperature of the pouring custard should not exceed 165° F. [75° C.]). Alternatively, the custard can be set on a trivet in a water bath—a large pan filled with just enough simmering water to immerse the bottom half of the custard pan. Wine custard, which is even more heat-sensitive, must be cooked above—not touching—water kept at a slow, steady simmer either in a double boiler or in a pan just large enough to hold the vessel containing the custard.

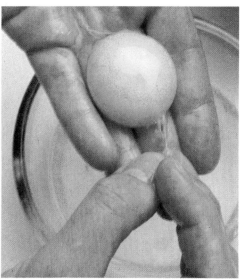

**1 Separating the eggs.** Crack each eggshell in half and slip the contents onto the palm of one hand, allowing all of the egg white to trickle through your fingers into a bowl. With your thumb and forefinger, gently remove from the yolk any clinging threads of albumen, then drop the yolk into another bowl.

**2 Mixing yolks and sugar.** Whisk the egg yolks lightly until they are smooth. Then add sugar to the yolks and beat the mixture vigorously so th the sugar is completely absorbed.

**3 Testing consistency.** Beat the mixture for about 10 minutes until it is pale and creamy, and reaches the ribbon stage. To test, lift some of the mixture on the whisk and dribble it into the bowl; it should form a trail, or ribbon, that is visible on the surface for a few seconds.

**4 Adding scalded milk.** Bring the milk almost to a boil over medium he When small bubbles appear around the edge of the pan, stir to prevent a s from forming. Slowly pour the scalde milk onto the yolk-and-sugar mixture whisking constantly but gently. Pour the mixture into a heavy saucepan.

**5 Cooking the custard.** Put the saucepan over low heat. Taking care to keep the custard below the simmering point, stir it in a figure-8 motion *(inset),* so that you pass the spoon through the middle — the hottest part — twice in each complete motion. A square-edged spoon will reach into the corners of the pan where the sides join the bottom and thus will prevent patchy thickening. The consistency is correct when the custard coats the spoon. At this point, dip the pan briefly into a bowl of ice *(above)* to stop the mixture from cooking further and possibly curdling.

**6 Smoothing the custard.** Strain the custard to remove any lumps. If you do not serve it immediately, keep the custard warm by placing the pan in hot water and stirring it often to distribute the heat. Alternatively, chill the custard over ice, stirring to prevent a skin from forming, or lay buttered wax paper on its surface and refrigerate the custard.

## A Foam of Eggs and Wine

**1 Whisking eggs and sugar.** In a large vessel — a sabayon pan is used here — beat egg yolks and sugar until they are pale and creamy. Meanwhile, fill a large pan partway with water and heat it to a simmer. Set the bowl or pan over — not in — the simmering water and continue to whisk.

**2 Adding the wine.** After about five minutes, when the yolks foam, pour in wine — here, Champagne — and add other flavorings, such as slivered lemon peel. Whisk 10 minutes more, until the mixture more than doubles in volume and froths up into a light custard. Remove the pan from the heat.

**3 Serving.** As a dessert, wine custard is usually eaten hot. Pour it into individual glasses *(above)* and serve it at once. As a sauce, wine custard may be used hot or cold. For a cold sauce, set the pan over ice to stop the cooking and to chill the custard before use.

# Lightly Set Confections Rich in Flavor

By combining a little egg white—which stiffens during cooking—with the yolks and milk that make a pouring custard *(pages 20-21)*, you can create lightly set baked custards such as the Peruvian cream demonstrated here *(recipe, page 90)*. A mixture that uses one whole egg to every five egg yolks for 2½ to 3 cups [625 to 750 ml.] of liquid produces a trembling, barely firm custard that is best cooked and served in individual ramekins or pots—which is why these desserts are known as *pots de crème*.

The basic custard cream mixture may be given many flavors. To extract the pure tastes of insoluble ingredients—such as the coffee and vanilla beans used here, or orange, lemon or lime peels—infuse them in the milk that later serves to make the custard *(Steps 1 and 2, right)*. Soluble flavorings—the chocolate and caramel in this demonstration, for example, as well as honey or clear fruit jellies—are added to the milk after the aromatic flavorings have been infused. In order to keep the mixture as smooth as possible, melt the chocolate very gently *(Step 3)*, and make the caramel *(pages 8-9)* fairly thin so that it will blend easily with the milk.

Custard combinations that include egg whites curdle so readily that it is difficult to make a smooth custard cream by cooking it over direct heat. A water bath provides a more gentle cooking medium. The ramekins, filled with the custard mixture, are placed in a large pan that is partly filled with hot water, covered, and set in a moderate oven or over low heat. The hot water diffuses the heat so that the custards cook slowly and evenly.

1 **Infusing the coffee.** Heat whole, roasted coffee beans in a 350° F. [180° C.] oven for a few minutes until they glisten with their aromatic oils. Bring milk to a boil in a pan over medium heat. Add the coffee beans. Snap or cut off a piece 2 or 3 inches [5 or 8 cm.] long from a vanilla bean and drop it into the milk. Remove the pan from the heat, covering it to keep the milk warm.

2 **Adding vanilla seeds.** After about 30 minutes, scoop out the van and coffee beans with a perforated spoon or skimmer. Split the vanilla be lengthwise and, with the tip of a shar knife, scrape its seeds into the milk; discard the pod and the coffee bean Sieve the milk into a bowl.

5 **Mixing the custard.** Place whole eggs and egg yolks—five yolks to every whole egg—in a mixing bowl and whisk them until they are smooth. Gradually pour in the hot, flavored milk, whisking it gently with the eggs.

6 **Skimming the custard.** To ensure that the custard is absolutely smooth strain it through a fine sieve into a clean bowl. Skim off any froth from th surface *(above)* so that bubbles will not spoil the appearance and texture the custard when it cooks. Then fill ramekins with the custard and place them in a wide, deep casserole.

**Melting the chocolate.** Drop chunks of semisweet baking chocolate into a pan. Set over very low heat and add enough milk to cover the bottom of the pan *(above)*. Stir the chocolate as it melts. When the mixture is a smooth paste, slowly stir in the remaining milk.

**Adding caramel.** In a small pan, make a little caramel *(pages 8-9)*. When it is a light golden color, remove the caramel from the heat. Immediately add a little hot water to soften the caramel, return it to low heat and stir until it is a smooth syrup. Stir into the milk.

**Baking.** Using a spatula to prevent splashing, pour hot water into the casserole to come two thirds of the way up the sides of the ramekins *(left)*. Cover and bake in a 300° F. [150° C.] oven for about 20 minutes, or until a knife inserted into one of the custards comes out clean. Chill the custards and serve them with cookies *(below)*.

# A Molded Custard with a Caramel Glaze

Baked custards firm enough to be served unmolded must include more egg-white stiffening than is used in custard-cream mixtures *(pages 22-23)*. The proportion of egg white to yolk is critical. Too much white will produce a coarse, rubbery-textured custard; too little will produce a custard that will collapse when it is unmolded. A ratio of one whole egg to one yolk will provide the correct balance for ½ to 1 cup [125 to 250 ml.] of liquid.

Such custards can be flavored with chocolate, finely grated orange or lemon peel, coffee or vanilla, and baked in an oiled mold. But the classic version of the dessert is caramel-coated custard, or *crème caramel*, demonstrated here *(recipe, page 94)*. *Crème caramel* is a vanilla custard that has been baked in a caramelized mold *(box, right)*. As the custard cooks, the hard caramel lining partly melts in the heat, allowing the cooked custard to slide easily out of the mold. The final product is a custard coated with firm caramel and presented in a sauce of caramel that has melted.

To ensure successful unmolding of the caramel-coated custard, bake it in a plain container with a smooth base and sides. Porcelain and glass molds or cups are suitable, but custard slips more readily from metal molds, such as the charlotte mold used here. How much caramel to make depends on how thin or thick you want the coating to be: ½ cup [125 ml.] of sugar and 2 tablespoons [30 ml.] of water will line a 4- to 6-cup [1- to 1½-liter] mold generously.

**1** **Adding custard to a mold.** In a bowl, beat the eggs, egg yolks, sugar and salt. Stir in hot milk flavored with vanilla bean *(page 22)* or — if you are in a hurry — with vanilla extract. Strain, then skim off any foam. Ladle the mixture into a caramelized mold *(box, below)* set in an ovenproof dish *(above)*.

**2** **Testing for doneness.** Pour warm water into the dish to immerse the mold two thirds of its depth. Cover the dish and bake the custard for one hour in a 350° F. [180° C.] oven. The custard is done when a knife inserted into it comes out clean; if the knife is wet, cook the custard for 10 minutes more, then rete

## Caramelizing a Mold

**1** **Making the caramel.** In a heavy pan over low heat, dissolve sugar in a little water. Cook over medium heat until the mixture is a light amber color. Stop the cooking by dipping the pan briefly in a bowl of ice cubes and water.

**2** **Coating the mold.** Immediately pour the caramel into a warm, dry mold. Using potholders, tilt and rotate the mold so that the caramel coats the sides completely. Brush almond oil or flavorless vegetable oil around the top edge if it is not fully coated.

3 **Loosening the custard.** Remove the mold from the oven and let it cool. When the custard feels tepid, insert the tip of a knife between the custard and the side of the mold and run the knife around the mold *(above)* to free the outside of the custard.

4 **Freeing the custard.** Hold the mold steady with one hand and use your other hand to press gently on the surface and ease the custard from the side of the mold. Rotate the mold and repeat the process until the custard does not stick to the mold at any point.

5 **Unmolding the custard.** Choose a serving plate deep enough to hold the liquid caramel that will run down the sides of the custard as you unmold it. Invert the plate on top of the custard and turn both over. Lift up the mold gently *(above)*. Serve the custard tepid, or chill it for a few hours in the refrigerator.

# Sculptures of Cream and Gelatin

When a dessert is to be chilled rather than cooked, whipped cream and gelatin can make it firm enough to hold even intricate shapes. Almond milk, thus enriched and stiffened, becomes a silky blancmange *(right, top; recipe, page 99)*. Pouring custard turns into a Bavarian cream, one of the most celebrated molded desserts *(right, bottom; recipe, page 101)*. And the same firming agents support a range of cold mousses and soufflés.

For all of these desserts, gelatin is added to a flavored base; when the gelatin begins to set, whipped cream is folded in and the mixture is molded and chilled. In the Bavarian cream demonstrated at right, two bases—raspberry purée and vanilla pouring custard—provide contrasting layers of color and flavor.

Timing is essential for success with these desserts: Dissolved gelatin *(page 16)* must be smoothly combined with the flavored bases, and whipped cream must be added at just the right moment. Because a gelatin mixture sets rapidly as it cools, the liquid gelatin must be warm when you add it to a flavored base—especially if the base is cold. Otherwise, the gelatin will set as soon as it touches the base and will form strings, a mishap termed roping by professional cooks.

Once the gelatin has been added to the base, the mixture should be chilled to speed setting. The consistency should be close to that of whipped cream if the two are to be combined successfully. If the gelatin mixture has not yet set sufficiently, it will be too liquid to blend easily with the cream; if it sets too much at this stage, its solidity will prevent you from folding in the cream evenly. To attain the right firmness, place the gelatin mixture over a bowl of ice cubes and water while you whip the cream; stir the gelatin mixture frequently until it just begins to set. Premature setting can be remedied by warming the mixture: Put the bowl over a pan of hot water for half a minute, stirring constantly.

For a pleasing visual effect, chill the dessert in a patterned mold brushed with almond oil or flavorless vegetable oil so that the Bavarian cream or blancmange will slip out effortlessly when it has set.

## An Almond-flavored Blancmange

1 **Preparing almond milk.** Pound blanched almonds to a paste with a little water. Mix the paste with milk and sugar, and heat to just below boiling. Pour the liquid into a strainer lined with a clean cloth and set over a bowl. Then gather up the cloth and twist *(above)* to wring out the almond milk.

2 **Stiffening the milk.** Soften gelatin *(page 16)*, place it in a pan with water to cover, and warm it gently. When the gelatin begins to dissolve, combine it with the warm almond milk. Add sugar to taste, and stir until the gelatin dissolves completely. Then pour the mixture into a bowl set over ice cubes. St the mixture as it cools.

## Contrasting Layers of Bavarian Cream

1 **Preparing fruit.** Make raspberry purée *(page 68)* and an equal quantity of medium-heavy sugar syrup *(pages 8-9)*. When the syrup boils, remove it from the heat and dissolve softened gelatin in it. Cool the syrup and blend it with the purée *(above)*. Refrigerate the mixture or stir it over ice to chill it.

2 **Starting the vanilla base.** Make a pouring custard *(pages 20-21)* flavore with vanilla. Stir the custard over low heat and add gelatin that has beer softened and then dissolved in warm water. Stir until the custard thickens enough to coat the spoon, remove it from the heat and stir it over ice.

3 **Adding whipped cream.** While the almond milk cools, whip heavy cream until it forms firm peaks. As soon as the gelatinized almond milk is thick and syrup-like, add the cream *(above)* and stir until it is thoroughly amalgamated with the almond milk. Pour the mixture into a lightly oiled mold. Cover and refrigerate for about five hours.

4 **Unmolding and serving.** Remove the cover and test the dessert: It should be firm to the touch. Loosen the edges of the blancmange with a knife and dip the bottom of the mold into a pan of hot water *(inset, above)* for one second. Unmold the loosened blancmange, using an inverted plate *(page 73)*.

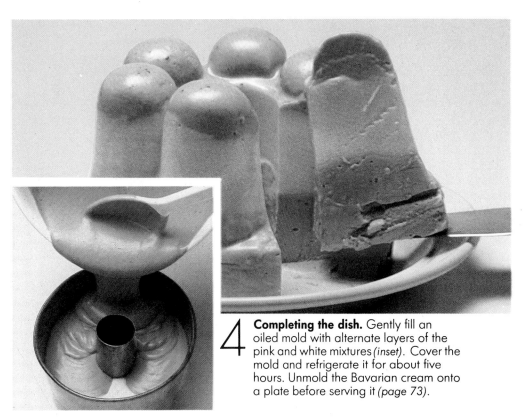

3 **Adding cream.** When the fruit and the custard mixtures begin to set, incorporate whipped, sweetened heavy cream *(box, page 15)* into each *(above)*. To keep the dessert layers separate, the purée and custard should have the same consistency: One may need more cream than the other.

4 **Completing the dish.** Gently fill an oiled mold with alternate layers of the pink and white mixtures *(inset)*. Cover the mold and refrigerate it for about five hours. Unmold the Bavarian cream onto a plate before serving it *(page 73)*.

# Puffs of Egg White, Crisp or Soft

## Piped and Baked Meringues

Egg whites play more than supporting roles when they are transformed into meringue: The whites inflate to become the airiest of desserts or dessert toppings.

A basic meringue mixture consists of no more than stiffly beaten egg whites and sugar *(pages 14-15)*; this simple alliance can be enlivened, of course, by additional flavorings—coffee or chocolate, for example. Depending on how it is cooked, the mixture can produce either of two quite different desserts. Baked meringues *(right; recipe, page 104)* are brittle shells that can sandwich whipped cream or ice cream. Poached meringues are fluffy and soft: They are usually served on custard to produce the dessert called floating island *(recipe, page 96)*, shown opposite in two versions.

Although simple in composition, the meringue requires about 15 minutes of vigorous beating. First the whites are whisked stiff, then sugar is beaten in. Too much sugar added at once will soften the whites: Beat it in a little at a time. Lastly, any flavorings are incorporated.

For baked meringues, place spoonfuls of the mixture on a lined baking sheet. More decorative shapes can be created by squeezing the meringue from a pastry bag fitted with a large, patterned tube, such as the star tube used here.

Slow, gentle drying is needed to produce baked meringues that are light and crisp, with no trace of stickiness. (Dry weather is a necessity, as well; high humidity prevents drying.) The meringues must be baked for two hours at very low heat, then left in the oven with the heat off to dry for one to two hours more.

To poach meringues, make the shapes by gently sliding spoonfuls of the mixture onto barely simmering sweetened milk. Because its sole purpose is to set the meringue, poaching is much briefer than baking; three to four minutes will produce firm, fluffy meringues.

For floating island, the poaching milk is used to make a pouring custard *(pages 20-21)* on which the meringues ride. In one version shown here, the meringues are piled up and decorated with wisps of caramel *(Step 3, opposite)*; in the other, they float on caramel-flavored custard *(box, opposite; recipe, page 165)*.

1 **Beating in sugar.** Beat whites into stiff peaks *(pages 14-15)*. Beat in sugar by the spoonful *(above)*; allow ¼ cup [50 ml.] of superfine sugar or ½ cup [125 ml.] of confectioners' sugar for each white. Fold in flavorings. Here, part of the mixture is flavored with unsweetened cocoa powder, part with strong, fresh coffee, and the rest is left plain.

2 **Filling a pastry bag.** Insert a patterned tube into a pastry bag. Turn the upper third of the bag inside out and spoon meringue into the lower two thirds, then fold back the upper third over the mixture. Twist the top of the bag to close it and to provide a handle. Squeeze the top gently until the meringue mixture starts to emerge from the tube.

3 **Forming the meringues.** Lightly oil a baking sheet and line it with wax paper or oiled aluminum foil. Pipe the meringue mixture in spirals *(above)*, using one hand to hold the top of the bag closed and the other to guide the tube.

4 **Serving the meringues.** Bake the meringues in a 200° F. [100° C.] oven for two hours, turn off the heat and leave them for one hour or longer, until they are dry enough to be lifted easily with a spatula and set on racks to cool. Serve them sandwiched in pairs with whipped cream, flavored, if you like, with praline powder *(page 13)*.

## Meringues Poached in Milk

### Islands in a Custard Lake

**Poaching meringues.** In a wide, shallow pan, heat sweetened milk until it is just at the simmering point. Scoop up a tablespoonful [15 ml.] of the meringue mixture and slide it onto the milk with a spatula. Poach the meringues three or four at a time for about three minutes, turning them once with a spoon. Lift out the meringues and drain them on a drum sieve or cloth.

1 **Flavoring the milk.** Poach the meringues *(Step 1, left)*, drain them and strain the milk. Dilute some caramel *(pages 8-9)* with warm water and then stir it into the still-hot milk *(above)*.

2 **Making custard.** When all of the meringues are poached, strain the milk *(above)* to remove fragments of egg white. Stir the milk into beaten egg yolks and sugar and gently cook the mixture to make a pouring custard *(pages 20-21)*.

3 **Assembling the dessert.** Pour the custard into a bowl, and cover it with meringue layers. If you like, top the meringues with caramel threads *(page 10)*, as shown here. Serve the dessert at once; or, to serve it cold, chill the components separately and assemble them at the last minute. This keeps the meringues from sinking.

2 **Adding the meringues.** Make a custard by cooking the caramel-flavored milk with beaten egg yolks *(pages 20-21)*. Pour the custard into a bowl. Using a spatula or large spoon, arrange the poached meringues in a pattern on the surface of the custard *(above)*.

# 2
# Soufflés and Puddings
## From the Ethereal to the Weighty

**olding in egg whites with a light touch**
**he quintessential chocolate mousse**
**tiered dessert from two molds**
**soufflé pudding based on nuts**
**aking the most of grains**

/hipped cream is squeezed from a astry bag to embellish a chocolate udding that was gently cooked in a old set in a water bath. To help the udding slip easily from its heavily uttered mold, it was left to firm up for 5 minutes before being turned out.

Soufflés and puddings represent the extremes of a spectrum of desserts ranging in character from airy and flamboyant to solid and hearty. Between them—and linked by related cooking techniques—lie mousses and hybrid soufflé puddings. Taken together, the group offers desserts for any mood, season or appetite.

Soufflés, the lightest of the group, acquire their airiness from stiffly beaten egg whites. The whites are folded into a flavored base that may be a simple fruit purée *(box, page 33)* or a complex mixture that includes flour, milk, egg yolks and butter. During baking, the air in the egg whites expands, raising the soufflé to startling heights. Once cooked, the soufflé waits for no man; it must be rushed to the table before its fragile form collapses.

A mousse *(pages 34-35)* also is composed of a flavored base lightened with beaten egg whites. However, a mousse is chilled, not cooked. As it cools, its texture becomes firmer; the whites do not expand, but the air bubbles they contain are trapped inside the dessert, giving it the characteristic spongy texture—not quite as light as that of a soufflé—from which its name ("foam" in French) derives.

A little further from the miraculous lightness of the classic soufflé is the soufflé pudding. It contains proportionately fewer egg whites than a soufflé, and it cooks in the moist heat of a water bath. As a result, it does not expand as dramatically as a soufflé, but neither does it fall so far when it cools. That means a soufflé pudding—such as a chocolate pudding *(opposite and box, page 35)* or a semolina *flamri (cover and pages 36-37)* —can be unmolded and decorated at leisure before it is served.

Without the airiness provided by beaten egg whites, semolina and other starchy ingredients make more substantial puddings. Rice, for example *(pages 38-39)*, simmered in sweetened, flavored milk, then baked with cream and egg yolks, becomes a rich and warming dessert.

When starchy ingredients are combined with fats, fruits and flavorings and then steamed, they become heavier puddings—cheerful, filling winter food. Plum puddings, traditional for English Christmases, belong to this group. These spicy, suet-based desserts *(pages 40-41)* may need as much as 12 hours' steaming, but some types will keep—and mature in flavor—for 18 months or more.

31

# Tactics for Entrapping Air

A soufflé acquires its taste from its sauce-like base, and its light texture from beaten egg whites. As the mixture is baked, the air trapped in the whites expands, giving the dessert a towering puff.

Most soufflé bases are made from flour, milk, egg yolks, butter and sugar, mixed with flavoring elements *(recipes, pages 105-108)*. In the soufflé demonstrated at right, the flavorings are vanilla and candied fruit. The lightest soufflés *(box, opposite; recipe, page 106)* have only sweetened fruit purées—raspberries, peaches or strawberries—for their foundations.

Whatever the base, beating the egg whites remains the most important step in making a soufflé. The cook must incorporate as much air as possible into them, and, if preparing a fragile fruit base, should provide extra support by beating the whites together with sugar *(Step 1, page 28)*. Do not let the beaten whites stand for more than a few minutes before combining them with the base; they will lose their air and deflate. To blend the ingredients smoothly, first mix a spoonful of whites into the base to lighten it; the base can then easily be folded into the rest of the whites.

Once the soufflé is assembled, it is best baked immediately, although a sauce-based mixture can wait up to 30 minutes if covered with an inverted pot to shut out drafts and left at room temperature. As a cooking vessel, use a straight-sided dish that will force the expanding soufflé upward. In the case of a delicate fruit soufflé, the dish should be metal for rapid cooking; to allow for this sort of soufflé's great expansion, wrap a paper collar around the dish, as shown opposite. With any soufflé, coat the dish—and the collar, if you use one—with butter and sugar to prevent the soufflé from sticking.

Most soufflés are baked at 350° F. [180° C.]. (The oven should, of course, be preheated so that the assembled mixture can be cooked promptly.) To help a fruit-based soufflé retain the freshest flavor, however, cook the mixture at a high temperature—450° F. [230° C.]—so that the whites set quickly. Either type of soufflé may be served slightly underdone, to give it the creamy center favored in Europe, or well done, to make it drier.

1 **Preparing the soufflé dish.** Coat a straight-sided, ovenproof dish with butter, and sprinkle a little sugar into it. Rotate the dish so that the sugar clings evenly to the buttered surfaces. Tap the sides of the dish to loosen surplus sugar, then shake out the loose sugar.

2 **Making the base.** In a bowl, make a thin paste from flour and cold milk. In saucepan, bring to a boil a mixture of milk and sugar, flavored with a vanilla bean. Stir in the paste. Whisk over low heat for two minutes, until the mixture thickens. Remove the pan from the heat; discard the vanilla bean.

3 **Adding the yolks.** After the thickened milk has cooled for three minutes, add egg yolks and softened butter. Whisk until the mixture is well blended, then stir in pieces of chopped, candied fruit.

4 **Folding in the egg whites.** Beat the egg whites until they form stiff peaks *(pages 14-15)*. Stir about a quarter of the whites into the base mixture to lighten its texture, then pour the mixture over the remaining whites. Using a spatula or your hands, fold the whites from the bottom of the bowl over the top of the mixture. Continue folding until the soufflé is nearly homogeneous.

# The Simplest Soufflé: Fruit and Egg Whites

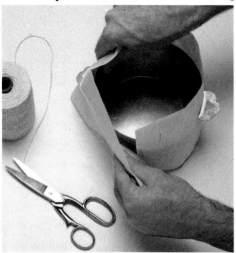

1 **Making a collar.** Wrap a double layer of wax or parchment paper around a charlotte mold or similar straight-sided metal dish. If necessary, cut slits in the paper where it passes over the handles. Keep the paper in place by tying string around it. Coat the mold and the paper collar with softened butter and sprinkle them with sugar *(Step 1, left)*.

2 **Filling the mold.** Following the directions in Step 4, opposite, combine egg whites that have been stiffly beaten with sugar with a sweetened purée of strawberries or other soft fruit to make an even-colored mixture. Spoon the mixture into the prepared dish; the soufflé should just reach the top of the dish below the paper collar.

3 **Baking the soufflé.** Cook the soufflé immediately in a preheated 450° F. [230° C.] oven for about 15 minutes. Test for doneness *(Step 5, below)*. The top should be brown but the center moist. Remove the soufflé from the oven and serve it at once.

5 **Filling the dish.** Immediately pour the mixture into the prepared soufflé dish and place it in a preheated 350° F. [180° C.] oven. After about 25 minutes, check the soufflé by inserting a knife through the side. The blade will be moist if the soufflé is slightly underdone, dry if it is well done. Serve the soufflé at once *(right)*. If it cools, it will collapse — especially if it is slightly underdone.

33

# The Special Demands of Chocolate

When it is chilled, a flavored base aerated with beaten egg whites becomes a smooth, light mousse *(below; recipe, page 111)*. Reducing the proportions of whites, adding flour and cooking the mixture yields a substantial pudding *(box, opposite; recipe, page 112)*.

These desserts may be made with a variety of flavorings, chocolate being a perennial favorite. Plain, unsweetened baking chocolate is traditionally chosen for its intensity of flavor, but semisweet or sweet baking chocolate can be used if you adjust the sugar called for in the recipe. Melting the chocolate requires gentle heat, since chocolate burns or hardens easily. Melt it in a double boiler over simmering water; in a slow oven; or, as here, in a heavy pan with a little liquid—water, rum or coffee—over low heat.

After you have combined the chocolate with butter and egg yolks to give it smoothness, stir in sugar, if you are u[sing] it, and any additional flavoring. T[he] chocolate mixture can then be folded in[to] the egg whites *(pages 32-33)*, but becau[se] chocolate is so dense this may produce a[ir] pockets that would give the dessert a[n] uneven texture and color. To achieve t[he] finest grain, blend a little of the chocola[te] into the whites and then fold this mi[x]ture into the remaining chocolate.

1 **Melting the chocolate.** Put pieces of chocolate into a heavy pan with just enough water to cover the bottom. Over a very low heat, stir with a wooden spatula until the chocolate blends with the water to form a smooth paste.

2 **Blending in butter and eggs.** Remove the pan from the heat. Add small pieces of butter a few at a time, stirring until they melt into the chocolate *(left)*. Separate the eggs, reserve the whites and add the yolks to the pan one by one *(right)*, stirring continuously. Stir the mixture until it is smooth and glossy, then add sugar to taste and a flavoring such as rum or brandy.

3 **Introducing chocolate into egg whites.** Whisk egg whites until they form fairly stiff peaks *(pages 14-15)*. To combine the whites evenly with the chocolate, leaving no unflavored pockets of egg white, spoon a little of the very dense chocolate mixture evenly over the surface of the beaten egg whites *(above)*. Whisk gently until the mixture is a uniform color.

4 **Blending egg whites and chocolate.** Pour the egg-white mixture into the pan containing the bulk of the chocolate. Fold th[e] chocolate into the egg-white mixture, using a whisk to lift and slide the chocolate gently from the bottom of the pan onto the top the mixture. Continue folding the mixture in this way until the mousse has a uniform color and consistency.

## Baking a Molded Chocolate Pudding

1 **Adding flour to chocolate.** Melt the chocolate and add butter and egg yolks *(Steps 1 and 2, opposite)*. Stir sugar into the chocolate, then blend in sifted flour *(above)*. Combine the chocolate mixture with beaten egg whites *(Steps 3 and 4, opposite)*.

2 **Molding and cooking.** Pour the chocolate mixture into a heavily buttered mold *(above)* to within 1 inch [2½ cm.] of the top, leaving room for the pudding to rise. Place the mold in a water bath and add hot water to two thirds the depth of the mold. Place in an oven preheated to 350° F. [180° C.].

3 **Serving the pudding.** After about 40 minutes, probe the pudding with a thin, dry skewer. If the skewer comes out clean, the pudding is cooked. Let it rest for a few minutes to firm; then, using an inverted plate, unmold the pudding. Set the pudding aside and let it cool before decorating it with whipped cream and serving it *(above)*.

5 **Serving the mousse.** Spoon the chocolate mousse into serving glasses *(left)* and chill for at least two hours to firm. Just before serving, decorate the mousse with whipped cream and, if you like, sugared orange peel *(page 11, top)*.

# Heavy Ingredients Lightly Treated

An egg-white-lightened dessert whose base includes rich, heavy ingredients is called a soufflé pudding, because it combines some of the lightness of the classic soufflé *(pages 32-33)* with the firmness of an orthodox pudding *(pages 38-41)*. In the *flamri* demonstrated at top right *(recipe, page 122)*, boiled semolina—fine grains milled from hard, durum-wheat berries—provides the base. In the nut loaf at bottom right *(recipe, page 119)*, ground almonds and pistachios are the foundation. Since desserts like these are not intended to be airy, the base mixtures are blended with just enough egg whites to soften their textures.

Instead of being baked quickly in the oven, a soufflé pudding is cooked in a mold in a water bath *(pages 22-23)*. Covered and partially immersed in water kept just below the boiling point—either in a moderate oven or on top of the stove—the pudding mixture will cook slowly and evenly. It will rise as it cooks, but not as dramatically as a classic soufflé. And although it will settle slightly when it is removed from the oven, it is dense enough so that there is no danger of its collapsing. In fact, a nut loaf can be kept for a day or two and actually will improve in flavor.

In most semolina soufflé puddings, the grains are cooked in milk as a first stage. However, in the *flamri* the semolina acquires more flavor by being simmered in white wine mixed with water. Adjust the amount of sugar according to the sweetness of the wine and your own taste. Whole eggs are included to enrich the semolina before the beaten whites are folded in. The pudding is easier to unmold if it is cooked in a fairly shallow dish; you can build a taller, more formal dessert by using two or more molds and turning them out one on top of the other, as shown here *(Step 4)*. *Flamri* is usually served with a tart sauce made from a purée of soft fruit, such as blackberries or raspberries.

The almond-and-pistachio loaf shown here also includes white wine and the yolks of eggs as well as their whites. Cooked orange and lemon peels added to the ground nuts help to balance the rich flavor of their aromatic oils.

## Wine-simmered Semolina

1 **Cooking the semolina.** Bring equal quantities of water and white wine to a rolling boil. Maintaining the same heat, sprinkle in semolina, stirring continuously with a whisk or spoon. Cover the pan, reduce the heat and simmer for 20 minutes, until the semolina cooks to a thick, smooth paste.

2 **Adding the eggs.** Remove the pan from the heat and let the semolina co for a few minutes. Beat in sugar to taste, a pinch of salt and the whole egg Whisk egg whites until they form stiff peaks *(pages 14-15)*. Use a spatula *(above)* to fold the whites gently but thoroughly into the semolina mixture.

## A Loaf of Pounded Nuts

1 **Making the nut paste.** Pound blanched almonds and blanched pistachios *(pages 12-13)* in a mortar until they are smooth, or use a food processor. Simmer strips of orange and lemon peels in a little sugar syrup *(pages 8-9)*, then add the peels and syrup to the pounded nuts *(left)*. Blend the peels and the nuts and alternately stir in small quantities of white wine and sugar *(center)*. Add the egg yolks and beat the mixture until stiff *(right)*.

3 **Cooking the mixture.** Turn the mixture into two buttered molds — one for the base, the other for a decorative top. Cover each mold with buttered wax paper and place it in a large pan *(above)*. Pour in hot water to reach two thirds of the way up the sides. Cover the pan and place it over low heat for 25 to 40 minutes, until the *flamri* is firm.

4 **Unmolding the pudding.** Let the molds stand until the soufflé pudding is lukewarm. Unmold the larger mold first, using an inverted plate. Place a wide spatula over the smaller mold, then turn over the mold and lower it gently onto the first soufflé pudding *(above)*. Carefully slide out the spatula before unmolding the top pudding.

5 **Decorating and serving.** Crown the *flamri* with whole blackberries, as here, or raspberries. Make a sauce by puréeing some of the fruit with sugar to taste. If fresh berries are out of season, use frozen ones, or substitute a purée of cooked, dried apricots.

2 **Folding in egg whites.** Whisk egg whites to stiff peaks. Blend a spoonful of the egg whites with the nut purée, then fold the purée into the remaining whites. Pour the mixture into a buttered mold. Set the mold in a water bath *(Step 3, above)* and bake it in a preheated 375° F. [190° C.] oven for 25 minutes, until the pudding has set.

3 **Serving the pudding.** Unmold the nut loaf, using an inverted plate. Let the loaf stand for a few minutes to allow it to settle, then decorate it with whipped cream. If you like, add strips of sugared orange peel *(page 11, top)*.

# Transforming Rice with Eggs and Cream

Heavier and heartier than soufflé puddings and mousses, starchy puddings are based on such ingredients as bread, rice, tapioca or flour, and are rarely lightened by egg whites. Among starchy pudding foundations, rice—cooked in milk, wine, hard cider or water—is the most versatile. Because of its unassertive taste, rice can accommodate many different flavorings. In this demonstration, the rice is perfumed by a bouquet of orange and lemon peels *(recipe, page 120)*. Among popular alternatives *(recipes, pages 120-121)* are cinnamon, cardamom, vanilla and even rose water.

Cooked, flavored rice may be served as soon as it has absorbed its cooking liquid, but it also lends itself to more elaborate treatments. It may be enriched with egg yolks and cream, as here, then baked to give it a brown crust. Or it can be blended with gelatin and whipped cream and chilled to produce a luxurious *riz à l'impératrice*, as shown on pages 86-87 *(recipe, page 153)*. The cooked rice even can be made into a soufflé pudding by combining it with beaten egg whites, then cooking the mixture in a mold in a water bath *(recipe, page 152)*.

No matter what dessert the rice is destined for, the initial steps for handling it are the same. You can use long-grain rice, as shown here, or medium- or short-grain rice. Long-grain rice stays intact during cooking, resulting in a pudding with clearly separated grains. Kernels of medium- and short-grain rice, with their higher gluten content, merge together to produce a more homogeneous pudding.

Before cooking any rice, wash it thoroughly to remove surface starch that could make the finished pudding gummy. Put the rice in a bowl, cover it with cold water and stir it for a few moments, then drain it. Parboil the rice *(Step 1, right)* for a few minutes, then drain it again and rinse it to wash away any remaining starch and to keep the rice from cooking further at this point.

During the next stage of cooking, the rice will absorb about three times its own volume of sweetened, flavored liquid. This process takes 20 to 30 minutes, depending on the rice you use; afterward, the rice is ready for the table—or for any elaboration you choose.

**1 Parboiling the rice.** Rinse the rice and put it in a heavy pan with plenty of cold water. Bring the water to a boil, stirring occasionally with a wooden spoon to keep the grains separate. Boil the rice for about five minutes, uncovered; then drain it in a strainer, rinse it under running water and let it drain again in the strainer.

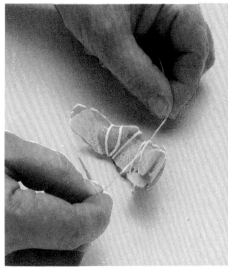

**2 Preparing the flavoring.** Set a pan of milk over medium heat. While the milk is heating, pare strips of peel from a lemon and an orange, cutting close the surface to avoid including the bitter pith in the strips. Tie the strips together with string to make a bundle, and set this bouquet aside.

**5 Cooling the rice.** Remove the pan from the heat and take out the bouquet of peels. Separate the rice grains by stirring them gently with a fork. Serve the rice immediately, if you wish. If you plan to enrich the dessert with cream and egg yolks, let the rice cool for five minutes; its heat would curdle the yolks.

**6 Adding the egg yolks.** Separate the egg yolks from the whites *(page 14)* and reserve the whites for other uses, such as meringues *(pages 28-29)*. Add the egg yolks to the rice *(above)* and stir the mixture—taking care not to crush the grains—until the rice is well coated.

3 **Adding sugar.** Pour sugar into the milk, and stir it to make sure the sugar dissolves thoroughly. Then add the bouquet of lemon and orange peels, some butter and a pinch of salt. For extra taste, remove the pan from the heat, set it aside and let the flavorings infuse in the milk for up to one hour.

4 **Adding the rice.** Bring the milk to a boil, add the parboiled rice *(above)* and stir well. Slowly bring the milk back to a boil, cover and cook in a 325° F. [160° C.] oven or over very low heat for about 30 minutes, until the rice absorbs the milk and is tender.

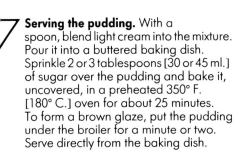

7 **Serving the pudding.** With a spoon, blend light cream into the mixture. Pour it into a buttered baking dish. Sprinkle 2 or 3 tablespoons [30 or 45 ml.] of sugar over the pudding and bake it, uncovered, in a preheated 350° F. [180° C.] oven for about 25 minutes. To form a brown glaze, put the pudding under the broiler for a minute or two. Serve directly from the baking dish.

# Steaming: An Age-old Way to Make a Pudding

Of all puddings, steamed ones are the richest and most dense. Composed of fats, starches, spices, dried fruits and usually spirits, they cook for long hours in humid heat that keeps them moist and melds their various flavors.

A splendid example of the breed is English Christmas pudding *(right; recipe, page 124)*. For fat, it contains suet, the hard fat that surrounds beef kidneys. Its starchy ingredient is bread crumbs, and the mixture is enlivened with generous amounts of dried and candied fruits, nuts and spices. Cooking the pudding is a simple matter of mixing the ingredients, molding them and steaming them.

Choose the suet carefully: It should be white, dry and crumbly. Buy it fresh from the butcher, and pick over it to remove any connective tissue and membrane before you chop it with a knife or grate it with an ordinary kitchen grater.

In the demonstration here, the pudding mixture is packed into a classic pudding basin; however, metal or ceramic molds or heatproof bowls could be used instead. Covered and set on a rack in a large, covered pot half-filled with water, the pudding will be fit to eat in one and one half hours. Most cooks, however, steam Christmas puddings for nine to 12 hours to blend the flavors thoroughly and to allow the dried fruit to spread its dark color throughout the dessert.

Owing to the excellent keeping properties of cooked suet and the preservative effects of sugar and alcohol, steamed puddings such as the one here can be made months—or even a year or two—in advance and stored; indeed, their flavors often will improve if they are left to mature in an airtight container *(box, opposite)*. When you are ready to serve the pudding, steam it for a couple of hours.

For a traditional presentation, pour a glass of warm brandy over the pudding and set it alight at the table. The time-honored garnish is hard sauce, made by beating together butter and confectioners' sugar and flavoring the mixture with dark rum or brandy *(recipe, page 163)*.

1 **Preparing the ingredients.** Chop blanched almonds *(box, page 13)* and candied fruit peel and cherries, and place them in a large bowl with soft dark brown sugar and dried fruit — here, currants and raisins. Grate the peel of an orange and a lemon over the mixture. Brush the remaining peel off the grater with a pastry brush. Add grated suet, bread crumbs and such spices as grated nutmeg and ground ginger. Mix thoroughly with your hands.

2 **Binding ingredients.** Pour beaten eggs into the mixture. Add whiskey, brandy or, as here, dark beer; stir well. Traditionally, cooks add coins or good-luck charms to a Christmas pudding. If you do so, first sterilize them for five minutes in boiling water, then wrap each one in foil.

**Preparing the basin.** Brush a pudding basin with vegetable oil. Line the base with a circle of wax or parchment paper, oiled on both sides so that the paper will not stick to the basin or the pudding. Pack the pudding mixture into the basin; level it with a spoon. Cover the pudding with another circle of oiled paper *(above)*.

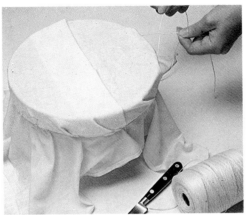

**Sealing the pudding.** Sprinkle dampened cloth with flour and place it over the basin, floured side down. Pleat the cloth so that the pudding has room to rise, and tie the cloth with string beneath the basin rim. Bring the cloth ends over the top of the basin and tie them together to form a handle.

**Steaming the pudding.** Place a trivet in a large pan and lower the pudding basin onto it. Pour boiling water into the pan until the pudding basin is half immersed. Cover the pan and simmer the pudding for about nine hours, adding boiling water as necessary.

**Serving.** Remove the basin from the pan, using the tied ends of the cloth as a handle. Uncover the pudding and unmold it onto an inverted plate. Decorate the pudding with holly. Just before serving, pour warm brandy over the top of the pudding; hold a lighted match near the pudding to ignite the brandy.

## A Wax Seal for Storage

**Brushing with wax.** Remove the cloth and paper from the cooked, cooled pudding. Brush parchment or wax paper with vegetable oil and tie it tightly, oiled side down, over the basin with string. To make an airtight seal, melt paraffin over simmering water; brush the paper on the top and around the sides with the melted wax. Stored in a cool, dry place, the pudding will keep for over a year. To serve the pudding, remove the paper, scrape any wax off the basin and steam for two hours.

# 3

# Crepes, Omelets and Fried Desserts
## Imaginative Uses of High Heat

Although pan frying and deep frying are commonly associated with savory dishes, these cooking methods can be used to make an array of delicate desserts. Pan frying—cooking food over high heat with a minimum of fat or oil—produces what are perhaps the most versatile desserts of all: souffléed omelets *(pages 48-49)* and the paper-thin pancakes called crepes *(pages 44-45)*. The basic composition of the desserts could hardly be more simple: An omelet contains nothing more than eggs and sugar, and a crepe is made from an egg, flour, milk and butter batter. However, both can be wrapped around a seemingly endless variety of fillings *(recipes, pages 126-131)*, including sugared fruit, fruit purées, preserves and chocolate. Crepes, in addition, can be folded over a soufflé and baked in the oven *(page 46)*, or they may be stacked in filled layers to form a kind of cake *(page 88)*.

Deep frying—immersing foods in bubbling oil—is a similarly productive method. While the best-known deep-fried desserts are pastries such as fritters *(recipes, pages 131-133)*, almost any food, including flower petals, pieces of fruit, custard and sweetened cheese, may be cooked this way. The only requirements are that the food be stiff enough to hold its shape as it cooks and that it be given a coating—batter or bread crumbs and egg—to keep it from disintegrating in the oil. During cooking, the coating hardens to a crisp crust—a pleasing contrast to the tender ingredients it encloses.

In pan frying and deep frying alike, proper equipment is the key to success. Crepes and omelets must cook quickly and evenly and—to prevent greasiness—should be fried with the absolute minimum of butter or oil. They are best made in cast-iron or carbon-steel pans that have been rendered slick by seasoning *(page 44)*. Inexpensive pans shaped especially for preparing either crepes or omelets are available, and many cooks keep them for no other purpose than the making of these desserts.

A deep-frying pan need only be tall enough to prevent the oil from splattering or spilling. Because the oil's temperature must be carefully regulated *(page 50)*, a deep-frying thermometer will prove a very useful tool. If you do not have a thermometer, test the oil by dropping a bread cube into it; when the oil is the right temperature, the cube of bread will brown in 60 seconds.

gleaming wine syrup drenches a
w of crepes rolled around poached
s. Peaches, apricots or plums may
e substituted for the figs, and the fruit
epes, once assembled, may be
rved with a sabayon or fruit sauce
stead of wine syrup; or they may be
mply dotted with sugar and butter and
azed quickly under the broiler.

# How to Achieve the Perfect Crepe

Whether crepes are served with a sprinkling of sugar and lemon juice, rolled or folded around a filling *(page 46)* or suffused with a warm sauce *(page 47)*, the ingredients for the batter remain the same: eggs, flour, milk and melted butter, which helps keep the thin pancakes from sticking as they cook. These ingredients should be whisked together just until they blend: Overbeating toughens the gluten in the flour, producing an elastic batter that spreads unevenly in the pan. For this reason, many cooks let the assembled batter rest for an hour to give the gluten time to soften—an essential step if the batter is mixed in a blender or food processor.

To ensure that the crepes cook evenly and can be easily turned, choose a heavy cast-iron or steel pan with sloping sides. Season a new, uncoated pan to give it a nonstick surface *(box, right)*.

As the crepes finish cooking, stack them in a plate over a pan of warm water *(Step 4)* to keep them hot and moist. If you do not plan to use them at once, remove the stack from the heat, cover it with plastic wrap and set it aside; the crepes will stay tender for up to six hours.

## Seasoning a Crepe Pan

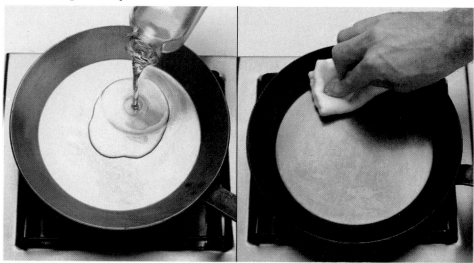

**Seasoning a new crepe pan.** Wash and dry the pan, pour in ¼ inch [6 mm.] of oil *(left)* and set the pan over low heat until the oil darkens and smokes. Remove the pan from the heat, let it cool, pour out the oil and wipe the pan dry with a cloth or paper towels *(right)*. The pan is now ready for use. Never wash the crepe pan; if you do, you will have to reseason it. If a crepe should stick during cooking, remove any batter residue by rubbing the pan with salt. To prevent rusting during storage, always wipe the crepe pan lightly with a well-oiled cloth before storing it.

1 **Forming the crepe.** Wipe the pan with an oiled cloth or paper towel. Set the pan over medium heat. When a light haze forms above the pan, ladle in a small amount of batter *(left)*; the batter should sizzle as it touches the hot metal. At once, tilt and roll the pan to spread the batter as thin as possible *(center)*, then pour any liquid, surface batter back into the mixing bowl *(right)*.

## A Well-blended Batter

1 **Blending the ingredients.** Sift flour and a pinch of salt into a mixing bowl. Form a well in the center of the flour, break eggs into the well and gradually whisk them into the flour, working outward from the center of the bowl. When the mixture is free of lumps, whisk in milk *(above)*.

2 **Flavoring the batter.** When the batter is smooth, add melted butter. If you like, pour in a dash of brandy or liqueur *(above)*. Add a little sugar, unless you intend to use a very sweet filling for the cooked crepes. Stir gently to blend the ingredients. Cover the bowl and let the batter rest for one hour.

3 **Testing the consistency.** Crepe batter should have the consistency of light cream and run freely from the spoon *(above)*. If the batter is too thick, gradually whisk in a little more milk. If the batter is thin, simply let it rest longer.

2 **Removing excess batter.** Use a narrow-bladed spatula to cut off any trail left on the pan when excess batter was poured out. Replace the pan over the heat and cook the crepe until its upper surface looks dry and almost opaque, and the edges begin to curl — after about 10 to 15 seconds.

3 **Turning the crepe.** Free the edges of the crepe by running the spatula around the sides of the pan. The edges will be cool enough to touch: Hold one side of the crepe with your fingers *(above)* and flip the crepe over. Alternatively, you can slide the spatula underneath the crepe to turn it.

4 **Stacking the crepes.** The second side of the crepe will cook in only eight seconds and will be paler. Slide the crepe onto a warmed plate. If the pan looks dry, oil it again. The batter tends to separate; stir it before making a fresh crepe. Stack the finished crepes in a dish over a pan of warm water.

## Rolling Crepes around Fruit

**A fruit filling.** Peel, core or pit the fruit as necessary; cut firm fruit, such as the tart app shown here, into thin slices. Simmer the fruit with a bit of butter until soft. Add sugar to tast Put a little fruit near one edge on the paler side of each crepe, roll up the crepe *(left)* a place it, flap side down, in a buttered bakin dish. Dot the crepes with butter and sprinkle them with sugar. Bake them in a 350° F. [180° C.] oven for approximately 10 minute: To serve each crepe, slip a spoon beneath and steady it with a fork *(below)*.

## Wrapping up a Soufflé

**A surprise soufflé filling.** Prepare a sweet soufflé mixture *(recipe, page 128)*, flavoring it with fruit liqueur. Put a heaping spoonful of the soufflé mixture onto the darker side of each crepe *(above)*; the filling will expand during cooking, so do not add too much. Fold each crepe in half over the filling and place it in a buttered baking dish. Sprinkle the crepes with sugar and bake them in a preheated 425° F. [220° C.] oven for seven or eight minutes. Serve at once *(right)* with a Champagne sabayon sauce *(box, page 21)*.

pes suzette *(recipe, page 126)*, per-s the most famous of crepe desserts, sesses elemental appeal. To make it, es *(pages 44-45)* are folded around auce of butter, sugar, orange juice orange liqueur. When the crepes are fly heated, the sauce suffuses them h a rich but delicate citrus flavor.

he chief challenge of this dessert lies in the preparation of the sauce. Butter, being a fat, does not absorb liquids easily. To incorporate the fruit juice and liqueur as smoothly as possible, you first must cream the butter—beat it with sugar to aerate and soften it. Creaming is easily done by hand, as shown below, or with an electric mixer or food processor. When the butter is fluffy, beat in the juice and liqueur, drop by drop, making sure each drop is absorbed before adding the next.

You can vary crepes suzette by using tangerine juice instead of orange juice. Although some cooks douse the crepes with spirits and set them afire, purists believe that this ruins the presentation. In the words of one famous chef, flaming crepes suzette are "operetta, not cuisine."

**1 Creaming the butter.** To make the butter pliable, press it against the sides of a mixing bowl with a wooden spoon while adding sugar gradually. When the mixture is soft, beat it with a whisk until it is pale and fluffy.

**2 Adding flavoring.** Drop by drop, whisk the orange juice into the creamed butter-and-sugar mixture, beating constantly. When the orange juice has been completely absorbed, gradually beat in the orange liqueur.

**3 Assembling the crepes.** Place a spoonful of the sauce on the paler side of each crepe. With the flat side of a knife blade, spread the sauce over the crepe.

**4 Folding the crepes.** Fold each crepe in half over the sauce to make a semicircle. Then fold the semicircle in half, corner to corner, to make a wedge. Place the folded crepe in a buttered pan, its point toward the center of the pan. Repeat with the rest of the crepes, overlapping them to cover the bottom of the pan.

**5 Heating and serving.** Dust the crepes with confectioners' sugar, then sprinkle them with orange liqueur and, if you like, strips of blanched orange peel *(page 11)*. Place the assembly in a preheated 350° F. [180° C.] oven for five to 10 minutes; serve the crepes as soon as they are heated through.

# The Dessert Omelet: A Stove-Top Soufflé

Fluffy dessert omelets—as quickly made and as readily varied as crepes—are essentially soufflés cooked on top of the stove rather than in the oven. As with ordinary omelets, eggs are the fundamental ingredient, but their treatment is quite different; the eggs are separated and the whites beaten to soft peaks, then gently incorporated into yolks that have been sweetened and perhaps flavored by vanilla, grated lemon peel or a liqueur. When the mixture is cooked, the air trapped in the egg whites expands, giving the omelet its pillowy puff.

As with a crepe, the dessert omelet's success depends on using the right pan and on carefully regulating the cooking heat. The pan should be a flat-bottomed one that heats evenly, and its surface should be very smooth, to keep the omelet from sticking. The pan used in this demonstration is a traditional omelet pan, seasoned as described on page 44; its curving sides make it easy to roll the finished omelet onto a plate. Any smooth, heavy pan with sides that slant outward will do, however.

Preheat the pan until it is hot enough to set the bottom of the omelet quickly, but not so hot that the bottom overcooks and the top loses its creaminess. Use a bit of butter, as described in Step 2, to test the temperature of the pan before adding the omelet mixture.

The actual cooking of the omelet is a brief affair indeed. A three-egg omelet, which will serve two people, should be done in no more than two to three minutes and should be served as soon as it is done; an overcooked omelet will be dry and heavy. To keep the mixture from deflating, touch it as little and as lightly as possible during cooking.

Once the basic omelet is cooked, it may be folded (Step 6) and served with only a sprinkling of sugar. Alternatively, it can be folded around any of a variety of fillings, from fresh or preserved fruit to melted chocolate. For an eye-catching finish, you can dust the omelet with confectioners' sugar and brand it with hot skewers, as in this demonstration. Or, for a more dramatic presentation, you can sprinkle the omelet with a little heated liqueur or brandy and ignite it.

1 **Combining the eggs.** Separate the eggs, and beat the yolks with sugar and a pinch of salt until the sugar dissolves. Beat the whites until they form soft peaks (pages 14-15). Pour the yolks onto the whites and, with a spatula, fold the mixture gently together until it becomes a streaky yellow-white.

2 **Heating the pan.** Place the omelet pan over moderate heat; after about ⊙ minute, drop a pat of butter into the pan. If the butter sizzles and immediat begins to brown, the pan is ready. Quickly wipe off the test butter with ⊙ paper towel and then wipe fresh butter over the bottom of the pan.

6 **Folding the omelet.** Slip a narrow, flexible spatula under the unfilled half of the omelet, and lift and fold the unfilled half over the filled one. Press the folded omelet halves gently together with the flat side of the spatula blade.

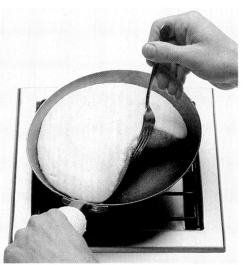

**3** **Adding the eggs.** Immediately pour the omelet mixture into the pan. Smooth the top of the mixture lightly with a fork so that the omelet is a uniform thickness, but do not let the fork touch the bottom of the pan; this would prevent the omelet from setting evenly.

**4** **Finishing the omelet.** After two minutes, when the edges of the omelet are dry and the center creamy, run the fork around its edges to loosen it. Then gently lift one edge of the omelet to inspect the bottom. It should be golden brown. Put the pan under a preheated broiler for 30 seconds to firm up the top.

**5** **Adding a filling.** Remove the pan from the heat and quickly spoon some of the filling — such as the sugared strawberries used here — in a line across the center of the omelet. Add the rest of the filling on one side of the line to ease the folding of the omelet.

**7** **Serving.** Tilt the pan over a warm plate and slide the spatula under the omelet so that you can ease the omelet gently onto the plate *(left)*. Sprinkle a thick layer of confectioners' sugar over the omelet and press a very hot metal skewer — preheated over a high flame or under the broiler — into the sugar to caramelize it and form an attractive surface design *(inset)*.

# A Deep-fried Cream in a Crisp Shell

Deep frying is enlisted to produce numerous desserts. Among the best-known are fritters—small pieces of fruit or even delicate flower petals *(recipe, page 131)* that are coated with a starchy batter, then cooked in deep, hot oil so that they will emerge crisp on the outside but still tender within. Less familiar are deep-fried desserts based on soft, creamy ingredients such as ricotta cheese or the custard used in this demonstration *(recipe, page 132)*. The principles for frying, however, remain the same. Fragile ingredients are covered with a protective coating—here, bread crumbs and beaten egg instead of batter—that hardens into a crisp shell during cooking and prevents the contents from disintegrating in the intense heat of the oil.

Creamy ingredients must, of course, be firm enough to form into small shapes that may easily be coated and fried. The custard shown here actually is almost as stiff as cream cheese: In addition to the egg yolks and milk most custards include, it contains flour, which gives it extra body. If ricotta is used instead, it should be drained of excess moisture *(page 82)* before it is shaped and coated.

For adequate protection, the custard must be completely covered by its egg-and-bread-crumb coating; otherwise, the dessert would absorb too much oil—and heat. Your fingers are the best tools for spreading the coating *(Step 5)*.

Another critical factor in the making of these desserts is the temperature of the frying oil; it must be kept between 365° and 375° F. [186° and 190° C.]. If the cooking medium is too cool, the dessert will absorb oil and emerge soggy and leaden; if it is too hot, the surfaces will burn. A deep-frying thermometer is the best defense against these problems. If you lack one, test the oil by dropping a bread cube into it; if the oil is the right temperature, the bread will brown in 60 seconds. Fry only a few custards at a time to keep the temperature from dropping below the proper level.

1 **Starting the custard.** Stir eggs, sugar and a pinch of salt together in a heavy saucepan until they are thoroughly blended. Then add sifted flour in small batches, stirring after each addition to make sure that the flour is thoroughly incorporated into the eggs.

4 **Chilling the custard.** Transfer the custard to a shallow, buttered pan small enough so that the custard reaches a depth of at least ½ inch [1 cm.]. Smooth the custard so that it is even throughout, and cover the custard — not just the pan — with plastic wrap to prevent a skin from forming. Cool, then refrigerate for at least two hours.

5 **Forming the coating.** Run a knife blade around the edges of the custard to loosen it from the pan. Then cut the custard into 2-inch [5-cm.] squares. Lift each square from the pan with a spatula. Use a fork to dip the square into beaten egg *(left)* and then drop it into fine, dry bread crumbs. Turn the square with your fingers to completely coat the surface with crumbs *(right)*.

**2** **Adding liquids.** In another saucepan, scald milk with a vanilla bean over medium heat until small bubbles form around the sides of the pan. Remove the vanilla bean and slowly pour the milk into the egg-and-flour mixture, whisking steadily *(left)*. Stir chunks of butter into the mixture, whisking until they melt *(right)*.

**3** **Cooking the custard.** Set the saucepan over medium heat and bring the custard to a boil, whisking steadily. Continue to whisk and cook the custard for a minute or two, until it is thick enough to stand up in stiff peaks when lifted on the whisk.

**6** **Frying.** Fill a deep skillet or pan half-full of oil and heat the oil over medium heat to about 365° F. [185° C.]. Put a few custard squares into the oil and deep fry them for two to three minutes, until they are a light golden brown. Use a skimmer to transfer them to paper towels to drain *(above)*. Sprinkle the squares with confectioners' sugar before serving them *(right)*.

# 4

# Frozen Desserts
## The Everyday Miracle
## of Ices and Ice Cream

Adorned with glazed gooseberries and the fragrant pulp of passion fruit, a mango parfait *(pages 58-59)* is sliced for serving. Egg yolks and cream give the parfait its luxurious texture; mango purée, blended into the basic mixture, contributes a rich, golden hue.

Ices and ice creams, a varied group of frozen delicacies that enjoy nearly universal esteem, are easy to make as long as the cook understands the effects of the freezing process. When these mixtures freeze, the water they contain forms crystals of ice. To make the desserts light and smooth, the mixtures must be stirred during the freezing process; this aerates them, preventing the formation of large ice crystals. The only exceptions to the stirring requirement are the very richest ice creams, French parfaits *(pages 58-59)*. Parfaits contain high proportions of egg yolks and cream, both already whipped full of tiny air bubbles that are sufficient to keep the ice crystals small.

For some desserts, such as the water ices demonstrated on pages 54-55, a pleasantly grainy texture is often considered desirable. These sherbets, sorbets, granitas or ices, as they are variously called, may be frozen in ice trays with only occasional stirring to break up the largest crystals. (With no stirring at all, of course, a water ice would emerge from the freezer as a leaden, rock-hard lump.)

Ice creams can be made in ice trays too, but for the proper silky texture, ice-cream mixtures should be continuously and rapidly agitated throughout the freezing process—as must a water ice, if you want a smooth rather than grainy result. The necessary equipment is a hand-operated or electrically powered ice-cream maker, consisting of a mixing container set inside a bucket of crushed ice and rock salt. Rock salt accelerates the melting of the ice and in the process draws heat rapidly from the mixture inside the container, hardening the ice cream more quickly than a freezer would. At the same time, a stationary paddle fitted inside the revolving container churns the mixture, aerating it, and scrapes the container walls—where the temperature is lowest—so that forming ice clusters are broken up and dispersed.

When you are making any frozen dessert, from a simple water ice to an elaborate molded bombe or frozen soufflé *(pages 62-65)*, bear in mind that coldness mutes taste. The mixtures, therefore, should be more strongly flavored than similar, unfrozen desserts. For perfect results, allow all frozen desserts to stand for 30 minutes or so in the refrigerator before serving them. They will soften slightly so that they can be sliced or scooped readily, and they will improve in taste and texture.

# Water Ices: Capturing Clean, Clear Flavor

Water ices, also known as sherbets, sorbets or granitas, are the simplest of frozen desserts, often constituted of nothing more complicated than fruit juices or purées mixed with a light sugar syrup. For extra flavor, some ices include wine or liqueur, and some are given an especially smooth texture by the addition of beaten egg whites *(recipes, pages 135 and 136)*.

Almost any fruit—for example, lemons, pineapples, pears or berries—can form the basis of an ice. An Ogen melon, which is available during the winter at specialty markets, is used in the melon-and-Champagne ice demonstrated here *(recipe, page 136)*, but it could easily be replaced by a cantaloupe or a honeydew melon. Whatever your fruit, it must be of the very best quality and at the peak of freshness if the ice is to have the clear, penetrating flavor that is distinctive of this light dessert.

The texture of the water ice depends on both the blending and the freezing of the ingredients. Begin by making medium sugar syrup *(pages 8-9)* far enough in advance so that it will have time to cool while you purée the fruit and mix it with the other flavorings. Cool syrup blends smoothly with the fruit, and the colder the mixture is when it goes into the freezer, the less time it will need to solidify.

For an ice with a uniform, slightly grainy texture, freeze the ingredients in a metal cake pan or ice tray, as shown here, removing the tray at intervals and stirring the mixture to break up and distribute the ice crystals that form around the edge. Or, for a velvet-smooth ice, freeze the mixture in an ice-cream maker, as described on pages 56-57.

Water ices made by either method may be stored in sealed containers in the freezer, but they are best eaten within a few days, before their fresh flavors fade. If you plan to eat the dessert promptly, an attractive presentation can be devised by serving it in the hollowed shells that the fruit was taken from, as shown opposite.

1 **Making melon purée.** Make a medium sugar syrup *(pages 8-9)* and set it aside to cool. Halve and seed ripe melons. Scoop out the flesh, and refrigerate the shells. Force the flesh through a sieve into a bowl *(above)*. Stir in a little lemon juice to bring out the fruit's flavor. Add about half as much chilled Champagne as you have purée.

2 **Adding sugar syrup.** Blend the cooled syrup into the melon-and-Champagne mixture *(above)*. Pour the mixture into a shallow ice tray and set it in the freezer or the freezing compartment of the refrigerator.

3 **Stirring the mixture.** After about 30 minutes, remove the tray and use a fork to stir the frozen edges of the mixture into the center *(above)*, breaking up any large crystals. Replace the tray in the freezer, and repeat the stirring procedure every hour.

4 **Whisking the ice.** After three to four hours of freezing, the ice mixture be granular and just firm enough to mound up on a spoon. Scrape the mixture from its tray into a chilled bowl, and whisk it until smooth.

## Carving a Natural Container

Hollowed-out oranges, grapefruits and large lemons or limes, as well as the small melon halves shown here, can be carved into perfect containers for individual portions of water ice made from the fruit. Large melons and pineapples will hold enough ice for several people.

Shaping the shells should be done when the fruit is whole. Because of a whole fruit's rigidity, the cuts can be made accurately. After hollowing out round fruit, trim a thin slice from the bottom so that the fruit stands upright. And when cutting out melon or pineapple flesh, leave a layer ¼ inch [6 mm.] thick to strengthen the shell.

Shell containers should be thoroughly chilled in the refrigerator before use. You can rinse the shells with a little brandy or rum just before filling them; incorporate the brandy into the ice as you give it a final whisking *(Step 4, left)*.

1 **Cutting the melon.** Score a line around the melon's circumference halfway between the ends. Cut deeply around this line in a zigzag pattern *(top)*. Separate the halves *(bottom)*.

2 **Removing the seeds.** With a spoon, scrape the seeds from each half. Then, with a sharp-edged spoon, remove most of the flesh to make the water ice. Refrigerate the shells.

5 **Serving the ice.** Spoon the ice mixture into the chilled melon shells *(right)*, and serve immediately on cracked ice. If you have made the dessert a little in advance, you can keep the filled melon shells in the freezer. Do not leave this particular water ice for more than one to two hours, however, or the Champagne will lose its sparkle and the dessert much of its charm.

# The Art of Ice-Cream Making

The simplest ice cream is just what the name suggests: frozen cream. Sweetened and flavored, heavy cream can be frozen either in an ice tray—as is water ice (*pages 54-55*)—or, for the smoothest texture, churned and frozen in an ice-cream maker, as demonstrated here.

The cream mixture (*recipe, page 166*) should be prepared at least an hour before churning. To blend tastes completely, the cream should be scalded to dissolve the sugar, honey or maple-syrup sweetener, then cooled to room temperature. While hot, the cream can be flavored with coffee beans or a vanilla bean (*page 22*), but extract will lose its taste unless it is added after the cream cools, and liqueurs will slow the freezing process unless they are added after the ice cream has been churned. Fruit purée may be added during churning. Solid flavorings such as chopped fruit or nuts should be folded into fully churned ice cream; otherwise they would impede the churn's dasher, or mixing paddle.

To speed the freezing, chill the sweetened cream before churning it. And refrigerate the metal canister and its dasher until they are frosty cold. Just before churning, crush the ice into chips that you can pack solidly around the canister. The tidiest way to do this is to put ice cubes into a canvas bag and pound them with a mallet or heavy saucepan.

Fill the canister with the cream mixture, set the canister in its place in the bucket and pack the space around it with ice. Add a handful of rock salt—available at hardware stores—for every few inches of ice, distributing the salt in layers. For 4 quarts [4 liters] of ice cream, plan on 15 pounds [7 kg.] of ice and about 1 cup [250 ml.] of salt.

The completed ice cream may be eaten in its soft state, immediately after churning. Or it may be hardened—or ripened—for two to three hours. To harden ice cream, cover the canister tightly and set it in a freezer, or repack the bucket with ice and salt and lay a heavy cloth or newspapers over it. In any case, homemade ice cream should be eaten within one week; after that, its flavor fades.

**1** **Assembling the ice-cream maker.** Pour chilled, sweetened cream into the canister until the canister is about two thirds full; this gives the ice cream room to expand as it is aerated and frozen. Seat the canister firmly in the bucket, place the dasher (*rear*) inside and fit on the canister lid and the crank or motor. Place the assembly on a tray to catch the drained brine.

**5** **Packing the ice cream.** Plunge the wooden spoon vigorously up and down in the ice cream to remove air pockets; the pockets might produce large crystals when the ice cream hardens. Smooth the surface of the ice cream.

**6** **Ripening the ice cream.** Seal the canister with a double layer of foil and the lid over it. Place it in the freezer for two to three hours to allow the ice cream to harden. About 30 minutes before serving, transfer the canister to the refrigerator to soften the ice cream.

2 **Adding ice.** To prevent pieces of ice from jamming the canister, switch on an electric ice-cream maker before packing it with crushed ice and rock salt. Add about 1 cup [¼ liter] of cold water *(above)* to start the freezing. If you use a hand churn, begin the cranking slowly so the canister does not jam.

3 **Testing consistency.** Keeping the bucket filled with ice and salt, churn the mixture for 20 to 30 minutes, until a hand churn becomes hard to crank or an electric motor sounds labored. Wipe off the canister top and remove it carefully. Lift out a spoonful of the mixture. It should have the consistency of very stiffly whipped cream.

4 **Adding fruit.** Remove the dasher and use a rubber spatula to push the clinging ice cream back into the canister. With a wooden spoon, gently stir chilled, crushed fruit — in this case, peaches mixed with a little lemon juice — into the ice cream.

7 **Serving.** Anchor the canister firmly with one hand, hold the scoop perpendicular to the surface and cut through the ice cream, around the circumference of the canister *(left)*. The ice cream will roll into the scoop to form a perfect globe *(above)*.

# An Egg-rich Mixture Frozen in a Mold

The richest, smoothest ice creams are frozen custards and mousses, which contain egg yolks as well as cream. A custard ice cream *(box, right, bottom)* is based on the pouring custard demonstrated on pages 20-21, but it is made with a lower proportion of egg yolks and substitutes cream for some or all of the milk.

Custard ice creams may be flavored in innumerable ways. Vanilla *(recipe, page 166)*, coffee and chocolate are classic additions; use the techniques described on pages 22-23 to flavor the cream or milk before you make the custard. Brandy, liqueur or pounded nuts, used in the almond ice cream shown here *(recipe, page 142)*, are also popular flavorings.

Custard ice creams may be frozen in ice trays as if they were water ices *(page 54)*, but an ice-cream maker *(pages 56-57)* yields smoother results. Mousse-based ice creams *(right)*, known in France as parfaits, are composed of sugar syrup *(pages 8-9)* beaten with egg yolks until the mixture triples in volume, then combined with an equal quantity of whipped cream. Parfaits may be flavored with liqueurs, coffee or puréed fruit; in the demonstration at top right, sieved, ripe mango provides a rich golden color and an exotic taste *(recipe, page 139)*.

Because a parfait mixture's ingredients are thoroughly aerated, the parfait may be frozen without further stirring. The mold should be metal; this material's efficient heat conduction will help the dessert set and will aid in unmolding. When filling the mold, allow room for the mixture to expand by about 10 per cent. Seal the mold airtight and freeze the mixture for several hours to harden it.

Before unmolding the parfait, soften it in the refrigerator for about 25 minutes; otherwise, the dessert will be hard to cut. To release the dessert, wrap the mold in a towel soaked in warm water; a towel that is too hot would melt the surface of the parfait and blur any decorative pattern.

1 **Beating syrup into yolks.** Make a medium-heavy sugar syrup *(page 9)*. In a pan placed above barely simmering water, beat the egg yolks with the syrup. Whisk steadily until the mixture is light, foamy and triple its original volume — about 10 to 15 minutes.

2 **Adding the flavoring.** Take the pan off the heat and set it in a bowl of ice cubes to stop the cooking process. Continue whisking until the mixture has cooled. Gradually whisk in the flavoring — here, puréed ripe mango. Add a pinch of salt and a little lemon juice to accentuate the flavor of the fruit.

## Churning a Custard Ice Cream

1 **Flavoring the custard base.** For almond ice cream, pound the nuts *(box, page 12)*, then add heated milk and cream. Beat together egg yolks and sugar, and add the almond mixture. Pour into a heavy pan and stir over low heat for five minutes, until the custard thickens *(Step 5, page 21)*.

2 **Preparing for freezing.** When the custard coats a spoon, remove it from the heat and then chill it: Refrigerate it or stir it over ice *(above)*. Strain the custard and pour it into an ice-cream maker or ice trays for freezing.

3 **Finishing the parfait.** Fold an equal volume of lightly whipped heavy cream into the mixture. Pour the mixture into a chilled metal mold to within ½ inch [1 cm.] of the top *(above)*. Cover the mold — with a lid, if it has one, or foil — and set it in a freezer for at least four hours, or until it is solid.

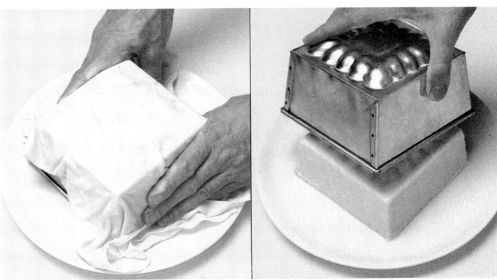

4 **Unmolding.** Soak a towel in warm water and wring it out. Remove the lid or foil from the mold, put a serving plate on top and invert mold and plate together. Wrap the warm towel around the mold for a few seconds *(left)*. Remove the towel and lift up the mold to free the ice cream without spoiling its shape *(right)*. If the surface has melted slightly, smooth it with the flat of a knife and refreeze the parfait for a few minutes.

3 **Freezing and churning.** Churn for about half an hour *(pages 56-57)*. Or freeze the ice cream in covered ice trays for about three hours, pouring it into a bowl and whisking it smooth at one-hour intervals. Serve the finished ice cream as it is or use it in a composite dish such as a bombe *(pages 62-63)*.

5 **Serving.** If you like, decorate the parfait with glazed fruit — here, gooseberries *(page 10)*. Pour over a fruit sauce — in this case, the scooped-out pulp of passion fruit (available at specialty shops in spring and fall) sweetened with light syrup.

# Inventive Interplays of Ice Creams and Sauces

Ice creams and sherbets form the bases of a wide range of assembled desserts *(pages 60-65)*. The simplest are sundaes —scoops of ice cream bathed in a sauce. When a sundae is made by layering the ice cream and sauce in a tall glass, as shown here, the result is called a parfait, although it is quite different from the classic French dessert *(pages 58-59)*. No matter how a sundae is assembled, the cook has a free hand in choosing ingredients; the dessert may include any ice cream or sherbet—or several different ones—and any of a plethora of sauces.

Two sorts of sauces—fruit purées and liqueurs—require no cooking. You can create a sundae by garnishing ice cream with coffee, almond or orange liqueur. Fruit sauces are almost as straightforward: Crush any soft fruit—peaches or raspberries, for example—and mix with sugar, allowing 2 to 4 tablespoons [30 to 60 ml.] of sugar for each cup of fruit.

Cooked sauces require a little more effort but, if well covered, will keep as long as two weeks in the refrigerator. Many consist of a sugar-syrup base *(pages 8-9)* mixed with fruits or nuts *(recipes, pages 163 and 164)*. Others are, in effect, liquid candy. They include sugar, water and often butter or cream plus such flavorings as chocolate *(recipe, page 163)* or coffee. Butterscotch sauce, based on brown sugar, corn syrup, butter and water *(demonstration, right; recipe, page 164)*, belongs to this group. The molasses in the brown sugar gives the sauce its characteristic taste, and the corn syrup contributes body; cream, added after the sauce is cooked, serves as further enrichment.

Temperature regulation is important when making butterscotch or any other sugar-based sauce. For a thin sauce, heat the ingredients until they reach 234° to 240° F. [112° to 115° C.]—the so-called soft-ball stage. For a thick butterscotch, heat the sauce to 244° to 248° F. [118° to 120° C.]—the firm-ball stage. The stages can be judged without using a candy thermometer *(Step 3)*.

Cool the sauce to room temperature before assembling a sundae: Butterscotch should not be so warm that it melts the ice cream. If the sauce has been chilled, remove it from the refrigerator and let it warm so that it pours easily.

1 **Starting the syrup.** In a saucepan, combine butter and sugar with water. Add brown sugar *(above)* that has been tightly packed in its measuring cup to eliminate any air pockets that might distort the measurement.

2 **Adding more sweetener.** Pour dark corn syrup into the pan and stir the mixture over moderate heat until t butter and sugar have dissolved. Let ▶ mixture cook, uncovered, until it boils.

5 **Adding cream.** Whisk light cream into the mixture until the cream is fully incorporated and the sauce is an even, tawny brown. Cover the sauce and set it aside to cool to room temperature for immediate use, or cover tightly and place it in the refrigerator.

6 **Assembling the sundae.** Put about 2 tablespoons [30 ml.] of butterscotch sauce into a tall, narrow glass and add a scoop of firm ice cream — here, vanilla. Alternate sauce and ice-cream layers to fill the glass, ending with ice cream.

**Testing consistency.** Stirring occasionally, boil the mixture for five to eight minutes until it reaches 234° to 248° F. [112° to 120° C.], depending on the consistency you desire. Lacking a candy thermometer, drop a bit of the mixture into ice water, then form it into a ball. The ball flattens of its own accord at the soft-ball stage, but at the firm-ball stage holds its shape unless pressed.

4 **Flavoring.** Immediately remove the pan from the heat and dip the pan bottom in ice water for a few seconds to arrest the cooking. Then stir in vanilla extract and add a pinch of salt to intensify the flavor of the sauce.

7 **Marbling.** You may leave the sundae in layers or marble it by sliding a knife blade up and down around the inner surface of the glass *(above)* to blur the boundaries between the ice cream and the sauce. Garnish the sundae with whipped cream *(right)*, nuts *(page 12)* or praline *(page 13)*.

# Packing Flavor within Flavor

A bombe, so called because of its traditional shape, is a layered and molded assembly of ices and ice creams that excites the palate with contrasts of texture as well as of flavor. The bombe here, called a New York ice cream *(recipe, page 142)*, is a concoction of liqueur-flavored fruit and chestnut parfait enclosed in a shell of almond-flavored custard ice cream *(box, pages 58-59)*. Other ingredients can produce equally pleasing results *(recipes, pages 142-144)*; the only rule for a bombe is that at least two textures and flavors of ice cream or water ice be used. You can prepare the components especially for this dessert—or make creative use of leftover ice creams or water ices.

Bombe molds are traditionally made of copper, a good heat conductor that facilitates both freezing and unmolding. If you cannot obtain such a mold, you can improvise with a deep metal mixing bowl or even a charlotte mold.

**1 Lining the mold.** Set a chilled mold in a bowl of ice. Line it with a ½-inch [1-cm.] layer of softened ice cream — in this case, almond —reserving some ice cream in the freezer for sealing the mold *(Step 6)*. Smooth the ice cream to cover the interior of the mold completely; return the mold to the freezer while you prepare the other ingredients.

**2 Making a chestnut parfait.** Sieve peeled, softened chestnuts *(pages 70-7* into a mixing bowl. Add egg yolks and sugar to the chestnut purée and place the bowl over a pan of water, heated to just below the simmering poi Whisk the mixture until it is smooth, glossy and doubled in volume *(above)* in about 10 to 15 minutes.

**5 Filling the bombe.** Take the mold from the freezer and again set it in a bowl of ice. Use the fruit to fill the mold to about half its depth, then add the chestnut parfait to within ¾ inch [2 cm.] of its top *(above)*. Cover the parfait with the remainder of the raspberries.

**6 Finishing the bombe.** Seal the mold with a final layer of the almond-flavored custard ice cream reserved for this purpose *(Ste 1)*. Smooth the custard ice with the back of a spoon *(above)*. Place a circle of wax paper on top of the ice cream, then put the on the mold or cover it tightly with aluminum foil. Freeze the bombe for four hours or, if you wish, overnight.

**3 Flavoring the parfait.** Take the mixing bowl from the heat and set it over a bowl of ice. Stir briskly with a spatula until the mixture is cold. Remove the bowl from the ice and beat in a liqueur or brandy flavoring, such as the Curaçao used here. Fold a roughly equal quantity of whipped cream into the parfait mixture and set the bowl aside.

**4 Preparing the fruit filling.** Sprinkle kirsch *(above)* and sugar over soft fruit — in this case, raspberries. Toss the fruit gently to coat every piece. You can include the fruit whole in the bombe, as here, or purée it first. If you use a fruit purée, freeze it until it is somewhat firm before you include it in the bombe.

**7 Unmolding and serving.** Take the mold from the freezer. Remove the lid or foil and the wax paper; wrap a towel soaked in warm water around the mold, and invert the mold onto a chilled plate. Remove the mold and let the bombe soften in the refrigerator for about 30 minutes before serving *(right)*.

# The Splendid Structure of a Frozen Soufflé

A frozen soufflé is a magnificent illusion. Although it is served in a soufflé dish—over which it rises proudly, like a perfectly baked soufflé—it is made entirely of a rich parfait mixture *(pages 58-59)* that is divided up into several variously flavored batches and frozen layer by layer.

The rainbow effect in this demonstration *(recipe, page 146)* is achieved by means of layers flavored with pistachio paste *(page 12)*, raspberry purée *(box, page 68)*, coffee and toasted, crushed hazelnuts and almonds *(page 12)*. You can, of course, substitute any flavorings you wish. The sides of the dish are extended with a paper collar to raise the frozen soufflé to an impressive height—up to three times that of the dish, depending on the size of your freezer and the time you allow for freezing. Each layer must be frozen firm before the next is added.

The parfait base can be made by beating sugar syrup into egg yolks over heat *(Step 1, page 58)*, or you can beat sugar directly into the yolks, as here.

**1 Adding sugar to egg yolks.** Place egg yolks in a bowl and set it over a pan of water kept at a low simmer. Slowly pour sugar onto the yolks. For extra flavor, include some vanilla sugar, made by burying a vanilla bean for about a week in a closed container of sugar.

**2 Whisking the mixture.** Whisk the egg yolks and sugar over low heat for about 10 minutes, until the sugar dissolves and no trace of graininess remains. At this point, the mixture will have tripled in volume, and will be pale, glossy and thick enough to form a ribbon *(Step 3, page 20)*. Remove the bowl and set it over ice to cool.

**3 Adding whipped cream.** Continue to beat the mixture over ice until it is so thick that it leaves the sides of the bowl. Remove the bowl from the ice. In a separate bowl, whip heavy cream until it forms soft peaks, then fold the cream into the egg mixture *(above)*.

**4 Flavoring the mixture.** Divide the mixture equally among as many bowls as you have flavorings. Fold each flavoring into a bowl of the mixture and chill in the refrigerator.

**Building up the layers.** Wrap a double layer of wax or parchment paper around a soufflé dish, securing it with paper clips or with string, as shown on page 33. Set the dish on a tray to minimize handling; add the first layer of flavored mixture *(right)*. Put the dish and tray in the freezer for 30 minutes, or until the first layer is firm to the touch, then add the next layer *(far right)*. Continue in this manner until you have completed the desired number of layers.

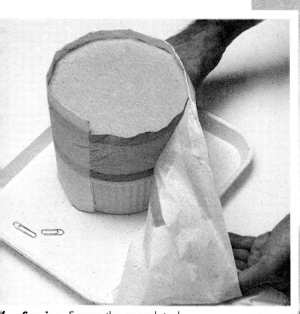

**Serving.** Freeze the completed frozen soufflé for three to six hours, then gently peel off its paper collar. Set the frozen soufflé in the refrigerator to soften for 30 minutes. Decorate the dessert with chocolate scrolls *(box, page 11)* and glazed pistachio nuts, as here, or any other garnish you prefer.

# Fruit
## A Prodigal Source of Color and Flavor

Fruits play a part in countless desserts, flavoring, coloring and garnishing all manner of assemblies. But no matter what its function, the fruit is subject to one overriding dictum: It must be perfect in quality and absolutely fresh and ripe if the dessert is to be superlative. For this reason, you should plan your desserts, whenever possible, according to the fruits that are in season in your area. In some cases, of course, local origin is not important: Citrus fruits, with their thick, protective skins, can be picked ripe and shipped long distances with little loss of quality. But most fruits—berries, peaches and plums among them—are soft when ripe; if picked green for transport, they will be dull tasting and mealy.

When choosing fruits to include in desserts, judge quality and ripeness by appearance, softness and fragrance. Apricots, for example, should look velvety and feel firm, but not rock-hard; peaches should have a rosy blush and a sweet scent. A ripe pineapple has a tangy odor, and its base is dry and yields to light pressure; similarly, a fully ripe melon is fragrant and feels slightly soft at the stem end.

If destined for a sauce or garnish *(pages 49 and 60)* or for a filling in molded desserts *(page 63),* fruit may simply be trimmed and sugared. In many desserts, however, fruit plays a more central role, and preliminary preparation becomes more elaborate. Fruits such as apples, pears, peaches or cherries can be poached in sugar syrup to soften and flavor them, then served alone or combined with meringues, custards and a wide variety of other ingredients.

Poached fruits, as well as very soft raw fruits such as berries, are frequently puréed to transform them into foundations for a range of attractive desserts. The simplest of these creations require no cooking. For the traditional English dessert known as a fool *(pages 68-69),* puréed fruit is folded into whipped cream; for a feathery whip *(page 69)* the purée is combined with stiffly beaten egg whites. Purées also can be incorporated into soufflés *(page 33)* or molded and conjoined with whole poached fruits *(pages 76-77).* And some of the most pleasing effects of all are achieved by combining puréed fruit with bread. If the bread-encased fruit is baked, it becomes a crisp-crusted charlotte *(page 74);* if it is weighted and chilled for several hours, the result is a juicy summer pudding *(page 75).*

avy cream garnishes a moist, fruit-
d summer pudding. To make this
glish dessert, raspberries and
rants were poached, then packed into
read-lined mold; overnight
igeration allowed the bread to
sorb their flavors and rosy colors.

# Fruit Purée: A Natural Fundament

The way to reduce fruit to a purée depends on both the nature of the fruit *(box, below)* and the texture you desire. Very soft fruits such as raspberries can be puréed raw, but many fruits must first be gently cooked to soften their tough fibers. To avoid watery results with a cooked-fruit purée, simmer the fruit with no more than a soupçon of butter or water—just enough to prevent scorching—and strain off any liquid the fruit releases. You can reclaim these juices by concentrating them over high heat and stirring them back into the fruit.

The puréeing operation itself determines the texture of the finished purée. If you want a relatively coarse texture—to add contrast to smoother ingredients, for example—purée the fruit through a food mill, using a coarse disk *(Step 2, right)*. For a smooth dessert such as the fruit-flavored Bavarian cream shown on pages 26-27, you can make a fine pulp by puréeing the fruit in an electric food processor or by forcing it through a strainer or a fine-meshed sieve.

Certain molded desserts such as apple charlotte *(page 74)* require a purée that is stiff and dry so that the dessert will not collapse when it is unmolded. Before adding the purée to the other ingredients, cook it over medium heat for at least 15 minutes to evaporate any excess liquid, stirring continuously to prevent the fruit from burning.

For most other desserts, the purée can be used as is. In the fool demonstrated at right *(recipe, page 98)*, a coarse-textured rhubarb purée is sweetened and folded into whipped cream. (The amusing name of this dessert is said to come from the French *fouler*, meaning "to crush.") An equally simple treatment is the whip—known as a huff in England—shown at right, opposite: Gooseberry purée, egg whites and sugar syrup are beaten into a snowy mass *(recipe, page 99)*. Either dessert can be made with any puréed fruit, raw or cooked, but the ideal candidates for use in fools are fruits that have sufficient acidity to counterbalance the richness of the cream.

## Mellowing with Cream

**Cooking the rhubarb.** Cut off rhubarb leaves and slice the stalks into 2 inch [5-cm.] pieces. Put the pieces in a heavy saucepan with about half of their volume of brown sugar and a knob of butter. Stir the rhubarb and sugar over low heat until they are well mixed. Cover the pan and cook the mixture until the fruit is tender—20 to 30 minutes.

## Choosing the Best Puréeing Method

**Puréeing soft fruits.** Delicate fruits such as bananas, melons or raspberries *(above)* may be puréed raw. Force them through a strainer, using a heavy pestle or the back of a spoon. For raspberries or any similarly acid fruits, use a strainer that has plastic or stainless-steel mesh; aluminum could interact with the acid, causing discoloration and an off taste.

**Puréeing hard fruits.** Apples, winter pears and any other fibrous fruits should be peeled, cored, simmered until tender, strained to remove excess liquid, and then pressed through a food mill or sieve. The drum sieve shown here is helpful for dealing with large quantities of fruit.

**Puréeing tough fruit.** Pineapple—too fibrous, even when cooked, to be puréed through a food mill—is easily reduced to pulp in an electric food processor. The machine can, of course, purée any firm-textured fruit in a few seconds, but its whirling blades would liquefy soft fruits.

**Puréeing the rhubarb.** Pour the cooked rhubarb into a colander and allow excess liquid to drain off. Then, using a food mill set over a bowl, purée the drained rhubarb a few ladlefuls at a time. Set the purée aside to cool.

**3 Adding the cream.** Beat heavy cream until it forms soft peaks, and stir in the cooled purée *(above)*. Add more sugar to taste and, if you like, a flavoring such as liqueur or almond extract. Spoon the rhubarb fool into individual glasses, cover tightly and refrigerate for about two hours. Then serve, accompanied by cookies such as the shortcake wedges shown at right.

## htening with Egg Whites

**Puréeing the fruit.** Put whole gooseberries in a pan with a little sugar and just enough water to cover the base of the pan; cook, covered, over low heat for 20 to 30 minutes, until the fruit is soft. Strain off any liquid. Purée the fruit in a food mill, then let it cool. Lightly beat egg whites until they are foamy. Add the purée to the whites *(above)*.

**2 Whisking the mixture.** Make a small-thread sugar syrup *(pages 8-9)* and allow it to cool. Whisk the gooseberry purée and egg whites together until the mixture forms soft peaks. Gradually pour in the syrup, whisking continuously to blend the mixture evenly.

**3 Serving the whip.** Continue whisking until the whip stands up in firm peaks; the sugar syrup will help to stabilize the puffy whites. Serve the whip at once in individual glasses or in a glass bowl *(above)*. If left to stand, the whip will slowly subside.

# A Rich, Moist Purée of Chestnuts

In culinary terms, chestnuts defy classification. They certainly are nuts, hard shells and all; but dessert cooks, guided by the tenderness and sweet flavor of chestnuts' meat, prefer to treat them as fruits. Chestnuts can be poached and served whole in syrup, for example *(recipe, page 117)*, or puréed and used as a flavoring for desserts such as candied-chestnut pudding *(recipe, page 118)*, or as a dessert in their own right *(demonstration, right; recipe, page 118)*.

No matter what their destiny, chestnuts must be cooked in two stages: the first to make peeling possible, and the second to tenderize the meat. Shelling chestnuts and removing the bitter inner skin that covers the meat cannot be accomplished when the nuts are raw, and is a tedious job even when they have been cooked. Before the preparatory cooking, make crossed slits in the shells. Then either parboil the nuts—as here—or roast them in a 350° F. [180° C.] oven for about 20 minutes. Remove the shells and skins while the nuts are still warm, then simmer the chestnuts in sweetened, vanilla-flavored milk until they are tender. The nuts are now ready to be eaten whole, or they may be puréed through a food mill.

You can serve a chestnut purée in a simple mound, but for a more inventive presentation, use a ricer—a food press available in kitchen-equipment shops—to shape the purée. When forced through the holes in the ricer *(Step 4, right)*, the purée emerges in long threads. Or shape threads by forcing the purée through the holes of a colander or a large-holed, flat grater with the back of a spoon.

Only a firm mixture can be formed into threads; if the purée seems too liquid after it has been through the food mill, dry it out by cooking it in a pan set over low heat *(Step 3)*. Adding a little sugar at this stage helps to thicken the purée.

Serve the purée either chilled or at room temperature. Topped with whipped cream, the dessert is called "Mont Blanc" after its resemblance to the snow-capped Alpine peak. If you like, you can mold the riced chestnuts into a more formal shape, as shown in the box on the opposite page.

**1** **Shelling the chestnuts.** With a small, sharp knife, cut a cross through the shell on the flat side of each chestnut. The longer the arms of the cross, the easier it will be to peel the chestnut. Parboil the chestnuts for 10 minutes. Take the pan off the heat. Lift out the chestnuts a few at a time, leaving the rest to soak. Cut away the shell from each chestnut *(left)*, and if the skin does not pull away with the shell, peel it off with a knife or your fingernails *(right)*.

**4** **Ricing the purée.** Using a spoon or a wooden spatula, fill a ricer with the chestnut purée. Hold the ricer over the center of a large serving plate. Press the handles together to force the purée through the holes in the bottom of the ricer; the purée will emerge in long threads. Repeat until all of the purée has been riced.

2 **Tenderizing the chestnuts.** Place the chestnuts in a pan and cover them with milk. Add sugar and a vanilla bean. Bring the milk to a boil, then cover the pan, reduce the heat and simmer until the milk has been absorbed — about 45 minutes. Remove the vanilla bean. Purée the chestnuts through a food mill.

3 **Drying the purée.** The chestnut purée should be smooth, but firm enough to hold together in a mass. If the purée is runny, put it in a pan over low heat. Add sugar to taste, and stir until the purée firms. If it becomes dry and crumbly, stir in a little milk.

## A Cream-capped Nut Mold

For a symmetric presentation, you can fill a ring mold—unoiled, since the soft purée will not stick—with unriced chestnut purée or, as here, you can rice the purée directly into the mold. To give the dessert extra richness, blend egg yolks and butter into the purée off the heat before you rice it. The purée can be unmolded at once, without refrigeration, by inverting the mold and giving it a sharp tap.

1 **Filling the mold.** Force the chestnut purée through a ricer set over a mold, distributing the threads as evenly as possible. Gently push the threads with a spatula to arrange them more uniformly, but avoid crushing them.

5 **Decorating and serving.** Leave the mound of riced purée untouched — manipulating it would mash the fragile threads and spoil the final presentation. Spoon sweetened whipped cream over the threads *(above)* and serve.

2 **Decorating.** Unmold the purée onto a serving plate. Fill the center cavity with whipped cream. Dip a metal spatula in hot water to prevent the cream from sticking to it, and shape the cream into a peak.

# Creating a Pure and Shimmering Jelly

The lightest of all gelatin-stiffened desserts are fruit jellies, simple mixtures of fruit juice and gelatin that, when turned out from a handsome, fluted mold, combine an imposing appearance with a welcome lightness. The translucent jelly in this demonstration is based on calf's-foot gelatin *(demonstration, pages 16-17; recipe, page 164)* mixed with fresh orange juice and garnished with orange segments *(box, below)*. Lime or grapefruit juice may be substituted for the orange juice. And you could replace the homemade gelatin with a commercial product *(recipe, page 147)*.

If you are using calf's-foot gelatin, simply melt it over low heat and stir in strained fruit juice. Add sugar to taste, then pour the mixture into the mold to set. Sweetening is more likely to be needed with commercial gelatin, which contains no sugar.

The flavored jelly should fill your mold almost to the brim; if the dessert must slide more than about ½ inch [1 cm.] when it is unmolded, it may be damaged on impact with the serving plate.

**1 Preparing the juice.** Squeeze the juice from several oranges and, for a tart accent, a lemon. Let the juice stand for 30 minutes, then pour it through a strainer lined with a doubled piece of dampened muslin or cheesecloth. The waiting time allows fragments of pulp to gather in a layer at the top of the juice *(inset)*; the thick layer collects in the cloth and assists the straining process.

## Flawless Orange Segments

**Slicing oranges.** Peel oranges with a knife, removing as much white pith as possible. To separate each segment of orange flesh from the membrane that encloses it, cut down both sides of the segment between the flesh and the membrane. Pull off any clinging bits of membrane and pith with your fingers.

**2 Flavoring the jelly.** Heat calf's-foot gelatin *(pages 16-17)* until barely melted, and measure into a bowl enough gelatin to fill the mold by slightly more than half. Stir in a little less than the same volume of strained juice.

**3 Setting the jelly.** Stand the bowl of jelly in a larger bowl of crushed ice. Stir constantly until the jelly just begins to thicken, then ladle it into a chilled mold. Cover the mold and refrigerate the jelly for at least four hours. Check its solidity by tilting the mold: When the jelly stays firm as the mold is tilted, it is ready to be turned out.

4 **Unmolding on a plate.** Run the tip of a knife around the inside rim of the mold, then dip the entire mold briefly in warm water to loosen the jelly. Invert a plate over the mold. Hold the mold firmly against the plate and smartly turn over the mold and plate together. Lift the mold away from the jelly.

5 **Decorating and serving.** The immersion of the mold will have melted the jelly slightly: Return the unmolded dessert to the refrigerator at once to firm. Garnish the jelly with fresh fruit — here, orange segments stripped of pith and membrane *(box, opposite)*.

# Bread Casings Baked or Chilled

Among the many types of bread pudding *(recipes, pages 108-109 and 160)*, molded ones containing fresh fruit are the lightest. If cooked in the mold, the bread becomes a rigid casing; if chilled rather than cooked, the bread sops up the fruit juices, yet stays firm enough to unmold.

In a charlotte *(right; recipe, page 160)*, buttered pieces of bread are arranged in an overlapping pattern in a mold. The bread case is filled with a very stiff fruit purée—in this instance, made from tart apples. When the charlotte is baked, the buttered bread case turns crisp and golden brown; once the dessert cools, it will slip easily from its mold.

For summer pudding *(opposite; recipe, page 117)*, a bread-lined mold is filled with soft fruits that have been cooked just enough to draw out their juices. The pudding is refrigerated overnight and compressed with a weighted plate so that the fruits, juices and bread merge in a moist, unified whole.

For both charlottes and summer puddings, use firm, homemade-type bread. The bread should be slightly dry to prevent it from disintegrating during cooking or chilling.

## Apple Purée in a Bread-lined Mold

1 **Forming the case.** Cut slices of dry, firm bread into narrow rectangles slightly longer than the mold is deep. Brush one side of the slices with melted butter, then place the buttered sides out, around the mold, overlapping them slightly. Line the base with overlapping bread triangles.

2 **Filling the case.** Make a stiff purée of cooked apples *(page 68)* flavored with sugar and lemon peel or ground cinnamon or cloves. Pack the purée in the bread case, mounding the purée in the center. Cut bread slices to make lid for the case. Brush the lid with melted butter *(above)* and set it in place.

3 **Unmolding.** Bake the charlotte in a preheated 375° F. [190° C.] oven for about 40 minutes, until the bread is golden brown. To check the color, pull back the side *(above)*. Let the charlotte cool for 20 minutes, then unmold it and serve with a puréed fruit sauce *(pages 68-69)* — in this case, apricot *(right)*.

## Absorbing the Juice of Summer Fruits

**Lining the pudding basin.** From a thick slice of firm, dry white bread, cut a circle to line the base of a pudding basin *(above)* or a mold. Cut wedges of bread to line the sides of the basin. Use scraps from the bread wedges to fill any gaps in the bread lining.

2 **Preparing the fruit.** Pick over the fruit — in this case, raspberries and black and red currants — and throw away any damaged specimens. Put the currants in a heavy pan, sprinkle them with sugar and cook gently for about five minutes. Then add the raspberries and cook for a further five minutes, or until the currants are tender but not soft.

3 **Filling the case.** With a small strainer or a slotted spoon, lift the fruit from the pan and fill the mold halfway to the top. Place a layer of bread on the fruit *(above, left),* then spoon the remaining fruit over it. Cover the fruit with a lid of bread and pour the juice from the pan over it so that the entire bread case is saturated *(right).*

4 **Weighting the pudding.** Place the basin on a tray or large plate to catch any juices that might overflow. Cover the basin with a plate that fits just inside the rim, and weight the pudding heavily *(above).* Use kitchen weights, as here, or unopened food cans. Refrigerate the dessert overnight.

5 **Unmolding.** Remove the weights and the plate. Gently loosen the pudding from the basin with a knife. Unmold the pudding onto a plate with a rim that will catch any escaping juices. Serve the pudding with heavy cream.

# Glowing Rings of Cooked Fruit

Virtually any fruit can be poached in syrup and served either alone or in combination with custard, meringue, ice cream, or perhaps a differently prepared fruit-based element. Here, a diverse array of poached fruits is paired with a ring of molded apple pudding to produce the glowingly colored assembly known, with good reason, as fruit supreme.

For the apple pudding *(recipe, page 113)*, sweetened, cinnamon-flavored apple purée is simmered until stiff and dry, then enriched and bound with eggs. The mixture is put in a ring mold and baked in a water bath, using the procedure for baked custard shown on pages 23-24.

When choosing the fruits that will be poached, seek a variety of sizes and colors. Here, fresh pears, peaches, apricots and nectarines are supplemented with dried currants and raisins. Both dried fruits and very firm, fresh fruits require preliminary poaching in medium sugar syrup *(page 9)* to soften them. The two types should be poached separately so that each becomes barely tender. In this demonstration, for example, the currants and raisins are cooked for 15 minutes and the peaches and pears—peeled, halved and pitted or cored—are cooked separately for 10 minutes.

Following any required preliminary cooking, the fruits are strained and combined *(Step 3)*. Then the poaching syrups are blended with the reserved fruit peels, reduced *(Step 4)* and used to cook all of the fruits together briefly. Strained and mixed with almond milk and butter, the syrup blend becomes a gleaming sauce for the fruits.

**1 Preparing the pudding.** Simmer sliced apples over medium heat with sugar and flavorings, then purée them *(box, page 68)*. Stirring constantly, cook the purée with butter and more sugar until it is stiff—about 15 minutes. Transfer the purée to a bowl, let it cool to room temperature, then beat in eggs.

**2 Molding.** Sprinkle a buttered ring mold with bread crumbs and shake out the excess. Spoon in the purée and cover with wax paper or foil. Bake the pudding in a water bath in a preheated 350° F. [180° C.] oven for 45 minutes, or until firm. Let it cool for 15 minutes before unmolding it onto a serving dish.

**5 Simmering the fruits.** Pour enough syrup over the fruits to just cover them. Return the pan to the heat and simmer gently for about 10 minutes, until the fruits are soft but still intact. Leave the pan uncovered so that the syrup reduces a little more as the fruits cook.

**6 Enriching the syrup.** Remove the pan from the heat. Add some thin slices of unsalted butter, and gently shake the pan to incorporate the butter into the warm syrup without breaking up the fruits. The butter will impart a sheen and a silky consistency to the syrup.

3 **Assembling the fruits.** Place poached peaches and pears in a sauté pan. Add poached currants and raisins and raw apricots and nectarines.

4 **Flavoring the syrup.** Simmer the fruit peels for 10 minutes in the syrup from the pears and peaches. Strain this syrup into that from the dried fruits *(above, left)*; discard the peels. Boil the mixture to reduce it by one third. Add almond milk *(page 26)* and boil briefly.

7 **Composing the supreme.** Arrange the poached fruits around the unmolded apple ring. Here, nectarines and dried fruits surround the ring; peaches, pears and apricots fill the center. Decorate the ring with uncooked fruit — in this case, prune and peach strips dipped in syrup *(above)*. Pour the syrup over the assembly and add slivers of almond *(right)*.

# 6
# Assemblies
## Studies in Dazzlement

Desserts invite elaboration and artifice, and dessert cooks have always delighted in creating magnificent displays from crepes, custards, meringues, fruits and other such fundaments of their art. For example, a dozen or more crepes can be baked in a mold with layers of fruit purée and custard to make *crêpes à la crème (page 88)* — a many-flavored cake fit for the most important occasion. Similarly, rice pudding, an unassuming if wholesome dish, acquires indubitable sophistication when the rice is molded with a liqueur-flavored Bavarian cream and decorated with gemlike pieces of candied fruit — the classic *riz à l'impératrice* shown opposite *(demonstration, pages 86-87)*.

Many another dazzling dessert has been produced by changing the contents rather than the concept of some humbler dish. Fruit charlotte and charlotte russe are related in this way. The former *(page 74)* is nothing more than a fruit purée encased in a crisp bread crust; in the latter *(pages 80-81)*, the fruit is replaced by a thick cream mixture, and delicate cookies called ladyfingers take the place of the bread. Although a charlotte russe retains the shape and contrasting textures that distinguish its progenitor, its luxurious richness places it on an altogether different plane.

A dessert need not, of course, be composed of rich ingredients to be considered sumptuous. Few confections are lighter than meringue, for example, yet meringue may be shaped into a decorative basket *(pages 84-85)* that can serve as a showy container for any of a myriad of ingredients — brightly colored poached fruits, perhaps, or pastel-hued sherbets. Whatever the filling, the dessert derives its distinction primarily from its color and form.

The same may be said of *paskha (pages 82-83)*, a Russian dessert traditionally served on Easter Sunday (the name literally means "Easter"). The components could hardly be more simple: a fresh curd cheese, such as ricotta or cottage cheese, plus sweetenings of sugar and fruit. But the *paskha* is molded into a pyramidal shape, then studded with candied fruit slices, achieving a visual effect few desserts can match. Indeed, the dessert is so impressive it is often used as a centerpiece during the Russian Easter meal. There, it delights the eye while tantalizing the palate with the promise of pleasures yet to come.

sauce of puréed raspberries
pplies a ruby backdrop for *riz à
npératrice,* a chilled dessert made
rice, custard, gelatin and whipped
eam *(pages 86-87).* The crowning
wels of the confection are translucent
vers of candied fruit and angelica.

# A Rich Cream Enclosed by Ladyfingers

The first desserts to be called charlottes were just simple fruit purées encased in bread and baked *(page 74)*. In the early 19th Century, the celebrated French chef Antonïn Carême created charlotte russe *(right; recipe, page 159),* a version that, once assembled, needed no baking. With its casing of airy ladyfingers and its center of cream stiffened with gelatin—the filling is similar to a Bavarian cream—charlotte russe retains the traditional contrast between crisp exterior and soft interior, but its ingredients are richer and its preparation is more exacting than that of a bread-and-fruit charlotte.

The light, crisp ladyfingers are made with eggs, sugar and flour *(Steps 1-3, right; recipe, page 167)*. After baking, they are trimmed so that they fit snugly together to line the base and sides of a deep, round mold; a traditional charlotte mold is used here, but any deep, straight-sided dish may be substituted.

Carême flavored his cream filling with vanilla alone, but you can add chocolate, coffee, praline *(page 13),* fruit juice or puréed fruit *(page 68);* or you can mix nuts or fruit into the cream.

Once you have spooned the filling into the cookie-lined mold, the charlotte russe will need at least four hours in the refrigerator to set. When you have turned it out of the mold, decorate the charlotte russe with whipped cream and candied fruit, or serve it, as here, with a sweetened fruit purée. Tart fruits such as blueberries or raspberries provide a pleasing foil for the creamy filling.

Many other desserts are constructed in the same way as charlotte russe; all of them begin with a ladyfinger-lined mold, but not all require a setting period in the refrigerator. *Charlotte à la chantilly,* for example, substitutes chilled, sweetened, vanilla-flavored whipped cream for the cream; the dessert is turned out as soon as the cream has been spooned into the mold. And for an ice-cream charlotte, the cookie-lined mold is filled with ice cream just before serving.

1 **Making the ladyfinger mixture.** Beat egg whites until they form stiff peaks *(pages 14-15)*. In a saucepan, combine the egg yolks with sugar and set the pan in a water bath placed over low heat. Beat the mixture until it is pale and frothy, then pour it into a large bowl and gradually fold in sieved flour *(left)*. When the mixture becomes heavier and difficult to work, stir with a spatula or a plastic disk *(right)*. Continue until thoroughly blended.

4 **Making the base.** Cut a circle of wax paper to fit the base of a charlotte mold. In the center of the paper, place a small circle cut out from a ladyfinger. To complete the base, trim the sides of other ladyfingers to make petal shapes that will fit closely together around the central circle *(above)*.

5 **Lining the mold.** Place the paper in the mold and arrange the cut cookies it, flat sides up. Fill spaces with ladyfinger scraps. Square off the ends more ladyfingers. Position them, flat surfaces inward, against the side of the mold, aligning the cookies on the side with those already on the base.

2 **Incorporating egg whites.** Fold a quarter of the beaten egg whites into the mixture *(above)*; this will lighten the mixture and make it easier to fold in the remaining whites. Add the rest of the whites, folding them in gently.

3 **Shaping the cookies.** Line a baking sheet with buttered parchment or wax paper. Fill a pastry bag *(page 28)*, fitted with a plain tube, with the ladyfinger mixture. Pipe the mixture out in ovals and dust them with sugar. Bake in a preheated 350° F. [180° C.] oven for 20 minutes, or until golden.

6 **Completing the assembly.** Prepare a gelatin-stiffened cream filling and flavor it to taste: Here, puréed dried apricots are used. Just before the cream sets, pour it into the mold. Cut off the projecting cookie ends *(above)*, cover the mold with wax paper and refrigerate.

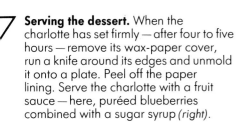

7 **Serving the dessert.** When the charlotte has set firmly — after four to five hours — remove its wax-paper cover, run a knife around its edges and unmold it onto a plate. Peel off the paper lining. Serve the charlotte with a fruit sauce — here, puréed blueberries combined with a sugar syrup *(right)*.

# A Bejeweled Edifice of Cheese

Unsalted fresh cheese such as ricotta can be turned into a soft, creamy dessert by the straightforward tactic of mixing the cheese with sugar, cream and flavorings—glacéed fruits or brandy, for example. This sort of cheese also lends itself to handsome, molded elaborations, perhaps enriched with eggs or butter (recipes, pages 109-110). The most famous mold of this type is *paskha*, the Russian Easter dessert.

Like many other molded cheese desserts, *paskha (recipe, page 151)* is served uncooked; its firm but creamy texture therefore depends on a thorough draining of the cheese before the dessert mixture is assembled. Let the cheese rest for several hours in a strainer over a bowl, then push it through a sieve to eliminate lumps *(Step 1)*, and beat it well before combining it with enrichments and flavorings. These usually include sugar, eggs, cream and butter, but chopped nuts and candied fruits also may be added. A final beating will make the *paskha* mixture as smooth as whipped cream and ready for molding.

The mold must have a perforated bottom that allows the *paskha* to drain further; otherwise, the dessert will remain too soft to hold its shape. Although Russians traditionally use a special wooden box as a mold, any perforated vessel will do; in this demonstration, a new clay flower pot serves the purpose. A flower pot should be scrubbed well and soaked in cold water for one hour to remove any clay flavor that might taint the *paskha*.

Line the mold with muslin or cheesecloth to prevent the mixture from escaping through the drainage hole. Then fill the mold and cover the cheese with a weighted plate, which will help force liquid from the dessert. The *paskha* should be refrigerated for no less than 12 hours to ensure its firmness. The molding period may be extended for as long as three days: *Paskha* improves with keeping.

Take the *paskha* out of the refrigerator half an hour before serving; it tastes best at room temperature. Slice it horizontally; if you plan to serve it again, reserve the fruit-adorned top slice to decorate the dessert when it reappears at the table.

**1 Preparing the cheese.** Pour the cheese into a strainer set over a bowl and let it drain at room temperature until no more liquid drips through. Discard the liquid. Using a plastic disk or wooden spoon, press the cheese through a sieve *(above)* to remove lumps, and beat it with an electric mixer until fluffy. Or, use a food processor to whirl the unsieved cheese briefly until smooth.

**2 Assembling the ingredients.** In a large bowl, beat eggs with sugar until the mixture is very pale. Chop almonds and candied fruit into coarse pieces, and add them to the egg mixture along with softened butter, the beaten cheese and a little grated lemon peel *(above)*. Stir in heavy cream and a few drops of vanilla extract, and beat the mixture until it is very smooth.

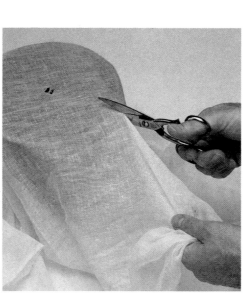

**3 Lining the mold.** Dampen a large square of muslin or a double thickness of cheesecloth. Drape it over the mold, slit the fabric from one edge to the center, and push it down into the mold. Starting at the slit, smooth the fabric against the mold; the slit lets the fabric overlap without making a bulky fold.

**4 Filling the mold.** Fill the lined mold with the cheese mixture, packing it firm. Tap the mold on a hard surface to settle the mixture. Fold the loose ends the fabric lining over the filling so that the mixture is completely covered.

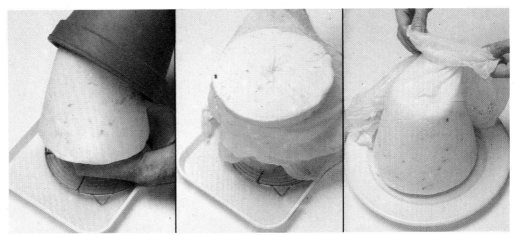

5 **Draining the paskha.** Place the pot on a rack with a tray underneath to catch drips. Put an inverted plate or saucer a bit smaller than the mold on top of the wrapped cheese. Place weights or heavy cans on the plate. Refrigerate for at least 12 hours.

6 **Unmolding the dessert.** Remove the weights and plate from the mold. Invert the mold onto your hand and gently lift the mold off the *paskha (left)*; then set the dessert upside down on the rack and peel away the cloth wrapping *(center)*. Place an inverted serving plate on the *paskha,* turn plate and *paskha* over together, and remove the cloth *(right).*

7 **Decorating.** Cut candied fruit peel into thin strips and use tweezers *(left)* to press the peel lightly onto the surface of the *paskha.* The traditional decoration includes the Cyrillic letters *XB,* which stand for the phrase *Christos voskres* ("Christ is risen"), but any attractive pattern may be used. Serve the dessert in horizontal slices *(below).*

# A Meringue Basket Brimming with Fruit

Among the many uses for a basic meringue mixture *(demonstration, page 28; recipe, page 104)*, baked Alaska and dessert baskets are the most imposing. For the Alaska *(box, opposite; recipe, page 150)*, meringue is used to coat a block of ice cream; a brief baking browns and lightly sets the meringue without melting the ice cream within. For a basket, rings of meringue are slowly baked to brittle stiffness, then glued together with more meringue to make an edible container for ice creams, sherbets and fruits.

A basket 4 inches [10 cm.] deep will require six meringue rings plus a base. The base and rings must be shaped and cooked on separate baking sheets, and the cooking and cooling process for meringue can take as long as four hours. For this reason, the basket is best assembled over a period of several days: Few cooks own seven baking sheets or could fit them into the oven at one time if they did. If the rings are stored in airtight containers that keep them from absorbing moisture, they will last for as long as a week.

**1 Making a pattern.** Cover a baking sheet with a piece of parchment or wax paper. Invert an 8- or 9-inch [20- or 23-cm.] plate on the paper and trace its rim with a pencil, pressing hard to leave a pattern on the other side: The paper must be reversed to avoid marring the meringue with graphite. Prepare six identical patterns.

**2 Forming the base.** Place a paper pattern, penciled side down, on a baking sheet. Using a pastry bag fitted with a ½-inch [1-cm.] plain tube, pipe a spiral of meringue mixture, beginning just inside the pattern line and working toward the center. Smooth the surface of the mixture with a spatula.

**5 Assembling the basket.** When all of the basket's components are baked and cooled, prepare some fresh meringue. Place the basket base on a baking sheet lined with fresh paper. Set the rings on the base, one on top of another *(above)*, using dabs of meringue to hold the rings in place. With a narrow spatula, spread more meringue around the outside of the basket, filling the gaps between rings.

**6 Decorating the basket.** Fit a fluted tube onto the pastry bag and fill the bag with meringue. Working from the base upward, pipe vertical lines of meringue on the outside of the basket *(above)*; pipe scrolls or rosettes on the rim. Bake for one and one half hours in a 200° F. [100° C.] oven. Cool the basket, then remove the paper as demonstrated in Step 4.

**7 Filling the basket.** Sprinkle chunks of fresh pineapple with sugar and soak them for about 30 minutes in kirsch. Just before serving, spoon softened ice cream into the basket. Drain the macerated pineapple chunks and put them on top of the ice cream.

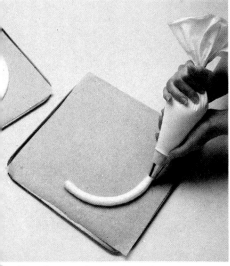

**3 Shaping meringue rings.** Line baking sheets with the remaining patterns. Pipe meringue around each pattern's inside edge *(above)*. Bake the meringues in a 250° F. [120° C.] oven for one to one and a half hours. Turn off the heat and leave the meringues in the oven until dry — one to two hours.

**4 Removing the paper.** Set the meringues, with the papers attached, on wire racks to cool for 20 minutes. Then place each meringue on a board with one side projecting over the board's edge. Steady the meringue with one hand and gently peel down the paper *(above)*, turning the ring until it is free.

## A Wrapping for Ice Cream

Served straight from the oven, the baked Alaska demonstrated below *(recipe, page 150)* yields an exciting surprise: an outer layer of hot meringue miraculously enclosing ice cream on a bed of spongecake. No magic is involved: The air trapped in the meringue insulates the ice cream and prevents it from melting during its brief spell in the oven. However, the ice cream must be frozen hard when it goes into the oven. Freeze it in a paper-lined mold so that it can be unmolded without using hot water.

**1 Piping meringue.** Unmold a block of ice cream — here, peach — on a spongecake cut larger than the block and placed on an ovenproof dish. Enclose the ice cream in a layer of meringue ¾ inch [2 cm.] thick.

**3 Serving the basket.** Purée soft fruits — in this case, raspberries. Sweeten the purée to taste, then pour it over the pineapple and ice cream. Decorate the basket with a few whole raspberries *(above)*. Serve immediately, cut into wedges.

**2 Baking and serving.** Cook the dessert in a preheated 450° F. [230° C.] oven until the meringue browns lightly — in about five minutes. Serve the baked Alaska immediately, cut into slices.

# An Opulent Amalgam of Rice and Custard

Cooked rice, the basis for the simplest of puddings, is also the foundation of a dessert that is elaborate enough to set before a queen: *riz à l'impératrice* — "empress rice" — named in honor of Eugénie, the consort of Napoleon III. This exalted creation *(recipes, pages 152-153)* combines rice with a gelatin-stiffened pouring custard *(pages 20-21)* that has been flavored with candied fruits, jam and liqueur. The rich mixture, lightened by the addition of whipped cream, is molded and refrigerated until the gelatin sets. After unmolding, it is decorated with glittering pieces of angelica and more candied fruit.

To ensure that the finished dessert has the proper silky texture, you must control temperatures carefully when assembling the components. The cooked rice must be cooled before you add the pouring custard: Heat from the rice might otherwise curdle the eggs in the custard. This mixture must be cooled still further *(Step 8)* so that it partly sets before you fold in the whipped cream. If the rice mixture is warm, the whipped cream will liquefy, losing the aeration that gives *riz à l'impératrice* its lightness. If, on the other hand, you allow the rice mixture to set firmly, you will not be able to incorporate the cream evenly.

The assembled rice mixture may be molded in any deep, smooth-sided dish; a charlotte mold is used in this demonstration. As with many other molded desserts, the bottom of the mold should be lined with wax paper to make unmolding easier. You can simply cut a piece of paper to fit, using the bottom of the mold as a guide. Or you can do the fitting by the quick and accurate technique that professional chefs use *(Steps 1-4)*.

To decorate the unmolded dessert, slice candied fruit and angelica to translucent thinness, then cut the slices into whatever shapes you desire and press them into the surface of the rice. You will need a very sharp knife to cut the sugary fruit; dip the knife in water between cuts to keep it from sticking to the fruit. Serve *riz à l'impératrice* with whipped cream, or a simple sauce made by combining fruit jelly and liqueur, or perhaps a more complex, purée-based sauce such as that shown on page 78.

**1** **Beginning the mold liner.** Fold a square piece of wax paper — at least 4 inches [10 cm.] larger than the base of the mold — in half and then into quarters to form a small square *(above)*. Fold the small square diagonally so that the folded edges meet to form a triangle.

**2** **Forming small triangles.** Press the folded edges of the triangle together repeatedly to form successively narrower triangles. Continue folding until the open end of the paper triangle is no more than 1 inch [2½ cm.] across.

**6** **Cooking the rice.** Combine milk, sugar, butter and a vanilla bean in the top of a double boiler. Simmer until the sugar dissolves and the butter melts, then set the pan over hot water and stir in rice prepared as for rice pudding *(page 38)*. Cover and cook gently for 25 to 30 minutes, until the rice is soft. Discard the vanilla bean.

**7** **Flavoring the dessert.** While the rice cooks, make a pouring custard *(pages 20-21)*. Stir in softened gelatin and, when it dissolves, add chopped candied fruit marinated in kirsch *(above)* and sieved apricot jam. Drain the rice in a strainer for 10 minutes. Gently fold the cooled rice into the custard.

**3** **Cutting to fit.** Lay the triangle on the inverted mold with the point at the center of the mold's base. With your nail *(above)*, mark the paper where it crosses the edge of the mold. Use scissors to cut through the folded paper about ⅛ inch [3 mm.] inside this mark.

**4** **Fitting in the liner.** Unfold the paper; it will form a circle slightly smaller than the base of the mold. Place the paper in the mold, smoothing out the folds with your fingers.

**5** **Oiling the mold.** Use a pastry brush or paintbrush to coat the paper circle lightly with almond or flavorless vegetable oil. Lightly oil the sides of the mold.

**8** **Adding whipped cream.** Place the bowl of rice custard in a bowl of ice. Stir the mixture until cool and slightly thick. Fold in softly whipped heavy cream.

**9** **Molding the rice.** Pour the mixture into the mold. Cover the mold with its lid or wax paper and refrigerate for at least six hours, or until the rice mixture is firm.

**10** **Decorating the dessert.** Unmold the rice onto a plate and decorate it with candied fruit and angelica. To avoid marring the surface, use a toothpick to pierce each piece of fruit and press it into the mold. Hold the fruit with a second pick while you extract the first.

# A Crepe-and-Custard Cake

One unexpected way to turn plain crepes into a dazzling dessert is to make a cake from them. You can simply stack the crepes on a plate alternately with fillings—such as fruit purées or whipped cream. Or, for the dessert called *crêpes à la crème (recipe, page 156)*, you can stack the crepes in a deep baking dish and cover each one with a custard mixture. After being baked to set the custard, the assembly is unmolded.

Richer, more intricately flavored versions of *crêpes à la crème* can be made by spreading each crepe with puréed fruit or pounded nuts before adding the custard. Here, both kinds of fillings—based on prunes and pistachios—are used.

To make a prune purée, simmer pitted prunes in water for about 25 minutes until soft, then drain them and pass them through a food mill. Add heavy cream, a pinch of salt, a dash of brandy and sugar to taste. For the pistachio filling, peel the nuts *(page 13)* and purée them in a food processor or mortar. Add sugar and enough cream to produce a thick paste.

1 **Layering the crepes.** Prepare the crepes *(pages 44-45)*. Butter a soufflé dish or straight-sided mold slightly wider than the crepes. Sprinkle in fresh bread crumbs and arrange decorative strips of angelica *(inset)* or candied fruit over them. Coat the crepes alternately with the prune and pistachio fillings, and stack them to within an inch [2½ cm.] of the top, ending with a plain crepe.

2 **Pouring the custard.** With a knife, push the crepes away from the dish's sides; pour custard mixture around and over the crepes to within ½ inch [1 cm.] of the rim. Cover with buttered wax paper and bake for 20 minutes in a preheated 375° F. [180° C.] oven.

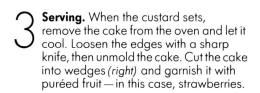

3 **Serving.** When the custard sets, remove the cake from the oven and let it cool. Loosen the edges with a sharp knife, then unmold the cake. Cut the cake into wedges *(right)* and garnish it with puréed fruit—in this case, strawberries.

# Anthology of Recipes

Drawing upon the cooking traditions and literature of more than 20 countries, the editors and consultants for this volume have selected 209 published dessert recipes for the Anthology that follows. The selections range from the simple to the elaborate—from fruit ices to a Dickensian trifle made with ladyfingers, two kinds of macaroons, sherry, brandy, jam, custard and whipped cream.

Many of the recipes were written by world-renowned exponents of the culinary art, but the Anthology, spanning nearly 1,000 years, also includes selections from now rare and out-of-print books and from works that have never been published in English. Whatever the sources, the emphasis is always on authentic desserts meticulously prepared with fresh, natural ingredients that blend harmoniously.

Since many early recipe writers did not specify amounts of ingredients, the missing information has been judiciously added. Where appropriate, clarifying introductory notes have also been supplied; they are printed in italics. Modern terms have been substituted for archaic language, but to preserve the character of the original recipes, and to create a true anthology, the authors' texts have been changed as little as possible. Some instructions have necessarily been expanded, but in any circumstance where the cooking directions still seem somewhat abrupt, the reader need only refer to the appropriate demonstrations in the front of the book to find the technique explained.

For ease of use, the dessert recipes are organized by types. Sauces and toppings are grouped separately. Recipes for standard preparations—basic ice cream, pouring custard and almond macaroons, for example—appear at the end of the Anthology. Cooking terms and ingredients that may be unfamiliar are explained in the combined General Index and Glossary.

Apart from the primary components, all recipe ingredients are listed in order of use, with both the customary U.S. measurements and the new metric measurements provided in separate columns. The metric quantities supplied here reflect the American practice of measuring such solid ingredients as flour or sugar by volume rather than by weight, as European cooks do.

To make the quantities simpler to measure, many of the figures have been rounded off to correspond to the gradations that are now standard on metric spoons and cups. (One cup, for example, equals 237 milliliters; wherever practicable in these recipes, however, a cup appears as a more readily measurable 250 milliliters.) Similarly, weight, temperature and linear metric equivalents are rounded off slightly. For these reasons, the American and metric figures are not equivalent, but using one set or the other will produce equally good results.

# Custards and Creams

*Recipes for basic custards appear in Standard
Preparations, page 165.*

## Peruvian Cream

### *Crème Péruvienne*

To serve 6

| | | |
|---|---|---|
| 2½ cups | milk | 625 ml. |
| ⅔ cup | freshly roasted coffee beans | 75 ml. |
| 2-inch | vanilla bean | 5-cm. |
| ⅓ cup | sugar | 75 ml. |
| 2 tbsp. | cold water | 30 ml. |
| 2 to 3 tbsp. | hot water | 30 to 45 ml. |
| 3½ oz. | semisweet chocolate, broken into 4 or 5 pieces | 100 g. |
| 5 | egg yolks | 5 |
| 1 | whole egg | 1 |

In a saucepan heat the milk to the boiling point. Meanwhile,
spread the coffee beans on a baking sheet and warm them in
a preheated 350° F. [180° C.] oven for a few minutes, or until
the beans start to sweat. Remove the milk from the heat and
add the coffee beans along with the vanilla bean. Cover, and
leave to infuse for 30 minutes over the lowest possible heat,
protecting the bottom of the pan with a fireproof pad.

Meanwhile, in a small saucepan, dissolve the sugar in
the cold water and cook over medium heat until the sugar
caramelizes and is very pale in color. Immediately immerse
the bottom of the pan in a bowl of cold water to arrest the
cooking. Add 2 to 3 tablespoons [30 to 45 ml.] of hot water to
dilute the caramel. Return the saucepan to very low heat
and stir the mixture until it turns into a smooth syrup. Set it
aside off the heat.

Place the chocolate in a saucepan and add enough of the
infused milk to cover it. Cover the pan and place it over
extremely low heat. When the chocolate has softened, after a
few minutes, work it with a wooden spoon until it becomes a
smooth paste. Remove the chocolate from the heat.

Pour the remaining infused milk through a strainer into
a clean bowl. Discard the coffee and vanilla beans. Stir in the
chocolate, then stir in the caramel syrup.

Place the egg yolks and the whole egg in a bowl and mix
them thoroughly with a whisk. A little at a time, add the
chocolate-and-caramel mixture, whisking gently to blend

the eggs and liquid thoroughly. Whisking too vigorously will
create an excessive amount of froth. Pour the mixture
through a strainer lined with dampened cheesecloth to remove any particles of egg.

Fill six individual ovenproof pots with the cream and
place them in a pan just large enough to hold them easily.
Pour into the pan enough boiling water to come two thirds of
the way up the sides of the pots. Put the pan in a preheated
300° F. [150° C.] oven and cover it with a close-fitting lid. The
oven should keep the water hot, but not boiling. Check the
pan frequently; as soon as you notice the slightest trembling
of the water, add a few spoonfuls of cold water.

The cooking time varies with the size of the pots used. For
3- to 3½-ounce [90- to 105-ml.] pots, allow 18 to 20 minutes.
For 4-ounce [125-ml.] pots, allow 23 to 25 minutes. To test
whether the cream is sufficiently cooked, tip one of the pots
slightly: the cream should tremble but remain firm.

Remove the pan from the oven. Leave the pots in the
water for a few minutes, then take them out and chill them
for about two and one half hours.

To serve, wipe the pots carefully and arrange them on a
napkin-covered serving dish or platter; the napkin will ensure that the pots do not slide around while being served.

MADAME SAINT-ANGE
LA CUISINE DE MADAME SAINT-ANGE

## Chocolate Custard Cream

### *Pots de Crème Panisse*

To serve 6

| | | |
|---|---|---|
| 6 oz. | semisweet baking chocolate, broken into pieces | 175 g. |
| 1 cup | water | ¼ liter |
| 1 | vanilla bean | 1 |
| 6 | egg yolks, well beaten | 6 |
| 1 cup | heavy cream, whipped | ¼ liter |

In a saucepan, combine the chocolate with the water and the
vanilla bean. Stirring occasionally, melt the chocolate over
low heat. When the chocolate is glossy and smooth, stir in
the egg yolks. Continue to cook, stirring constantly, until
the chocolate cream thickens and is perfectly smooth. Remove the pan from the heat, take out the vanilla bean and let
the mixture cool a little, stirring constantly. Pour the chocolate cream through a fine sieve into six ramekins, or *petits
pots,* filling them three quarters full. Cool, then top each
serving with a dome of whipped cream before serving.

ÉDOUARD NIGNON
LES PLAISIRS DE LA TABLE

## Burnt Cream

### *Crème Brûlée*

*This recipe was taken from The Ocklye Cookery Book (1909) by Eleanor L. Jenkinson.*

To serve 4 to 6

| | | |
|---|---|---|
| 2½ cups | heavy cream, or 1¼ cups [300 ml.] heavy cream mixed with 1¼ cups light cream | 600 ml. |
| 4 | large egg yolks, well beaten | 4 |
| ¼ to ⅓ cup | superfine sugar | 50 to 75 ml. |

Bring the cream to a boil, and boil it for about 30 seconds. Pour it immediately into the egg yolks and whisk them together. (At this point, although the recipe does not say so, I return the mixture to the pan and cook it without allowing it to boil, until it thickens and coats the spoon.) Pour the mixture into a shallow baking dish. Refrigerate it overnight.

Two hours before the meal, sprinkle the chilled cream with the sugar in an even layer, and place it under a broiler preheated to the maximum temperature. The sugar will caramelize to a sheet of brown smoothness; you may need to turn the dish under the grill to achieve an even effect.

JANE GRIGSON
ENGLISH FOOD

## Burnt Cream with Brown Sugar

### *Crème Brûlée*

To serve 6

| | | |
|---|---|---|
| 2½ cups | heavy cream | 625 ml. |
| 6 | eggs | 6 |
| 6 tbsp. | sugar | 90 ml. |
| 1 tsp. | cornstarch | 5 ml. |
| 1 tsp. | almond extract | 5 ml. |
| 1 cup | light brown sugar, sieved before measuring | ¼ liter |

In the top of a double boiler, heat the cream slowly just until a light skin forms on the top. Remove the pan from the heat and set the cream aside to cool.

Beat the eggs until thick and light colored. Mix the sugar with the cornstarch and add to the eggs gradually, beating constantly. Add the cream to the beaten egg mixture very slowly, stirring briskly. Pour this custard into the double-boiler top and cook over simmering—not boiling—water. Stir constantly until the custard will coat a metal spoon with a light layer. As soon as the custard coats the spoon, take it off the heat. Stir in the almond extract.

Strain the custard through a sieve into a 1-quart [1-liter] heatproof serving dish or six individual heatproof dishes.

Stir it gently twice during the first 10 minutes of cooling to prevent a surface skin from forming. When the custard is lukewarm, put it into the refrigerator to chill. Large dishes should be chilled at least six to eight hours; small ones need only three to four hours to chill thoroughly.

Just before serving, sprinkle the top of the custard with the brown sugar. Stand the dish in a pan of ice (to avoid the chance of breaking the dish because of a sudden change in temperature) and place the pan, ice and all, under a preheated broiler for two or three minutes, or until the sugar bubbles. Watch carefully: sugar has a tendency to burn. Serve the custard immediately.

ELEANOR GRAVES
GREAT DINNERS FROM LIFE

## Plum Custard

### *Oeufs à l'Anglaise*

To serve 8 to 10

| | | |
|---|---|---|
| 2 cups | brandied plums in syrup | ½ liter |
| 18 | eggs | 18 |
| | salt | |
| 1 tsp. | ground cinnamon | 5 ml. |
| 1 cup | sugar | ¼ liter |
| ½ cup | candied citrus peel, diced | 125 ml. |
| ¾ cup | raisins, soaked in warm water for 15 minutes and drained | 175 ml. |
| 1 cup | crumbled almond macaroons *(recipe, page 167)* | ¼ liter |
| 1 cup | heavy cream | ¼ liter |
| 1 tbsp. | orange-flower water | 15 ml. |

Beat the eggs well with the salt, cinnamon and all but 1 tablespoon [15 ml.] of the sugar. Mix in the plums along with their liquid, the candied peel, raisins, crumbled macaroons and cream. Pour the mixture into a large buttered baking dish, place in a shallow pan partly filled with boiling water and bake in a preheated 325° F. [160° C.] oven for 50 minutes, or until the custard is just set. When the custard is done, sprinkle over it the orange-flower water and the remaining sugar, and put it under the broiler to glaze the top.

PIERRE DE LUNE
LE NOUVEAU CUISINIER

## Little Pots of Pistachio Cream

### Petits Pots aux Pistaches

*The technique of blanching pistachio nuts is demonstrated on page 12. To obtain the spinach juice used as a coloring in this recipe, parboil a few leaves of spinach for one minute, drain them and squeeze out any excess liquid. Pound or purée the leaves, and squeeze their juice through a cloth.*

| | To serve 8 | |
|---|---|---|
| ⅔ cup | pistachio nuts, blanched and pounded fine | 150 ml. |
| 2½ cups | heavy cream | 625 ml. |
| ½ cup | sugar | 125 ml. |
| 1 | egg | 1 |
| 4 | egg yolks | 4 |
| 1 tsp. | spinach juice | 5 ml. |

Bring the cream to a boil in a saucepan. Add the sugar and stir until dissolved, then mix in the ground pistachio nuts, bring the cream to a boil again, remove the pan from the heat and let the mixture cool.

Combine the egg and egg yolks in another saucepan, mix, then stir in the cream-and-pistachio mixture, and add the spinach juice. Pour this custard mixture through a fine strainer into a bowl. Pour the mixture into eight small, oven-proof pots or ramekins, set the pots in a shallow pan partly filled with boiling water, and cook the mixture over low heat for about 20 minutes, or until the custard is set.

MM. VIARD ET FOURET
LE CUISINIER ROYAL

---

## Coconut Pudding

*For instructions on how to make coconut milk, see the demonstration on page 13.*

| | To serve 4 | |
|---|---|---|
| 1 cup | coconut milk, made from the flesh of half a fresh coconut and 1 cup [¼ liter] boiling water | ¼ liter |
| ½ cup | freshly grated coconut | 125 ml. |
| 2 | eggs, lightly beaten | 2 |
| 1½ tbsp. | sugar | 22 ml. |
| 1 | banana, peeled and mashed | 1 |
| ¼ tsp. | ground cinnamon | 1 ml. |

Beat together the eggs and sugar. Add the coconut milk slowly, beating continuously. Beat in the banana and then the grated coconut. Pour the custard into a buttered baking dish and sprinkle with the cinnamon. Bake in a preheated 350° F. [180° C.] oven for 45 minutes. Serve hot or chilled.

MONICA BAYLEY
BLACK AFRICA COOK BOOK

## Special Coconut Custard

*The technique of making coconut milk appears on page 13; the technique of caramelizing a mold is shown on page 24.*

| | To serve 6 to 8 | |
|---|---|---|
| 2 cups | thick coconut milk, made from the flesh of a fresh coconut and 2 cups [½ liter] boiling water | ½ liter |
| 1 cup | brown sugar | ¼ liter |
| ¼ cup | water | 50 ml. |
| 6 | egg yolks | 6 |
| 4 | egg whites, lightly beaten | 4 |
| 1 cup | granulated sugar | ¼ liter |
| 1 tbsp. | grated lime or lemon peel | 15 ml. |

In a saucepan, dissolve the brown sugar in the water and cook the mixture over medium heat until it browns, or caramelizes. Evenly line a 1-quart [1-liter] mold with three quarters of the hot caramelized syrup and set the mold aside. Stir the coconut milk into the remaining caramelized syrup. Place this over low heat and stir continuously until all the caramel has dissolved. Set aside.

Add the egg yolks to the beaten egg whites, and beat them lightly together to mix them thoroughly. Add the granulated sugar and grated lime or lemon peel. Then add the coconut-milk mixture and beat well.

Strain this custard through cheesecloth or muslin and pour it into the caramel-lined mold. Place the mold in a pan, fill the pan with hot water to come halfway up the sides of the mold, and cook the custard slowly in a preheated 300° F. [150° C.] oven without allowing the water to boil.

After about one and one half hours' cooking—or when a small knife inserted in the custard comes out clean—place the mold under a preheated broiler to brown the top of the custard. Cool the custard and unmold it before serving.

HELEN OROSA DEL ROSARIO (EDITOR)
MARIA Y. OROSA: HER LIFE AND WORK

## Tea Custards

*Crème au Thé*

To serve 12

| | | |
|---|---|---|
| 1 cup | freshly made strong black tea | ¼ liter |
| 1 quart | heavy cream | 1 liter |
| ½ cup | sugar | 125 ml. |
| 4 | egg yolks, lightly beaten | 4 |
| 6 | eggs, lightly beaten | 6 |
| | **Orange flower sauce** | |
| 1 tbsp. | orange-flower water | 15 ml. |
| ¼ cup | sugar | 50 ml. |
| 1 cup | heavy cream | ¼ liter |
| 2 | egg yolks, lightly beaten | 2 |

In a saucepan, reduce the cream by half by boiling it over high heat, stirring often. Gradually beat in the tea and sugar, then the egg yolks and whole eggs. Pass the custard mixture through a fine strainer. Beat the mixture and strain it again. Divide the custard mixture among 12 small custard pots, place the pots in a shallow pan partly filled with boiling water, and cook in a preheated 300° F. [150° C.] oven for 20 to 25 minutes, or until set.

Cool the pots of custard until tepid, then refrigerate them until they are cold.

For the sauce, dissolve the sugar in the cream over low heat. Whisk in the orange-flower water and gradually add the egg yolks. Stir over low heat, without allowing the sauce to boil, until it lightly coats a spoon. Cool the sauce to tepid.

Invert the pots onto a chilled serving platter and pour the sauce over the cold custards.

JULES BRETEUIL
LE CUISINIER EUROPÉEN

## Coffee Cream Custard

To serve 6

| | | |
|---|---|---|
| 1 cup | strong, freshly made coffee | ¼ liter |
| ½ cup | heavy cream | 125 ml. |
| 2 cups | milk | ½ liter |
| 3 | eggs | 3 |
| 3 | egg yolks | 3 |
| ¾ cup | sugar | 175 ml. |
| 1 tsp. | vanilla extract | 5 ml. |

Pour the milk into a 1-quart [1-liter] nonaluminum pot. Stir the coffee into the milk and slowly bring the milk mixture to the boiling point. Meanwhile, put the eggs and yolks in a large mixing bowl and beat together thoroughly with a wire whisk. Then beat in the cream and sugar.

When the milk mixture reaches the boiling point, slowly pour it into the egg mixture, beating with the whisk. Add the vanilla and beat again.

Pour half of the coffee cream into a 10-inch [25-cm.] pie dish or a 6-cup [1½-liter] soufflé dish. Set the dish in a shallow pan filled with boiling water to reach halfway up the side of the dish. Place the pan in a preheated 350° F. [180° C.] oven. Pour into the soufflé dish the rest of the coffee cream, or enough to fill the dish to the top. Reduce the heat to 325° F. [160° C.] and bake the coffee cream for about one and a quarter hours, or until a knife plunged into the center will come out clean and dry. Remove the custard dish from the pan of water and cool, then cover and refrigerate for at least three hours. The coffee cream must be served icy cold.

CAROL CUTLER
THE SIX-MINUTE SOUFFLÉ AND OTHER CULINARY DELIGHTS

## Caramel Custard

*Crème au Caramel*

To serve 6

| | | |
|---|---|---|
| ¾ cup | sugar | 175 ml. |
| 3 tbsp. | water | 45 ml. |
| 5 cups | milk | 1¼ liters |
| 1 | egg | 1 |
| 2 | egg yolks | 2 |
| 1 tsp. | vanilla extract | 5 ml. |

In a heavy saucepan boil ¼ cup [50 ml.] of the sugar with the water until the sugar caramelizes and is amber brown. Set aside to cool.

Scald the milk, allow it to cool slightly and pour it into the pan with the caramelized sugar. Stir over low heat until the caramel is completely dissolved in the milk. Beat the egg with the yolks, and add the remaining sugar and the vanilla. Gradually pour in the caramelized milk, stirring to blend.

Pour the custard into individual cups, or into one 1½-quart [1½-liter] mold. Place in a shallow pan partly filled with boiling water and bake in a preheated 325° F. [160° C.] oven for 30 to 40 minutes, or until set. This can be tested by inserting a silver knife into the custard; if the knife comes out clean, the custard is set. Serve warm or chilled.

CHARLOTTE TURGEON
TANTE MARIE'S FRENCH KITCHEN

## Caramel-Water Custard

*Oeufs à l'Eau au Caramel*

To serve 4 to 6

| | | |
|---|---|---|
| ½ cup | sugar | 125 ml. |
| 2½ cups | water | 625 ml. |
| 2-inch | cinnamon stick | 5-cm. |
| 10 to 15 | coriander seeds, lightly crushed | 10 to 15 |
| | peel of 1 lemon | |
| 6 | egg yolks, lightly beaten | 6 |

Boil the sugar in ½ cup [125 ml.] of the water until the syrup becomes caramel colored. Moisten promptly with the remaining water. Add the cinnamon, coriander and lemon peel, and boil gently for 30 minutes. Strain the syrup and, when half-cooled, pour it slowly over the egg yolks in a mixing bowl, whisking at the same time.

Strain, and pour the custard mixture into a 1-quart [1-liter] mold or into individual ramekins set in a shallow pan partly filled with boiling water. Poach the custard over low heat until set—allow up to 40 minutes for a single mold, about 15 to 20 minutes for ramekins. Serve hot.

MENON
LES SOUPERS DE LA COUR

## Caramel-coated Custard

*Crème Renversée à la Vanille*

*The technique of caramelizing a mold is shown on page 24.*

To serve 3

| | | |
|---|---|---|
| ⅓ cup | granulated sugar | 75 ml. |
| ⅓ cup | cold water | 75 ml. |
| 1 tsp. | strained fresh lemon juice | 5 ml. |
| 2 | eggs | 2 |
| 2 | egg yolks | 2 |
| 1 tbsp. | superfine sugar | 15 ml. |
| about ½ tsp. | vanilla extract | about 2 ml. |
| | salt | |
| 1¼ cups | milk | 300 ml. |

Put the granulated sugar, cold water and lemon juice into a small, enameled or tin-lined saucepan and let them cook until they are a light coffee color. Watch this caramel carefully, as it is apt to burn. When it is ready, pour the caramel into a plain, dry, 2-cup [½-liter] soufflé mold or dish that has straight sides and a flat bottom. Turn the mold around and

around until the caramel coats it uniformly. It is a good plan to warm the mold first. Allow the caramel to become cold while you are making the custard.

Put the eggs and egg yolks into a bowl with the superfine sugar, vanilla extract to taste and a pinch of salt, and mix them to a cream with a wooden spoon. Heat the milk and pour it slowly into the egg mixture, stirring all the time. Strain this custard into the prepared mold and cover the mold with wax paper.

Steam *very* slowly for about an hour until a knife inserted in the center comes out clean, or bake in an oven, preheated to 350° F. [180° C.], with some warm water round the mold.

Let the custard stand until tepid before turning it out. The pudding will have a glaze of caramel over the top and some of the caramel will run round the sides as a sauce. Serve tepid, or chill and serve cold.

FLORENCE B. JACK
COOKERY FOR EVERY HOUSEHOLD

## Old-fashioned Cinnamon Custard

*Lattaiolo*

To serve 6

| | | |
|---|---|---|
| ½ tsp. | ground cinnamon | 2 ml. |
| 5 cups | milk | 1¼ liters |
| | salt | |
| 1 | small piece lemon peel | 1 |
| 1 | small piece vanilla bean | 1 |
| 2 | eggs | 2 |
| 6 | egg yolks | 6 |
| 2 tbsp. | flour | 30 ml. |
| | grated nutmeg | |
| ½ cup | confectioners' sugar | 125 ml. |

Put the milk in a saucepan along with a pinch of salt, the lemon peel and the vanilla bean, then set the saucepan on medium heat. When the mixture reaches the boiling point, reduce the heat and simmer very slowly for 30 minutes. Using a wooden spoon, keep removing the skin that will form repeatedly on top of the milk. Remove the saucepan from the heat and let the milk cool completely.

Preheat the oven to 300° F. [150° C.]. Place the eggs and egg yolks in a bowl, then add the flour and whisk very well. Add a pinch of nutmeg and the cinnamon. When the milk is cool, pour it into the bowl and whisk thoroughly. Pass the contents of the bowl through a piece of cheesecloth into another bowl. Butter a loaf pan 9 by 5 by 2¾ inches [23 by 13 by 7 cm.] and pour in the contents of the bowl. Bake in the preheated oven for 40 to 50 minutes, then remove from the oven and allow the custard to cool for one hour.

Cover the loaf pan with aluminum foil and chill the custard in the refrigerator for at least four hours. Then unmold the custard onto a serving dish, sift the confectioners' sugar over the top and serve.

GIULIANO BUGIALLI
THE FINE ART OF ITALIAN COOKING

---

## Royal Eggs
### *Huevos Reales*

To serve 6 to 8

| | | |
|---|---|---|
| 3 | egg whites | 3 |
| 12 | egg yolks | 12 |
| ½ cup | sweet sherry | 125 ml. |
| 2 tbsp. | seedless raisins | 30 ml. |
| 2 cups | sugar | ½ liter |
| 1 cup | cold water | ¼ liter |
| 2-inch | stick cinnamon | 5-cm. |
| ¼ cup | pine nuts | 50 ml. |

Preheat the oven to 325° F. [160° C.]. In a large mixing bowl, beat the egg whites until they are stiff enough to form soft peaks. In another bowl, beat the egg yolks until they thicken enough to fall back in a ribbon when the whisk or beater is lifted out of the bowl. Then, thoroughly mix the whites into the yolks and pour the mixture into a buttered shallow baking dish about 8½ to 9 inches [21 to 23 cm.] square. Smooth the top with the spatula.

Place the baking dish in a large shallow pan in the middle of the oven and pour enough boiling water into the pan to come halfway up the sides of the dish. Bake for 10 to 15 minutes, or until the eggs are firm. Remove the dish and cool to room temperature. Then, with a knife dipped in hot water, cut the baked eggs into 1½-inch [4-cm.] squares.

Combine ¼ cup [50 ml.] of the sherry and the raisins in a small bowl, and set aside to soak. In a small saucepan, bring the sugar, water and cinnamon stick to a boil over high heat, stirring only until the sugar is dissolved. Boil briskly, undisturbed, over high heat for five minutes. Discard the cinnamon and pour the syrup into a shallow heatproof dish or pan.

With a spatula, place the egg squares in the dish one at a time and, when they are almost entirely saturated with syrup, transfer the squares to individual dessert dishes or a deep platter, arranging them side by side in one layer. Strain the remaining syrup through a fine sieve into a small bowl, stir in the remaining ¼ cup of sherry and pour as much of the mixture as you like over the egg squares. Then sprinkle the tops evenly with the presoaked raisins and the pine nuts.

FOODS OF THE WORLD/LATIN AMERICAN COOKING

---

## Celeriac Custard
### *Crème au Céleri*

To serve 14 to 16

| | | |
|---|---|---|
| 1 | celeriac, peeled and quartered | 1 |
| 1½ quarts | heavy cream or half-and-half cream | 1½ liters |
| 8 | large egg yolks | 8 |
| 1 cup | sugar | ¼ liter |

Boil the cream. Add the celeriac, reduce the heat and simmer gently for about 20 minutes, or until the cream takes on the flavor of the celeriac. While the mixture is infusing, whisk the egg yolks until smooth; add the sugar to them.

After removing the quarters of celeriac, gradually stir the hot cream into the egg yolks. Strain, pour the custard mixture into small porcelain cups and stand them in a shallow pan partly filled with boiling water. Cover the pan and place it over low heat or in a preheated 325° F. [160° C.] oven, and bake until the custard is set, about 15 to 20 minutes.

L. E. AUDOT
LA CUISINIÈRE DE LA CAMPAGNE ET DE LA VILLE

## Ginger Custard

To serve 6

| | | |
|---|---|---|
| | preserved ginger, cut into thin strips | |
| ½ tsp. | ground ginger | 2 ml. |
| 4 | eggs | 4 |
| ½ cup | sugar | 125 ml. |
| 2 cups | milk | ½ liter |
| ¼ tsp. | salt | 1 ml. |
| 2 tbsp. | rum | 30 ml. |
| | pouring custard (recipe, page 165), flavored with preserved ginger syrup | |

Place the strips of ginger on the sides of six buttered 1-cup [¼-liter] molds. Beat the eggs lightly, add the sugar, milk, salt, ground ginger and rum and strain into the greased molds. Set in a shallow pan partly filled with hot water and bake in a preheated 325° F. [160° C.] oven until firm—about 40 minutes. Serve with custard sauce.

AMY B. W. MILLER AND PERSIS W. FULLER (EDITORS)
THE BEST OF SHAKER COOKING

## Sultan's Cream

### Crème à la Sultane

*A recipe for ladyfingers appears on page 167.*

To serve 4 to 6

| | | |
|---|---|---|
| ⅔ cup | milk | 150 ml. |
| 1¼ cups | heavy cream | 300 ml. |
| 2-inch | stick cinnamon | 5-cm. |
| 6 | coriander seeds | 6 |
| 1 | strip fresh lemon peel | 1 |
| ¼ cup | sugar | 50 ml. |
| 6 | egg yolks, lightly beaten | 6 |
| 4 | chocolate ladyfingers, chopped fine (about ¾ cup [175 ml.]) | 4 |
| 4 | almond-flavored ladyfingers, chopped fine (about ¾ cup [175 ml.]) | 4 |
| | crystallized orange flowers or violets, crushed (about 2 tbsp. [30 ml.]) | |
| 2 tbsp. | candied lemon peel, chopped fine | 30 ml. |
| ¼ tsp. | ground cinnamon | 1 ml. |

Boil the milk and cream together with the cinnamon stick, coriander seeds, fresh lemon peel and sugar. When the mixture has come to a boil, allow it to cool partially, then mix in the egg yolks and pour this custard through a fine strainer. To the cream mixture, add the ladyfingers, orange flowers or violets, candied lemon peel and cinnamon. Pour into a 1-quart [1-liter] ovenproof dish and place it in turn in a shallow pan partly filled with boiling water. Bake in a preheated 325° F. [160° C.] oven for 30 to 45 minutes, or until set. Let the custard cool before serving it.

LE CUISINIER GASCON

## Milk and Egg Sweet

### Tyropatinam

*This recipe is based on one written by a Roman gourmand, Apicius, in the First Century.*

To serve 4

| | | |
|---|---|---|
| 2½ cups | milk | 625 ml. |
| 5 | eggs, lightly beaten | 5 |
| ½ cup | honey | 125 ml. |
| | freshly ground pepper | |

Mix the milk with the honey, then add the eggs. Work the eggs with the milk into a smooth mixture. Strain the mixture into a 1-quart [1-liter] earthenware pot, set it in a pan partly filled with boiling water and cook it in a preheated

325° F. [160° C.] oven for about 30 minutes, or until set. Grind pepper over the custard and serve.

BARBARA FLOWER AND ELISABETH ROSENBAUM
THE ROMAN COOKERY BOOK

## Floating Island

### Oeufs à la Neige

*The technique of making a pouring custard is demonstrated on pages 20-21.*

To serve 6

| | | |
|---|---|---|
| 8 | eggs, the yolks separated from the whites | 8 |
| 1 quart | milk | 1 liter |
| 1½ cups | granulated sugar | 375 ml. |
| 1 | vanilla bean, split lengthwise | 1 |
| 4 cups | confectioners' sugar, sifted | 1 liter |

Bring the milk to a boil with half of the granulated sugar and the vanilla bean. Remove the pan from the heat, cover and allow to infuse for 10 minutes, then remove the vanilla bean.

Beat the egg whites until they stand stiffly in peaks, then gradually beat in the confectioners' sugar. Return the pan of milk to the heat. Scoop up the egg-white mixture a spoonful at a time, rounding it into egg shapes with another spoon, and poach these eggs in the simmering milk, turning them so that they cook for about one minute on each side. (The number of meringues will depend on the size of the spoons you use.) When the poached meringues are firm, drain them and arrange them in a deep dish. Reserve the hot milk.

Make a pouring custard with the egg yolks, the remaining granulated sugar and the reserved milk. Pour the custard into the serving dish, around—but not over—the meringues. The meringues should float on the custard. Serve the dish warm or cold.

RAYMOND OLIVER
LA CUISINE

## Wine Cream

### Crème Bachique

To serve 6

| | | |
|---|---|---|
| 2 cups | good white wine | ½ liter |
| ½ cup | sugar | 125 ml. |
| 1 | strip lemon peel or ½ stick cinnamon | 1 |
| 7 or 8 | egg yolks | 7 or 8 |

Pour the wine into a saucepan; add the sugar and lemon peel or cinnamon. Bring the wine to a boil, then remove the pan from the heat and cover it to allow the ingredients to infuse, until tepid. Remove the peel or cinnamon stick.

In a bowl, stir the egg yolks with a spoon to mix them well. Add the wine slowly, stirring constantly. Pour the mixture through a fine strainer into individual ramekins, and set these in a shallow pan partly filled with boiling water. Bake the creams in a preheated 325° F. [160° C.] oven for about 20 minutes, or until set.

L. E. AUDOT
LA CUISINIÈRE DE LA CAMPAGNE ET DE LA VILLE

## Iced Zabaglione
### *Zabaglione Gelato*

*To serve 8*

| | | |
|---|---|---|
| 8 | egg yolks | 8 |
| ½ | lemon, the peel sliced | ½ |
| ½ cup | sugar | 125 ml. |
| 1 cup | dry Marsala wine | ¼ liter |
| 1 tsp. | unflavored powdered gelatin, softened in 1 tbsp. [15 ml.] cold water | 5 ml. |
| 2 tbsp. | boiling water | 30 ml. |
| 3 tbsp. | Cognac or other brandy | 45 ml. |
| 2 cups | heavy cream, whipped stiff with ½ tsp. [2 ml.] vanilla and 1 tbsp. [15 ml.] sugar | ½ liter |

Beat the egg yolks, lemon peel and sugar for three minutes with an electric beater or nine minutes with a hand beater. Remove the lemon peel and fold in the Marsala wine. Place the egg mixture in the top of a double boiler. (The water in the bottom of the double boiler should be boiling slowly.) Cook for about six minutes, continuing to beat with the beater. Zabaglione is cooked when it stands in soft peaks. Remove from the heat.

Dissolve the softened gelatin in the boiling water and add it to the zabaglione, stirring slowly. When the zabaglione is at room temperature, fold in the Cognac and whipped cream. Place the zabaglione in individual glasses, or in a crystal or silver bowl, and chill in the refrigerator for four to five hours. Serve with cookies or French pastry.

MARIA LUISA TAGLIENTI
THE ITALIAN COOKBOOK

## Crème Carême

This dessert takes its name from the great 19th Century chef—Antonïn Carême—who created it.

*To serve 8*

| | | |
|---|---|---|
| 8 | egg yolks | 8 |
| ¾ cup | sugar | 175 ml. |
| 1 tbsp. | rice flour or 2 tsp. [10 ml.] cornstarch | 15 ml. |
| 3 cups | hot milk | ¾ liter |
| ⅓ cup | maraschino or 3 tbsp. [45 ml.] kirsch | 75 ml. |
| ¾ cup | heavy cream, whipped | 175 ml. |

In a bowl, whisk the egg yolks with the sugar and rice flour or cornstarch until the mixture is pale yellow. Add the hot milk very slowly. Put the mixture in a saucepan over very low heat, stirring with a wooden spoon until the spoon is thickly coated. Remove this custard from the heat, stirring occasionally until it is cold. Put it in the refrigerator. (Carême says put it on ice, surrounded by ice.) Remove it from the refrigerator from time to time to stir it.

Just before serving, stir in the maraschino and whipped cream. You will then have (these are Carême's words) a light, velvety, mellow cream.

ALICE B. TOKLAS
THE ALICE B. TOKLAS COOK BOOK

## Wine and Lemon Cream
### *Berliner Luft*

*To serve 4*

| | | |
|---|---|---|
| ¾ cup | wine | 175 ml. |
| 2 tsp. | freshly grated lemon peel | 10 ml. |
| 1 cup | heavy cream, whipped | ¼ liter |
| 2 tbsp. | unflavored powdered gelatin, softened in ½ cup [125 ml.] hot water | 30 ml. |
| 4 | eggs | 4 |
| 5 tbsp. | strained fresh lemon juice | 75 ml. |
| 1 tbsp. | Cognac or other brandy | 15 ml. |
| | macaroons or wafers (optional) | |

Add the wine and the lemon peel to the softened gelatin. Stir until the gelatin dissolves. In a heatproof bowl set in a pan partly filled with hot but not boiling water, whisk the eggs until they begin to thicken slightly. Remove the bowl from the heat. Strain the gelatin mixture into the eggs, and add the lemon juice and the Cognac. Beat the mixture until it cools. Finally, fold in the whipped cream. Serve in glasses and garnish with macaroons or wafers.

GRETE WILLINSKY
KOCHBUCH DER BÜCHERGILDE

# Red Wine Froth

*To serve 4*

| | | |
|---|---|---|
| 1 cup | Burgundy, Bordeaux or other dry red wine | ¼ liter |
| 4 | egg yolks, lightly beaten | 4 |
| ½ cup | sugar | 125 ml. |
| ½ tsp. | finely grated lemon peel | 2 ml. |
| 1 tbsp. | raspberry or red currant jelly | 15 ml. |

In an enameled or stainless-steel saucepan, whisk all the ingredients over low to medium heat until the mixture thickens: it must not boil. Remove from the heat and keep on beating vigorously until the mixture is cold. Serve in a glass dish or in small, individual dishes.

INGA NORBERG
GOOD FOOD FROM SWEDEN

# Rhubarb Cream

*To serve 4*

| | | |
|---|---|---|
| 1 lb. | rhubarb, cut into 1-inch [2½-cm.] lengths (about 4 cups [1 liter]) | ½ kg. |
| ½ cup | heavy cream, whipped | 125 ml. |
| ⅓ cup | apple juice | 75 ml. |
| ½ cup | light brown sugar (or to taste) | 125 ml. |
| ¼ tsp. | ground cinnamon | 1 ml. |
| 2 | eggs, the yolks separated from the whites | 2 |

Place the rhubarb and apple juice in a stainless-steel or enameled saucepan. Bring to a boil, reduce the heat, cover and allow to simmer for about 10 minutes, or until the rhubarb is tender.

Pass the mixture through a food mill, or blend it until smooth in an electric blender. Return it to the saucepan.

Beat all but 1 tablespoon [15 ml.] of the brown sugar into the rhubarb, or sweeten it to taste. Add the cinnamon.

Beat the egg yolks with the remaining brown sugar and stir them into the fruit mixture. Heat briefly, stirring, until the mixture thickens slightly; do not allow it to boil.

Cool and chill the mixture. Beat the egg whites until they are stiff but not dry, and fold them into the chilled rhubarb mixture. Fold in the whipped cream.

JEAN HEWITT
THE NEW YORK TIMES WEEKEND COOKBOOK

# Apricot Whip with Madeira

*The technique of blanching almonds is demonstrated on page 12. To toast almonds, place the blanched nuts in a shallow pan in a 350° F. [180° C.] oven for 10 minutes, turning them frequently to brown them evenly.*

*To serve 6*

| | | |
|---|---|---|
| 1½ cups | dried apricots, soaked in water overnight | 375 ml. |
| ⅔ cup | Madeira | 150 ml. |
| ¾ cup | sugar | 175 ml. |
| 2 | egg whites | 2 |
| 1 cup | heavy cream, stiffly whipped | ¼ liter |
| ¼ cup | almonds, blanched, sliced and toasted | 50 ml. |

Place the apricots and their water in a saucepan. Add half of the sugar and additional water, if necessary, to just about cover the fruit. Bring to a boil and simmer, uncovered, for about 25 minutes, or until the apricots are tender.

Drain the fruit and reduce the remaining liquid until it is a syrupy glaze. Add this to the cooked apricots and set them aside to cool. Purée the fruit and syrup in a blender with ½ cup [125 ml.] of the Madeira.

Beat the egg whites until they are stiff. Beat in the remaining sugar, a little at a time. Continue to beat the egg whites until the sugar has dissolved. Fold the stiffly beaten egg whites and half of the whipped cream into the apricot purée. Pour the mixture into a serving dish and sprinkle with the almonds. Chill well before serving. Beat the remaining Madeira into the remaining whipped cream and serve with the apricot whip.

PAULA PECK
PAULA PECK'S ART OF GOOD COOKING

# Gooseberry Fool

Rhubarb fool is made in just the same way as gooseberry fool, but it needs an even larger proportion of sugar, preferably dark brown; and it is necessary, when the rhubarb is cooked, to put it in a colander or sieve and let the excess juice drain off before the cream is added. The brown sugar gives rhubarb a specially rich flavor and color.

*To serve 6 to 8*

| | | |
|---|---|---|
| 2¼ quarts | gooseberries (about 2 lb. [1 kg.]) | 2¼ liters |
| 1 cup | superfine sugar | ¼ liter |
| 1 to 2 cups | heavy cream, whipped to soft peaks | ¼ to ½ liter |

Wash the gooseberries; there is no need to top and tail them. Put them with the sugar in the top half of a double boiler, over, and steam them for about 30 minutes, or until they are quite soft. Strain off the surplus liquid (which would make the fool watery) and purée the gooseberries through a food mill. When the purée is quite cold, add the cream. More sugar may be necessary.

ELIZABETH DAVID
SYLLABUBS AND FRUIT FOOLS

## Gooseberry Huff

*The technique of cooking sugar syrup to the small-thread stage is shown on page 9. To make an apple huff, substitute 1½ cups [375 ml.] of puréed apples for the gooseberries.*

| To serve 4 to 6 | | |
|---|---|---|
| 5 cups | gooseberries (about 1¼ lb. [⅔ kg.]), boiled until tender and puréed through a strainer or food mill | 1¼ liters |
| 1 cup | sugar | ¼ liter |
| ½ cup | water | 125 ml. |
| 3 | egg whites | 3 |

Prepare a syrup with sugar and water, cooking it to the small-thread stage. Let the syrup get almost cold. Beat the egg whites to a froth, combine them with the gooseberry purée and beat until the mixture looks white. Add the syrup to the gooseberry mixture and beat together until it is all froth. Pour into individual cups or glasses and serve.

J. STEVENS COX (EDITOR)
DORSET DISHES OF THE 17TH CENTURY

## Quince Blancmange

| To serve 8 | | |
|---|---|---|
| 8 or 9 | ripe quinces (2 to 2½ lb. [1 kg.]), peeled and cored | 8 or 9 |
| 2 quarts | water | 2 liters |
| 1½ cups | superfine sugar | 375 ml. |
| 6 tbsp. | unflavored powdered gelatin, softened in ½ cup [125 ml.] cold water | 90 ml. |
| 1 cup | heavy cream | ¼ liter |

Put the quinces with the water into a stainless-steel, enameled or tin-lined saucepan, and simmer gently until they are beginning to disintegrate but are not reduced to a pulp — after about 20 minutes. Strain the quince liquor through a

jelly bag or dampened cheesecloth into another pan, discarding the quince pulp. Add the sugar and stir the mixture over brisk heat, boiling it until it reaches the thread stage. Skim it carefully. Add the gelatin and stir until it dissolves.

Pour the mixture into a bowl, allow it to cool until tepid and stir in the cream. Continue stirring until the mixture is nearly cold, then with cold water rinse out a 2½-quart [2½-liter] mold. Pour in the blancmange, and refrigerate until it is quite cold and set.

When you are ready to serve the blancmange, turn it out of the mold onto a fancy dish.

OSCAR TSCHIRKY
THE COOK BOOK BY "OSCAR" OF THE WALDORF

## Almond Blancmange

*Blanc-manger aux Amandes*

*The original version of this recipe specified bitter almonds. To give sweet almonds a slightly bitter flavor, add ¼ teaspoon [1 ml.] of almond extract to the almond-milk mixture.*

| To serve 5 | | |
|---|---|---|
| 1 cup | blanched almonds | ¼ liter |
| ½ cup | cold water | 125 ml. |
| ½ cup | milk | 125 ml. |
| 1 cup | sugar | ¼ liter |
| 2 tbsp. | unflavored powdered gelatin, softened in 1 cup [¼ liter] cold water | 30 ml. |
| 2 cups | heavy cream | ½ liter |

In a large mortar or heavy bowl, pound the almonds as fine as possible, adding the water very gradually. Then add the milk and continue crushing the almonds by rotating the pestle. Put this almond milk into a saucepan with the sugar. Heat the mixture gently for two to three minutes over low heat, taking care not to let it reach a boil.

Remove the pan from the heat. Place a cloth napkin over a large bowl and pour the almond milk, little by little, into the napkin, twisting the napkin tightly in order to extract all of the almond milk. Warm the softened gelatin over low heat until it dissolves in its soaking water, then add it to the almond-milk mixture.

Whip the cream until it stands in firm peaks. Cool the almond-milk mixture to tepid; at this point, and no sooner, blend in the whipped cream. Pour the mixture into an oiled 5-cup [1¼-liter] mold and put in a cool place, or refrigerate, for about five hours. To serve, unmold the blancmange.

J. B. REBOUL
LA CUISINIÈRE PROVENÇALE

## A West Country Syllabub

*The original instructions in this recipe, which dates from 1800, called for the bowl to be filled with warm milk straight from the cow. If desired, 2 cups [½ liter] of white wine can be substituted for the mixture of port and sherry.*

To serve 6 to 8

| | | |
|---|---|---|
| 1¼ cups | port | 300 ml. |
| 1¼ cups | medium-dry sherry | 300 ml. |
| 2 to 3 tbsp. | sugar | 30 to 45 ml. |
| 2½ cups | milk | 625 ml. |
| ½ cup | heavy cream, whipped | 125 ml. |

Pour the port and sherry into a 1¾-quart [1¾-liter] glass or pottery bowl: the bowl should be about one third full. Stir in the sugar according to taste. Add the milk and stir a little. Leave to stand for about 20 minutes, or until the curd of the milk separates from the wine. Pour the syllabub into individual glasses, spooning the curd on top, and put a spoonful of whipped cream on each serving.

ELISABETH AYRTON
THE COOKERY OF ENGLAND

## Everlasting Syllabub

*The original version of this recipe called for double cream—the English equivalent of heavy cream, but higher in butterfat than its American counterpart. For best results, use cream that has not been ultra-pasteurized.*

In their heyday syllabubs were regarded as a refreshment to be offered at card parties, ball suppers and public entertainments, rather than just as a pudding for lunches and dinners. These syllabubs can be made at least two days in advance; they will keep well in a cool place.

To serve 4 to 6

| | | |
|---|---|---|
| 1 | lemon, thinly peeled and the juice strained | 1 |
| ½ cup | white wine or sherry | 125 ml. |
| 2 tbsp. | brandy | 30 ml. |
| ¼ cup | sugar | 50 ml. |
| 1¼ cups | heavy cream | 300 ml. |
| | grated nutmeg | |

The day before the syllabub is to be made, put the lemon peel and juice in a bowl with the wine and brandy and leave overnight. Next day, strain the wine-and-lemon mixture into a large and deep bowl. Add the sugar and stir until it has dissolved. Pour in the cream slowly, stirring all the time. Grate in a little nutmeg. Now whisk the mixture until it thickens and will hold a soft peak on the whisk. This process may take five minutes, or it may take as long as 15: it de-

pends on the cream, the temperature and the method of whisking. Unless you are dealing with a large quantity of cream, an electric mixer can be perilous: a couple of seconds too long and the cream is a ruined and grainy mess. For a small amount of cream, a wire whisk is perfectly satisfactory and just as quick as an electric beater. The important point is to learn to recognize when the whisking process is complete.

When the cream is ready, spoon it into syllabub or custard cups or sherry glasses, which should be of very small capacity—2 to 2½ ounces [60 to 75 ml.]—but filled to overflowing. Once in the glasses, the cream will not spoil or sink or separate. A tiny sprig of rosemary or a little twist of lemon peel can be stuck into each little filled glass. Keep the syllabubs in a cool place—not in the refrigerator—until you are ready to serve them.

ELIZABETH DAVID
SYLLABUBS AND FRUIT FOOLS

## Syllabub for Six

Recipes for syllabub vary in detail from place to place, and many include egg whites in the ingredients. This one does not and is said to be all the lighter for it.

To serve 6

| | | |
|---|---|---|
| ⅔ cup | medium-dry white wine | 150 ml. |
| 2 tsp. | finely grated fresh lemon peel | 10 ml. |
| ⅓ cup | superfine sugar | 75 ml. |
| 2 tbsp. | strained fresh lemon juice | 30 ml. |
| 1¼ cups | heavy cream, chilled | 300 ml. |

Put all but the cream into a bowl and set in a cool spot for no less than three hours. Better still, leave overnight. Then add the cream, and whip and beat and beat and whip until the mixture stands in soft, seductive peaks. The syllabub will keep like this for several days, but never lasts that long! It looks its best when piled high into wine or sundae glasses.

JOYCE DOUGLAS
OLD PENDLE RECIPES

## Strawberry Cream

To serve 4

| | | |
|---|---|---|
| 1½ cups | strawberries, hulled | 375 ml. |
| 1¼ cups | heavy cream, chilled | 300 ml. |
| ¼ cup | sugar | 50 ml. |
| 2 tbsp. | strained fresh lemon juice | 30 ml. |
| 2 tbsp. | unflavored powdered gelatin, softened in ¼ cup [50 ml.] water | 30 ml. |
| ½ cup | milk | 125 ml. |

Pass the strawberries through a nylon sieve into a bowl, and add the sugar and lemon juice to the strawberry pulp. In a saucepan over low heat, dissolve the gelatin in the milk, then strain it into the strawberry pulp. Whip the cream and blend it with the strawberry mixture. Mix together thoroughly, and pour into a 4-cup [1-liter] mold. Refrigerate until wanted, then unmold and serve.

A. KENNEY HERBERT
FIFTY DINNERS

## Striped Bavarian Cream

*A striped Bavarian cream is made by alternating layers of vanilla cream with layers of cream of a contrasting flavor and color. The strawberry cream used here can be varied by substituting puréed fresh raspberries or currants, or puréed, cooked dried apricots. To make a coffee-flavored cream, follow the instructions in this recipe for vanilla cream, but first infuse the milk for 15 minutes with ⅓ cup [75 ml.] of freshly ground coffee, mixed with just enough boiling water to make a smooth paste, then strain the milk through several thicknesses of cheesecloth.*

To serve 12

### Strawberry cream

| 2½ cups | strawberries, rubbed through a fine nylon sieve to yield about 1¼ cups [300 ml.] purée | 625 ml. |
|---|---|---|
| 1 cup | granulated sugar | ¼ liter |
| ⅔ cup | water | 150 ml. |
| 2 tbsp. | unflavored powdered gelatin, softened in ¼ cup [50 ml.] water | 30 ml. |
| ½ | lemon, the juice strained | ½ |
| 1¼ cups | heavy cream, whipped to soft peaks | 300 ml. |

### Vanilla cream

| 2 cups | milk, brought to a boil, and infused for 10 minutes with a vanilla bean, or mixed with 1 tsp. [5 ml.] vanilla extract | ½ liter |
|---|---|---|
| ¾ cup | granulated sugar | 175 ml. |
| 6 | egg yolks | 6 |
| | salt | |
| 3 tbsp. | unflavored gelatin, dissolved in 6 tbsp. [90 ml.] water | 45 ml. |
| 2 cups | heavy cream, whipped to soft peaks with ¼ cup [50 ml.] confectioners' sugar | ½ liter |

First prepare the strawberry cream. Make a heavy syrup by boiling the sugar in the water over medium heat for one to two minutes. Off the heat, add the gelatin, stirring until it dissolves completely. Add the lemon juice to the strawberry purée. Pour in the warm syrup, stirring until thoroughly blended. Set the mixture aside to cool while you prepare the

vanilla cream. As soon as the strawberry purée begins to set, fold in the whipped cream.

Using a wooden spoon, make the vanilla cream by first blending together the sugar, egg yolks and a small pinch of salt in a heavy saucepan over very low heat. When the mixture becomes quite smooth, gradually stir in the milk, then add the gelatin. Stirring all the time, keep the mixture on the heat until it coats the spoon, but do not allow it to boil. Transfer the vanilla cream to a bowl and cool by stirring over ice. As soon as it begins to set, fold in the whipped cream.

Choose a 2-quart [2-liter] mold, preferably a tube mold, and brush the inside with sweet almond oil, or rinse the mold in ice water. Fill the mold with alternate layers of the two creams, chilling each layer before adding the next one. Cover the mold and refrigerate it for about five hours.

To serve, dip the mold quickly into warm water and wipe the outside dry. Unmold the dessert onto a serving dish, which may be covered with a folded napkin or a paper doily if you like, or into a shallow glass dish.

PROSPER MONTAGNÉ
THE NEW LAROUSSE GASTRONOMIQUE

## Raspberry Cream

*Crème Celesta*

*For instructions on making sugar syrup, see pages 8-9.*

To serve 6 to 8

| 1 cup | puréed raspberries, made from 2½ to 3 cups [625 ml. to ¾ liter] fresh raspberries and flavored with kirsch or maraschino liqueur | ¼ liter |
|---|---|---|
| 1 cup | medium sugar syrup, made from ½ cup [125 ml.] sugar and ¾ cup [175 ml.] water | ¼ liter |
| 10 | egg yolks | 10 |
| 1 | vanilla bean | 1 |
| 1 cup | heavy cream | ¼ liter |
| ¼ cup | confectioners' sugar | 50 ml. |

Pour the syrup into a medium-sized, well-tinned copper saucepan placed inside a larger pan of simmering water. Add the egg yolks and beat well. Add the vanilla bean and cook, stirring constantly, until the mixture is smooth and glossy. When the mixture has the consistency of a hollandaise sauce, remove the vanilla bean. Transfer the mixture to an enameled bowl and whisk until it cools.

Add the raspberry purée and pour the mixture into six or eight individual cups or ramekins, filling them two thirds full. Chill in the refrigerator for one hour. Whip the cream with the sugar to make Chantilly cream. Fill the cups or ramekins to the top with the Chantilly cream and chill again in the refrigerator until ready to serve.

ÉDOUARD NIGNON
LES PLAISIRS DE LA TABLE

## Bavarian Cream Perfect Love

A chocolate cream can be made by melting 3 ounces [90 g.] of semisweet baking chocolate in the milk, a coffee cream by substituting freshly made strong black coffee for the milk.

*To serve 8 to 10*

| | | |
|---|---|---|
| 2 cups | sugar | ½ liter |
| 8 | egg yolks | 8 |
| 2 cups | milk | ½ liter |
| 6 | whole cloves | 6 |
| 2 tbsp. | unflavored powdered gelatin, softened in ¼ cup [50 ml.] cold water | 30 ml. |
| 3 cups | heavy cream, whipped | ¾ liter |
| 1½ tbsp. | finely grated lemon peel | 22 ml. |

Beat the sugar and egg yolks until the mixture is lemon-colored. Heat the milk with the cloves. When the milk reaches a boil, remove the cloves and slowly stir the milk into the egg yolks and sugar. Put this mixture in a saucepan and set it over very low heat. With a wooden spoon, stir the mixture continuously until the spoon remains thickly covered. Do not allow the mixture to boil.

Remove the pan from the heat and pour the mixture into a bowl. Add the gelatin and stir until it is completely dissolved, then strain and stir from time to time until the mixture is cool. When it begins to thicken, fold in the whipped cream and the grated lemon peel.

Pour the Bavarian cream into a lightly oiled 4-cup [1-liter] mold and chill in the refrigerator for four hours. Unmold onto a serving dish.

ALICE B. TOKLAS
THE ALICE B. TOKLAS COOK BOOK

## French Flummery

*This recipe is adapted from a book published anonymously in 1747, but attributed to the English writer Hannah Glasse.*

*To serve 6 to 8*

| | | |
|---|---|---|
| 1 quart | heavy cream | 1 liter |
| about ⅓ cup | sugar | about 75 ml. |
| 4 tbsp. | unflavored powdered gelatin, softened in ½ cup [125 ml.] water | 60 ml. |
| 1 tbsp. | rose water | 15 ml. |
| 1 tbsp. | orange-flower water | 15 ml. |

Place the cream in a saucepan and boil gently over low heat for 15 minutes, stirring all the time. Remove the pan from the heat, sweeten the cream with sugar to taste, add the gelatin and stir until it is dissolved. Add the rose water and orange-flower water. Strain the flummery mixture into a 5-cup [1¼-liter] mold. Refrigerate the flummery for 1½ hours or until set. Unmold the flummery onto a serving dish and, if liked, arrange baked pears around it. Serve with cream.

THE ART OF COOKERY MADE PLAIN AND EASY

## Queen Mab's Pudding

*The original version of this recipe specifies bitter almonds. To give sweet almonds a slightly bitter flavor, add ¼ teaspoon [1 ml.] of almond extract to the almond-and-cream mixture.*

In this recipe, preserved ginger may be substituted for the glacéed cherries, and blanched, chopped pistachio nuts for the candied orange peel. Currants also may replace the cherries, but they must be steamed for 15 minutes before being used. Ginger syrup or a sweetened purée of raspberries or strawberries or other fresh fruit may be served as a sauce.

*To serve 6*

| | | |
|---|---|---|
| 6 | blanched almonds, lightly crushed | 6 |
| 1 | lemon, peeled very thin | 1 |
| 1 quart | heavy cream, or 2½ cups [625 ml.] milk combined with 1½ cups [375 ml.] heavy cream | 1 liter |
| ⅔ cup | sugar | 150 ml. |
| 6 | egg yolks, well beaten | 6 |
| 2 tbsp. | unflavored powdered gelatin, softened in ½ cup [125 ml.] cold water | 30 ml. |
| | salt | |
| ½ cup | glacéed cherries | 125 ml. |
| ⅓ cup | candied orange peel, cut into shreds | 75 ml. |

Put the almonds and lemon peel into a saucepan with 2½ cups [625 ml.] of the cream or the milk-and-cream mixture. Stir over very low heat until the mixture is on the point of boiling and the flavor of the lemon and almonds is well drawn out. Strain through a fine strainer or cheesecloth into another saucepan. Add the sugar and the remaining 1½ cups [375 ml.] of the cream or the milk-and-cream mixture. Bring just to a simmer. Turn the heat to low, then quickly stir in the beaten egg yolks, adding them in a slow stream.

Stirring constantly and carefully to prevent curdling, cook gently until the mixture becomes the thickness of a good custard. Add the soaked gelatin and stir until dissolved. Strain the mixture into a bowl. Continue stirring until nearly cold. Mix in the cherries and orange peel. Rub a drop of oil over a 5-cup [1¼-liter] mold, pour in the mixture and leave to set in the refrigerator for about one and one half hours. Unmold onto a dish and serve.

MARY JEWRY (EDITOR)
WARNE'S MODEL COOKERY AND HOUSEKEEPING BOOK

## Cold Lemon Soufflé

If you like, decorate the top of the soufflé with swirls of piped whipped cream and press some chopped, toasted nuts around the exposed sides.

| | To serve 4 or 5 | |
|---|---|---|
| 4 | large lemons, the peel grated fine and the juice strained | 4 |
| 4 | eggs | 4 |
| 2 tbsp. | unflavored powdered gelatin, softened in 5 tbsp. [75 ml.] cold water | 30 ml. |
| ½ cup | superfine sugar | 125 ml. |
| 1¼ cups | heavy cream | 300 ml. |

Around a 3-cup [¾-liter] soufflé dish, fit a standing collar of wax paper to come at least 3 inches [8 cm.] above the rim. In an ovenproof cup, sprinkle the gelatin over the cold water and leave to soften.

Select two bowls, one larger than the other, and a deep saucepan whose diameter is somewhat smaller than that of the larger bowl, so that the bowl can be set securely in the pan. Make quite sure that the smaller bowl is perfectly clean and dry. Pour 2 to 3 inches [5 to 8 cm.] of water into the saucepan and put it over medium heat. Separate the eggs, dropping the yolks into the larger bowl and the whites into the smaller one.

Add the sugar to the egg yolks. Fit the larger bowl over the pan of water, which should be barely simmering. Whisk the egg-yolk mixture vigorously until it is thick and light and leaves a trail on the surface when the whisk is lifted. Gradually whisk in the lemon juice and continue to whisk until the mixture thickens again. This time it will just manage to hold a trail on the surface. Remove the pan from the heat and lift off the bowl.

Stand the cup containing the softened gelatin in the pan of hot water; stirring occasionally, dissolve the gelatin. Meanwhile, continue to whisk the egg-yolk mixture until just lukewarm. When the gelatin has completely dissolved, remove the cup from the water. Allow the gelatin to cool slightly. Whisk the gelatin into the egg-yolk mixture. Fold in the lemon peel.

In a chilled bowl, whisk the cream until a trail just holds its shape on the surface, being careful not to let the cream get too stiff, or it will be difficult to fold into the soufflé base. The texture should approximate that of the egg-yolk mixture.

Make sure your whisk is perfectly clean and dry. Whisk the egg whites until they form floppy peaks. With a large metal spoon or a rubber spatula, fold the cream into the egg-yolk mixture, followed by the egg whites; work as lightly and quickly as possible.

Stand the prepared soufflé dish on a plate. Pour in the soufflé mixture, taking care not to dislodge or crumple the paper collar. Let the soufflé firm slightly for 15 to 20 minutes before refrigerating the dish. Chill the soufflé for two to three hours until firmly set. Just before serving, peel off the paper collar and decorate the top if desired.

ROBERT CARRIER
THE ROBERT CARRIER COOKERY COURSE

## Honeycomb Cream

*The name of this dessert derives from its honeycomb texture.*

When flavored with lemon, Honeycomb Cream is delicious as a sweet in its own right. Alternatively, it may be flavored with a vanilla bean to make a perfect accompaniment to any of the berry fruits, which can be piled high on a serving dish as a foil to the cream. When served with a real egg custard, into which a little whipped cream has been folded at the last minute, Honeycomb Cream becomes a really exotic dessert. It is best served on the same day it is made.

To flavor with vanilla, put a vanilla bean into the milk at least half an hour before you boil the milk. Remove the bean before pouring the hot liquid into the egg-yolk mixture.

| | To serve 6 to 8 | |
|---|---|---|
| ⅞ cup | light cream | 200 ml. |
| 1 | lemon, the peel grated and the juice strained | 1 |
| 1⅞ cups | milk | 450 ml. |
| 3 | large eggs, the yolks separated from the whites | 3 |
| ¼ cup | sugar | 50 ml. |
| 2 tbsp. | unflavored powdered gelatin, softened in ½ cup [125 ml.] cold water | 30 ml. |

Add the grated lemon peel to the cream and milk. Bring these slowly to a boil over low heat, thus allowing time for the lemon to flavor the liquid.

In a bowl, whisk together the egg yolks, sugar and lemon juice; add the gelatin. Whisking briskly, pour in the heated cream and milk.

Now stand the bowl in a sink of cold water, taking care that no water gets into the bowl. Stir the mixture from time to time as it cools, keeping the cream at the sides well stirred into the rest, because the honeycomb cream will start setting first on the sides of the bowl.

While the cream is still cooling, whisk the egg whites until they just stand in peaks. Carefully, but fully, incorporate the egg whites into the now cold, but not set, cream.

Pour the mixture into a wetted 1-quart [1-liter] mold or soufflé dish. Leave it in a cool place such as a pantry or cellar until you need it. Try not to put this pudding into a refrigerator unless the weather, or your kitchen, is very warm. All gelatin sweets are better unrefrigerated, as they can turn rubbery if they are left too cold for more than a few hours.

MICHAEL SMITH
FINE ENGLISH COOKERY

## Almond Cream

*Hsing Jen Lou*

This dessert can be made in advance, reheated and served hot. It can also be served cold, if you prefer.

| | To serve 6 to 8 | |
|---|---|---|
| ¾ cup | blanched almonds | 175 ml. |
| 1½ tbsp. | long-grain or short-grain rice | 22 ml. |
| 4 cups | cold water | 1 liter |
| about 6 tbsp. | sugar | about 90 ml. |
| 1 tbsp. | almond extract | 15 ml. |

Rinse the almonds and rice together. Soak them in 2 cups [½ liter] of the cold water for at least four hours. Pour the almonds and rice with the water into a blender. Blend them for five minutes or until the liquid is no longer grainy.

Set a bowl underneath a 12-by-14-inch [30-by-35-cm.] muslin bag and pour the almond-cream liquid into the bag. Twist the top to close the bag, then squeeze the bag to force the almond cream into the bowl. Put half of the remaining water (1 cup [¼ liter]) in another bowl, mix the contents of the bag with the water, pour the mixture into the bag and squeeze again to extract more cream. With the remaining 1 cup of water, repeat the process once more. You should have a total of 4 cups [1 liter] of almond cream. Pour this into a saucepan. Discard the residue in the bag.

Heat the pan of almond cream. Add sugar to taste and the almond extract, and slowly bring to a boil over medium to low heat, stirring constantly. This takes about 15 minutes. It is important to heat the cream slowly; otherwise, it will curdle. Remove the cream from the heat and serve it hot.

FLORENCE LIN
FLORENCE LIN'S CHINESE VEGETARIAN COOKBOOK

## Tea Cream

| | To serve 3 or 4 | |
|---|---|---|
| 2½ tbsp. | Hyson or other green tea | 37 ml. |
| 1¼ cups | heavy cream | 300 ml. |
| 1¼ cups | milk | 300 ml. |
| 1 | rennet tablet, dissolved in 1 tbsp. [15 ml.] cold water | 1 |
| ¼ cup | sugar | 50 ml. |

Heat the tea with the milk; strain off the leaves, then add to the milk the cream, dissolved rennet and sugar to taste. Set it in a warm place in the dish it is to be served in and cover it with a plate. When it is thick, it will be sufficiently done. Garnish with sweetmeats.

MARY JEWRY (EDITOR)
WARNE'S MODEL COOKERY AND HOUSEKEEPING BOOK

# Meringues

## Meringues

*Meringues Ordinaires*

These meringues may be flavored by carefully folding in 1 tablespoon [15 ml.] of strong black coffee or unsweetened cocoa into the beaten meringue mixture.

| | To make 3 to 4 dozen meringues, depending on size | |
|---|---|---|
| 8 | egg whites | 8 |
| 4 cups | confectioners' sugar | 1 liter |

Whisk the egg whites until very stiff, then sift in the confectioners' sugar, whisking all the time. Continue whisking for about 10 minutes longer. Put spoonfuls of the meringue mixture on an oiled baking sheet and place in a 200° F. [100° C.] oven to dry—not to bake—for several hours.

EUGÉNIE BRAZIER
LES SECRETS DE LA MÈRE BRAZIER

## Meringue Baskets

| | Makes one 9-inch [23-cm.] basket | |
|---|---|---|
| 4 | egg whites | 4 |
| 2 cups | confectioners' sugar, sifted | ½ liter |
| | vanilla extract | |

Line a large baking sheet with wax or parchment paper. Trace a circle 9 inches [23 cm.] in diameter on the paper lining. Preheat the oven to 250° F. [120° C.].

In a heatproof bowl, beat the egg whites with a wire whisk or rotary beater until they are frothy, but not stiff. Place the bowl on a trivet set in a pan of simmering water over low heat and gradually whisk in the sugar. Add two drops of vanilla extract and continue whisking until the meringue is very thick. Remove the bowl from the heat.

Using a pastry bag fitted with a plain tube, pipe out the meringue in concentric rings to fill the circle traced on the paper and form the base of the basket. Then pipe the remaining meringue around the edge of the circle to make the sides.

Bake for about one and one half hours. Gently peel off the paper, then cool the basket on a wire rack. If not used at once, the basket may be stored in an airtight container.

ZOË CAMRASS
THE ONLY COOKBOOK YOU'LL EVER NEED

## Pistachio Meringues

### Meringues aux Pistaches

*To make about 20 meringues*

| | | |
|---|---|---|
| ⅔ cup | white pistachio nuts, blanched and dried in a 325° F. [160° C.] oven for 10 minutes | 150 ml. |
| 6 | egg whites | 6 |
| ½ cup | superfine sugar | 125 ml. |

Pound the pistachio nuts in a mortar, adding a little egg white from time to time, until a fine paste is formed. In an ovenproof bowl, beat the remaining egg whites until stiff. Set the bowl over a saucepan of simmering water and gradually add 6 tablespoons [90 ml.] of the sugar, beating continuously. When the meringue mixture is stiff and shiny, fold in the pistachio paste.

Line baking sheets with buttered or oiled wax paper and, using a sifter, sprinkle the paper with the remaining sugar. Place spoonfuls of meringue ½ inch [1 cm.] apart on the paper and bake in a very cool oven—200° F. [100° C.]—for several hours or until the meringues are thoroughly dried but not colored.

With a spatula, remove the meringues from the paper and place them on wire racks. Set the racks in the oven until the bottoms of the meringues are thoroughly dried. Store the meringues in a dry place until ready to use.

MM. VIARD ET FOURET
LE CUISINIER ROYAL

## Molded Poached Meringue

### Oeufs à la Neige Moulés

*Molded poached meringue is often served as an island floating on a lake of chilled pouring custard (recipe, page 165). To make the fruit purée called for in this recipe, use about 3 cups [¾ liter] of raspberries, 1 cup [¼ liter] of strawberries and ¾ cup [175 ml.] of fresh currants. Force the fruit through a nylon sieve and sweeten the purée to taste with about ⅓ cup [75 ml.] of sugar.*

*To serve 4*

| | | |
|---|---|---|
| 4 | egg whites | 4 |
| ½ cup | vanilla-flavored confectioners' sugar, or sugar flavored with orange or lemon peel | 125 ml. |
| 2 cups | puréed, mixed raspberries, strawberries and red currants | ½ liter |

Beat the egg whites until stiff. Continuing to beat, gradually add the flavored sugar in a fine stream. Liberally butter a 3-cup [¾-liter] plain or fluted tube mold and sprinkle it with sugar. Fill the mold with the meringue mixture to within 1 inch [2½ cm.] of the brim. Place the mold in a pan and pour in hot water to reach halfway up the sides of the mold. Bake in a preheated 400° F. [200° C.] oven for at least 15 minutes, or until the meringue is firm to the touch and shrinks away from the sides of the mold. Remove the pan from the oven, take out the mold and let the meringue cool in a draft-free place for a few minutes. Unmold the meringue onto a plate and let it cool completely. Serve with the cold fruit purée.

JEAN DE GOUY
LA CUISINE ET LA PÂTISSERIE BOURGEOISES

# Soufflés and Puddings

## Apricot Omelet Soufflé

*To serve 6*

| | | |
|---|---|---|
| 1½ cups | apricot jam | 375 ml. |
| 4 tbsp. | butter | 60 ml. |
| 1 cup | flour | ¼ liter |
| 1 tbsp. | sugar | 15 ml. |
| 1¼ cups | cream | 300 ml. |
| ¾ cup | milk | 175 ml. |
| 6 | eggs, the yolks separated from the whites | 6 |
| 1 tsp. | vanilla extract | 5 ml. |
| | whipped cream | |

Blend together the butter, flour, sugar, cream and milk in the top of a double boiler. Heat over, but not in, boiling water, stirring constantly until the mass leaves the sides of the pan. Cool the mixture.

Preheat the oven to 325° F. [160° C.]. Add the egg yolks one at a time to the mixture, beating after each addition; add the vanilla. Beat the egg whites until they are stiff but not dry, and fold them in.

Pour the omelet mixture into two buttered, 9-inch [23-cm.] round pans with removable rims, and bake for 25 to 30 minutes. While the omelet is baking, heat the apricot jam in the top of a double boiler, over simmering water.

Have ready a heated serving dish on which to reverse one of the omelet layers. Cover the layer lightly with the jam. Reverse the second layer over it. Cover the second layer with jam and serve the omelet soufflé with whipped cream.

IRMA S. ROMBAUER AND MARION ROMBAUER BECKER
JOY OF COOKING

# Normandy Soufflé

## Soufflé à la Normande

To serve 4

| | | |
|---|---|---|
| 2 | apples, peeled, cored, diced and steeped for about 2 hours in about 3 tbsp. [45 ml.] Calvados sweetened with a little sugar | 2 |
| ½ cup | milk | 125 ml. |
| 3 tbsp. | superfine sugar | 45 ml. |
| 1 tbsp. | flour, blended with a little cold milk | 15 ml. |
| 1 tbsp. | butter | 15 ml. |
| 2 | egg yolks | 2 |
| 2 tbsp. | Calvados (or substitute another apple brandy) | 30 ml. |
| 3 | egg whites | 3 |
| 1 tbsp. | confectioners' sugar | 15 ml. |

Butter a 1-quart [1-liter] soufflé dish and dust it with sugar. Put the milk and superfine sugar into a saucepan and bring to a boil. Add the flour and cook over medium heat, stirring with a wooden spoon, for a few minutes or until the mixture thickens. Off the heat, stir in the butter, egg yolks and Calvados. Whisk the egg whites until they stand in stiff peaks and fold them into the mixture.

Spoon a layer of the mixture into the soufflé dish. Sprinkle in about 2 tablespoons [30 ml.] of diced apple. Add another layer of the soufflé mixture, and continue adding alternate layers of apple and soufflé mixture, finishing with a layer of soufflé mixture. Smooth the top of the soufflé and cook in a preheated 350° F. [180° C.] oven for 25 to 30 minutes. Two minutes before the end of the cooking time, sprinkle the soufflé with confectioners' sugar and raise the oven temperature to 450° F. [230° C.] to form a glaze.

PROSPER MONTAGNÉ AND A. GOTTSCHALK
MON MENU

# Prune Soufflé

*Dried apricots or dried peaches may be substituted for the dried prunes called for in this recipe.*

To serve 4 to 6

| | | |
|---|---|---|
| ½ lb. | pitted, dried prunes (about 1 cup [250 ml.]), soaked in water overnight and drained | ¼ kg. |
| 1¼ cups | water | 300 ml. |
| ½ cup | superfine sugar | 125 ml. |
| 5 | egg whites | 5 |
| | whipped cream | |

Cook the prunes in the water for about 10 minutes, or until they are very tender. Drain the prunes, then chop them fine and mix them with the sugar. Beat the egg whites until stiff and stir them into the prunes with a knife. Pour the mixture into a buttered 1-quart [1-liter] soufflé dish. Bake in a preheated 375° F. [190° C.] oven for about 10 minutes. Serve at once with whipped cream.

INGA NORBERG
GOOD FOOD FROM SWEDEN

# Strawberry Soufflé

*This is a modern version of a recipe by Carême, inventor of the classic soufflé. The mixture is so simple that the flavor of the soufflé depends largely on the strawberries, which should be highly perfumed. If they are not, add a little kirsch or lemon juice to the purée. This soufflé can be baked in as few as 15 minutes if the oven is preheated to 450° F. [230° C.].*

To serve 4

| | | |
|---|---|---|
| 1 pint | strawberries, hulled | ¼ kg. |
| ½ to ¾ cup | granulated sugar | 125 to 175 ml. |
| | kirsch or lemon juice (optional) | |
| 5 | egg whites | 5 |
| 1 to 2 tbsp. | confectioners' sugar | 15 to 30 ml. |

Purée the strawberries in a blender or work them through a sieve. Add about ¼ to ½ cup [50 to 125 ml.] of the granulated sugar, depending on the sweetness of the berries. If desired, add kirsch or lemon juice to taste. Butter the inside of a 1½-quart [1½-liter] soufflé dish and sprinkle it with sugar, discarding the excess. Preheat the oven to 350° F. [180° C.].

Whip the egg whites stiff. Add ¼ cup [50 ml.] of granulated sugar and beat until this meringue mixture is glossy and forms a tall peak. Stir a little meringue into the strawberry purée, mixing it well, then add the purée to the remaining meringue, folding them together as lightly as possible.

Spoon the soufflé mixture into the prepared dish (the mixture should reach the top of the mold) and bake it in the preheated oven for 25 to 30 minutes, or until puffed and brown. The center should still be slightly concave. Sprinkle the top with the confectioners' sugar and serve. A sauce of fresh strawberry purée is an excellent accompaniment.

ANNE WILLAN
GREAT COOKS AND THEIR RECIPES FROM TAILLEVENT TO ESCOFFIER

---

## Chocolate Soufflé

*To serve 3 or 4*

| | | |
|---|---|---|
| 3 oz. | semisweet chocolate, finely grated | 100 g. |
| 4 | eggs | 4 |
| 3 tsp. | sugar | 15 ml. |
| 1 tsp. | flour | 5 ml. |
| | superfine sugar | |

Break the eggs and separate the whites from the yolks, putting them into different bowls. Add to the yolks the sugar, flour and chocolate, and stir these ingredients for five minutes. Then whisk the egg whites until they are stiff, and fold them into the yolks until the mixture is smooth. Butter a 6-inch [15-cm.] round cake pan, put in the mixture and bake in a preheated 350° F. [180° C.] oven for 15 to 20 minutes.

Pin a white napkin around the pan, sift some superfine sugar over the top of the soufflé and send it immediately to the table. The proper appearance of this dish depends entirely on the expedition with which it is served; if it is allowed to stand after it is taken out of the oven, it will be entirely spoiled, as it falls almost immediately.

MRS. ISABELLA BEETON
THE BOOK OF HOUSEHOLD MANAGEMENT

---

## Toasted Almond Soufflé

*Serve the soufflé with wine custard sauce (recipe, page 165).*

*To serve 6 to 8*

| | | |
|---|---|---|
| 1½ cups | blanched almonds (about ½ lb. [¼ kg.]), coarsely chopped | 375 ml. |
| 1 cup | sugar | ¼ liter |
| 2 tbsp. | strained fresh lemon juice | 30 ml. |
| 7 | egg whites, beaten until stiff | 7 |
| 1 tbsp. | flour (optional) | 15 ml. |

Mix the almonds with the sugar, and toast in a skillet on top of the stove until nicely browned. Sprinkle the lemon juice

over the almonds and let stand until cool. Grind the mixture with a mortar and pestle, or in a blender or food processor.

Fold the almond mixture lightly into the egg whites. If the eggs are very large, fold in the flour.

Turn the mixture into a buttered and floured 1-quart [1-liter] soufflé dish and place in a shallow pan partly filled with warm water. Bake in a preheated 375° F. [190° C.] oven for 40 to 45 minutes, or until the soufflé is puffed and brown on top. Serve immediately.

JOSEPH PASTERNAK
COOKING WITH LOVE AND PAPRIKA

## Frangipane Soufflé

*Soufflé de Frangipane*

*Bitter-almond macaroons are not commonly available in America. Here, a few drops of almond extract provide the bitter-almond flavor. The original recipe also calls for 1 tablespoon [15 ml.] of powdered caramelized orange flowers; a like amount of orange-flower water may be added to the egg mixture as an alternative.*

*To serve 8*

| | | |
|---|---|---|
| 1 | whole egg | 1 |
| 8 | egg yolks | 8 |
| ⅓ cup | water | 75 ml. |
| 2¼ cups | heavy cream | ½ liter |
| 5 | almond macaroons | 5 |
| 1 | stale ladyfinger | 1 |
| ¼ cup | superfine sugar | 50 ml. |
| | almond extract | |
| 5 | egg whites | 5 |

Put the whole egg and four of the egg yolks in a saucepan and mix them with the water. Stir in the cream. Place the mixture over low heat and stir constantly until it thickens. Remove from the heat and allow the mixture to cool.

Crush the macaroons and ladyfinger very fine. Add them to the cooled egg mixture along with the superfine sugar and a few drops of almond extract. Mix together well, then add the remaining four egg yolks. (More egg yolks may be added if your mixture is too thick to stir easily.) Beat the egg whites stiff and fold them into the mixture.

Pour the soufflé mixture into a buttered 5-cup [1¼-liter] charlotte mold or soufflé dish and cook in a preheated 350° F. [180° C.] oven for about 35 minutes, or until the soufflé is well risen and lightly browned.

MM. VIARD AND FOURET
LE CUISINIER ROYAL

7/2020

# Vanilla Soufflé

*Soufflé à la Vanille*

*The author suggests the following variations: flavoring the soufflé with a liqueur, such as chartreuse, Grand Marnier, kirsch or Curaçao; with chocolate, by adding 2 ounces [50 g.] of melted semisweet chocolate; or with praline, by adding ¼ cup [50 ml.] of praline almonds (page 13). You also may add 2 or 3 tablespoons [30 or 45 ml.] of chopped candied fruit, plain or soaked in brandy.*

To serve 4

| ½ cup | milk | 125 ml. |
|---|---|---|
| 2 tbsp. | superfine sugar | 30 ml. |
| 1 | vanilla bean | 1 |
| 1 tbsp. | flour, mixed with a little cold milk | 15 ml. |
| 2 tsp. | butter | 10 ml. |
| 2 | egg yolks | 2 |
| 3 | egg whites | 3 |
| 1 tbsp. | confectioners' sugar | 15 ml. |

In a small saucepan, bring the milk to a boil, along with the superfine sugar and the vanilla bean (or any other flavoring of your choice). As soon as the milk reaches a boil, add the flour-and-milk mixture. Cook for two minutes, whisking constantly. Take the pan off the heat, remove the vanilla bean and add the butter and egg yolks. Mix thoroughly. Beat the egg whites until they form stiff peaks and fold them into the soufflé-base mixture.

Butter a 3-cup [¾-liter] soufflé dish and dust it with superfine sugar. Pour in the soufflé mixture and smooth the surface. Cook in a preheated 350° F. [180° C.] oven for about 25 minutes, or until the soufflé is well risen. Two minutes before removing the soufflé from the oven, sprinkle the confectioners' sugar over the surface to glaze it.

PROSPER MONTAGNÉ AND A. GOTTSCHALK
MON MENU

# Bread Pudding with Cognac Sauce

To serve 4 to 6

| 4 cups | cubed day-old French bread | 1 liter |
|---|---|---|
| 2 cups | milk | ½ liter |
| 4 tbsp. | butter | 60 ml. |
| ½ cup | sugar | 125 ml. |
| ½ cup | raisins, soaked in warm water for 15 minutes and drained | 125 ml. |
| 2 | eggs, lightly beaten | 2 |
| ⅛ tsp. | salt | ½ ml. |
| ½ tsp. | grated nutmeg | 2 ml. |
| 1 tsp. | vanilla extract | 5 ml. |
| ¼ cup | shredded coconut (optional) | 50 ml. |

**Cognac sauce**

| ¼ cup | Cognac or other brandy | 50 ml. |
|---|---|---|
| 8 tbsp. | butter | 120 ml. |
| 2 cups | confectioners' sugar | ½ liter |

Scald the milk. Melt the butter in the milk and stir in the sugar. Pour the mixture over the bread and raisins. Let them stand for 15 minutes. Add the beaten eggs, salt, nutmeg, vanilla and coconut. Bake in a well-greased 1½-quart [1½-liter] dish in a preheated 350° F. [180° C.] oven for 35 to 45 minutes, or until the top is browned and a knife inserted into the center of the pudding comes out clean.

Meanwhile, make the Cognac sauce by creaming the butter and sugar, then gradually adding the Cognac.

Serve the pudding warm, topped with Cognac sauce.

THE JUNIOR LEAGUE OF NEW ORLEANS
THE PLANTATION COOKBOOK

# Bread and Butter Pudding

To serve 4 to 6

| 4 | very thin slices bread, buttered | 4 |
|---|---|---|
| ½ cup | dried currants, washed and picked over | 125 ml. |
| 3 | eggs | 3 |
| 1 | egg yolk | 1 |
| ½ cup | sugar | 125 ml. |
| | grated nutmeg | |
| 2½ cups | milk | ½ liter |

Strew a few of the currants on the bottom of a 1¼-quart [1¼-liter] dish. Layer the buttered bread and remaining currants alternately on top. Put the eggs and egg yolk into a bowl and beat them well. Add the sugar and a pinch of nutmeg. Then add the milk and stir well together. About 10 minutes before putting the pudding in the oven, pour the egg mixture over the bread and butter. Set the dish in a pan partly filled with boiling water and bake in a preheated 350° F. [180° C.] oven. The pudding will take 45 minutes to bake.

MRS. RUNDELL
MODERN DOMESTIC COOKERY

# Hungarian Bread Pudding

### *Máglyarakás*

*To serve 6 to 8*

| | | |
|---|---|---|
| ½ lb. | brioche or other sweet yeast bread, 1 or 2 days old, cut into thin slices | ¼ kg. |
| 3 | eggs, the yolks separated from the whites | 3 |
| ½ cup | sugar | 125 ml. |
| 2 tbsp. | butter, melted | 30 ml. |
| 2 cups | milk | ½ liter |
| ⅔ cup | seedless white raisins, macerated in about 4 tbsp. [60 ml.] rum | 150 ml. |
| 1 cup | walnuts, pulverized with a mortar and pestle or in a food processor | ¼ liter |
| 3 or 4 | medium-sized apples (1 lb. [½ kg.]), peeled, cored and thinly sliced | 3 or 4 |
| 3 tbsp. | apricot jam, puréed through a food mill | 45 ml. |

Beat the egg yolks with the sugar until creamy, and mix in the melted butter. Add the milk and pour the mixture over the sliced bread. Set aside until the slices become soaked.

Butter a shallow ovenproof dish and place half of the soaked bread mixture in the bottom. Sprinkle with the raisins and the walnuts. Cover with the remaining bread mixture. Then top with the apple slices, sticking them in vertically. Bake for 30 minutes in an oven preheated to 375° F. [190° C.]. Meanwhile, beat the egg whites until they are stiff and fold in the puréed apricot jam.

Pour this egg-white meringue over the partly baked pudding. Smooth the surface with a knife. Return the pudding to the oven, reduce the heat to 325° F. [160° C.], and bake for 10 to 15 minutes or longer, until the topping rises well and browns a little. To serve, cut the pudding into large blocks.

FRED MACNICOL
HUNGARIAN COOKERY

# Ricotta Pudding

### *Budino di Ricotta*

Some ricottas are softer and moister than others. This pudding requires dry ricotta; it may be advisable to line a strainer with cheesecloth and place the moist ricotta in it to drain.

*To serve 4 to 6*

| | | |
|---|---|---|
| 2 cups | ricotta cheese | ½ liter |
| 1 | whole egg | 1 |
| 4 | eggs, the yolks separated from the whites, and the whites stiffly beaten | 4 |
| ½ cup | sugar | 125 ml. |
| ¼ cup | flour | 50 ml. |
| ¼ tsp. | grated nutmeg | 1 ml. |
| ¼ cup | glacéed orange peel, finely diced | 50 ml. |
| ¼ cup | glacéed citron, finely diced | 50 ml. |
| 1 | lemon, the peel grated | 1 |
| ¼ cup | rum (or substitute maraschino liqueur or kirsch) | 50 ml. |
| | confectioners' sugar | |
| | ground cinnamon | |

Put the ricotta into a large bowl. Beat in, one at a time, the whole egg and the four egg yolks, beating well after each addition. Beat in the sugar, flour, nutmeg, glacéed fruits, fresh lemon peel and rum, and continue beating until very smooth. Fold the egg whites into the ricotta mixture.

Generously butter a 2-quart [2-liter] mold that has smooth sides. Spoon in the ricotta mixture; the mold should not be more than half-full. Bake in a preheated 350° F. [180° C.] oven for about 30 minutes, or until the pudding is well puffed and golden. Sprinkle with confectioners' sugar and a little ground cinnamon, and serve hot. Or cool and then sprinkle with the confectioners' sugar and cinnamon.

NIKA HAZELTON
THE REGIONAL ITALIAN KITCHEN

# White Cheese Pudding

## *Pudding de Fromage Blanc*

This pudding can be flavored according to taste with grated orange or lemon peel, vanilla extract, orange-flower water or a fruit-flavored white liqueur of one's choice.

*To serve 4 to 6*

| | | |
|---|---|---|
| 1 cup | cottage cheese, sieved, or ricotta | ¼ liter |
| ½ cup | sugar | 125 ml. |
| ½ cup | heavy cream | 125 ml. |
| | salt | |
| 5 | eggs, the yolks separated from the whites | 5 |
| 2 tbsp. | seedless raisins, soaked in warm water for 10 minutes and drained | 30 ml. |
| 5 or 6 | almond macaroons, finely crushed | 5 or 6 |
| about 2 cups | puréed raspberries or apricots, or a mixture of raspberries, red currants and strawberries | about ½ liter |

In a large bowl, combine the cheese, sugar, cream and a pinch of salt. Whisk together well, incorporating the egg yolks one by one. Flavor to taste. Beat until the mixture is light, then add the raisins and crushed macaroons.

In another bowl, beat the egg whites until stiff, then fold them carefully into the cheese mixture. Pour into a well-buttered, floured 1-quart [1-liter] savarin mold and bake in a preheated 325° F. [170° C.] oven for 45 minutes, or until the pudding puffs up and is firm to the touch at the center. Turn the pudding onto a heated dish and serve it immediately, with the fruit purée presented separately.

JEAN DE GOUY
LA CUISINE ET LA PÂTISSERIE BOURGEOISES

# Chilled Cheese Dessert

## *Crema di Mascarpone*

*The mascarpone called for in this recipe is a fresh cream cheese made in Lombardy, Italy. Similar to ricotta, it has a soft texture and slightly acid taste.*

*To serve 4 to 6*

| | | |
|---|---|---|
| 1 lb. | *mascarpone*, ricotta or cream cheese | ½ kg. |
| ½ cup | sugar | 125 ml. |
| 4 | egg yolks, lightly beaten | 4 |
| 2 tbsp. | heavy cream | 30 ml. |
| 2 tbsp. | Cognac or other brandy | 30 ml. |
| | raspberries or strawberries | |

Blend the cheese in an electric blender until very smooth, or force the cheese through a sieve. Beat in the sugar, egg

yolks, cream and Cognac, beating until the dessert is very smooth and thick. Pour the dessert into a serving dish and chill it. Before serving, add a garnish of raspberries or of strawberries.

ROMEO SALTA
THE PLEASURES OF ITALIAN COOKING

# Cottage Cheese Pudding

## *Ofenschlupfer mit Quark*

*To serve 6*

| | | |
|---|---|---|
| 1 cup | cottage cheese | ¼ liter |
| | salt | |
| 3 tbsp. | sour cream | 45 ml. |
| ⅓ cup | superfine sugar | 75 ml. |
| ⅓ cup | seedless white raisins, soaked in warm water for 15 minutes and drained | 75 ml. |
| 4 or 5 | soft bread rolls, crusts removed, thinly sliced | 4 or 5 |
| 2 or 3 | medium-sized apples, peeled, cored and thinly sliced (about 2 cups [½ liter]) (optional) | 2 or 3 |
| 2 | eggs | 2 |
| ⅔ to 1 cup | milk | 150 ml. to ¼ liter |
| 1 to 2 tsp. | grated lemon peel | 5 to 10 ml. |
| 2 tbsp. | butter, cut into small pieces | 30 ml. |

Mix the cheese with a pinch of salt, the sour cream and 2 tablespoons [30 ml.] of the sugar, then mix in the raisins. Line the bottom of a buttered oven dish with the bread slices, then cover with the cheese mixture. A layer of thinly sliced apples may be added at this stage. Cover with the remaining slices of bread. Whisk the eggs with the milk, the grated lemon peel and half of the remaining sugar, and pour the mixture over the pudding. Sprinkle with the remaining sugar, dot with the butter pieces and bake in a preheated 350° F. [180° C.] oven for about 45 minutes or until brown and the custard has set.

HERMINE KIEHNLE AND MARIA HÄDECKE
DAS NEUE KIEHNLE KOCHBUCH

# Chocolate Mousse, Normandy-Style

*Mousse au Chocolat Normandie*

To serve 6 to 8

| | | |
|---|---|---|
| 8 oz. | semisweet baking chocolate, broken into small pieces | ¼ kg. |
| 24 | ladyfingers *(recipe, page 167)* or other crisp, sweet, finger-length cookies | 24 |
| ⅓ cup | water | 75 ml. |
| 16 tbsp. | unsalted butter, softened | 240 ml. |
| ⅔ cup | sugar | 150 ml. |
| 3 | eggs, the yolks separated from the whites, and the whites stiffly beaten | 3 |
| 1 cup | ground blanched almonds | ¼ liter |
| | salt | |
| 2 cups | heavy cream, 1 cup [¼ liter] whipped without sweetening, 1 cup whipped and flavored with 1 tbsp. [15 ml.] confectioners' sugar and ½ tsp. [2 ml.] vanilla extract | ½ liter |

Have ready a 5-cup [1¼-liter] charlotte mold and 2 feet [60 cm.] of ¼-inch [6-mm.] satin ribbon. Line the bottom of the mold with a round of white paper. Line the sides of the mold with the ladyfingers or other cookies.

Put the chocolate in a pan with the water and stir over low heat until the chocolate melts. Immediately take the pan off the heat and let the chocolate cool a little. Put the butter in a mixing bowl and beat with the sugar until light and fluffy. One at a time, beat in the egg yolks. Add the ground almonds and a pinch of salt to the butter-and-egg mixture. Mix in the cool melted chocolate, then fold in the beaten egg whites. Last, carefully and smoothly fold in the unsweetened whipped cream.

Fill the mold, cover it with plastic wrap and put it in the freezer to set for about 90 minutes. When the mousse is well set, carefully turn it onto a flat serving plate and remove the paper. Put the flavored whipped cream in a pastry bag fitted with a star tube, and pipe rosettes and scallops on top of the mousse. Tie the ribbon around the middle of the mousse with a little bow, and serve.

DIONE LUCAS AND MARION GORMAN
THE DIONE LUCAS BOOK OF FRENCH COOKING

# Chocolate Mousse

*Mousse au Chocolat*

*The author suggests two possible additions to this mousse: 2 tablespoons [30 ml.] of finely chopped toasted almonds, or 1 tablespoon [15 ml.] of chopped, candied orange peel.*

To serve 4 to 6

| | | |
|---|---|---|
| 8 oz. | semisweet baking chocolate, broken into pieces | ¼ kg. |
| 2 tbsp. | butter | 30 ml. |
| ¼ cup | water | 50 ml. |
| 5 | eggs, the yolks separated from the whites | 5 |
| 1 tbsp. | rum | 15 ml. |

Put the chocolate in a saucepan with the butter and water. Cook over very low heat until the mixture becomes a smooth paste. Off the heat, work in the egg yolks, one by one, using a wooden spoon. Then add the rum.

Beat the egg whites until they stand in stiff peaks, then fold them gently into the chocolate mixture. Pour the mousse into a deep 5-cup [1¼-liter] mold and leave overnight in the refrigerator.

EUGÉNIE BRAZIER
LES SECRETS DE LA MÈRE BRAZIER

# Chocolate Dream

To serve 6 to 8

| | | |
|---|---|---|
| 1¼ cups | grated unsweetened baking chocolate | 300 ml. |
| 8 | eggs, the yolks separated from the whites | 8 |
| 1 cup | confectioners' sugar | ¼ liter |
| ½ cup | hot, freshly made strong, black coffee | 125 ml. |
| 1 tsp. | rum | 5 ml. |

Melt the chocolate in the coffee. Place the egg yolks and sugar in the top of a double boiler, over simmering water. Beat constantly. When foamy, add the chocolate mixture. Continue to beat and heat slowly, until the custard begins to thicken. Add the rum and remove the custard from the heat.

Beat the egg whites until stiff, then fold in the custard. Serve at once in sherbet glasses, or chill and serve with heavy cream flavored with a little rum.

AMY B. W. MILLER AND PERSIS W. FULLER (EDITORS)
THE BEST OF SHAKER COOKING

## Molded Chocolate Loaf with Whipped Cream

*Gâteau Moulé au Chocolat, Crème Chantilly*

|  | To serve 4 |  |
|---|---|---|
| 3 oz. | unsweetened baking chocolate, broken into small pieces | 100 g. |
| 1 cup | heavy cream | ¼ liter |
| ¼ cup | water | 50 ml. |
| 6 tbsp. | unsalted butter, softened | 90 ml. |
| 3 | eggs, the yolks separated from the whites | 3 |
| 1 cup | sugar | ¼ liter |
| 2 tbsp. | flour | 30 ml. |
| 1 tsp. | vanilla extract | 5 ml. |
|  | salt |  |

Stir the water and chocolate pieces together over low heat in a round-bottomed metal mixing bowl until the chocolate has melted. Remove the bowl from the heat, whip in the butter, then the egg yolks, and finally ¾ cup [175 ml.] of the sugar, the flour and half of the vanilla. If at this point the mixture seems to curdle or disintegrate (it is only the action of the chocolate rehardening in contact with colder ingredients), place the bowl in another bowl filled with warm water and continue stirring; the mixture will come back together.

Beat the egg whites with a pinch of salt until they stand stiffly in peaks. Gently fold about one third of the entire volume of egg whites into the chocolate mixture, then fold in the remainder. Pour the pudding mixture into a buttered 1-quart [1-liter] mold (a savarin mold or a decorative jelly mold with a central tube). Place the mold in a pan filled with hot water to approximately the same level as the pudding's surface, and cook in a preheated 350° F. [180° C.] oven for 40 minutes. Leave to cool slightly, then turn the mold onto a serving plate, leaving the mold over the pudding until serving time. Chill in the refrigerator for about one hour.

Whip the cream with the remaining sugar and vanilla. Serve the chilled pudding either with the whipped cream presented separately, or with the central well of the pudding filled with the whipped cream and a decorative ribbon of cream piped around the base.

RICHARD OLNEY
THE FRENCH MENU COOKBOOK

## Chocolate Cream Pudding

*Suave*

|  | To serve 8 |  |
|---|---|---|
| 8 oz. | unsweetened baking chocolate, grated | ¼ kg. |
|  | pouring custard (recipe, page 165), flavored with coffee |  |
| 16 tbsp. | butter (½ lb. [¼ kg.]) | 240 ml. |
| 1 cup | superfine sugar | ¼ liter |
| 1 tbsp. | flour | 15 ml. |
| 5 | eggs | 5 |

In a heavy saucepan, melt the butter and the chocolate over low heat without letting them boil. When the chocolate is completely melted and very smooth, add the sugar.

Mix the flour with the eggs and add to the chocolate. Beat the mixture with a small whisk as you would an omelet. Line a 1-quart [1-liter] mold with buttered paper. Pour in the chocolate mixture and cook for 45 minutes in a bain-marie on top of the stove or in a preheated 350° F. [180° C.] oven. Refrigerate the pudding overnight. Unmold and serve cold with the coffee-flavored pouring custard.

LES PETITS PLATS ET LES GRANDS

## Mocha Mousse with Tía María Sauce

*Instructions on how to make custard appear on pages 20-21.*
Whenever a sauce should be clear, as in this recipe, arrowroot is preferable to cornstarch. But cornstarch may be used if arrowroot is not available.

|  | To serve 8 |  |
|---|---|---|
| 1½ cups | freshly made strong black coffee | 375 ml. |
| 6 | egg yolks, lightly beaten | 6 |
| ¾ cup | sugar | 175 ml. |
| 4 tbsp. | unflavored powdered gelatin | 60 ml. |
| ½ cup | cold water | 125 ml. |
| 3 cups | heavy cream | ¾ liter |
|  | **Tía María sauce** |  |
| ¼ cup | Tía María or other coffee-flavored liqueur | 50 ml. |
| 3 cups | freshly made strong black coffee | ¾ liter |
| 1½ cups | sugar | 375 ml. |
| 2 tbsp. | arrowroot or cornstarch | 30 ml. |
| ¼ cup | cold water | 50 ml. |

Make a soft custard by beating the egg yolks with first the sugar and then the coffee. Soften the gelatin in the cold water and add it to the custard. Stir, and refrigerate until the mixture begins to set. Whip the cream and fold it into the custard. Pour the mixture into a 2-quart [2-liter] melon-shaped mold, and chill.

To make the sauce, heat the coffee with the sugar. Stir the arrowroot or cornstarch into the cold water to dissolve it, and add the combination to the coffee mixture. Simmer and stir until thickened. Add the Tía María and chill.

Unmold the mousse and pour the Tía María sauce over it before serving.

EDITORS OF HOUSE & GARDEN
HOUSE & GARDEN'S NEW COOK BOOK

## Molded Apple Pudding

*Gâteau de Pommes*

*Two tablespoons [30 ml.] of all-purpose flour may be substituted for the single tablespoon [15 ml.] of potato flour called for in this recipe.*

To serve 6

| 12 | medium-sized apples, peeled, cored and sliced | 12 |
|---|---|---|
| 2 cups | sugar | ½ liter |
| 2-inch | stick cinnamon | 5-cm. |
| 3 to 4 tbsp. | strained fresh lemon juice | 45 to 60 ml. |
| 1 tbsp. | potato flour | 15 ml. |
| 2 tbsp. | butter | 30 ml. |
| 6 | eggs | 6 |
| 3 to 4 tbsp. | dry bread crumbs | 45 to 60 ml. |

Put the apples in a saucepan with the sugar, cinnamon stick and lemon juice. Cover and cook over medium heat until the apples begin to soften; reduce the heat and stir the apples until they become a thick purée. Strain the purée through a sieve into another saucepan. Add the potato flour and the butter. Reduce the purée over low heat, stirring all the while, until it is quite firm. Set the purée aside to cool.

Beat the eggs, one at a time, into the cooled purée. Prepare a 1½-quart [1½-liter] mold as follows: Butter it and sprinkle in the bread crumbs, then turn the mold upside down and let any loose crumbs fall out. Pour the pudding mixture into the mold to within 1 inch [2½ cm.] of the top. Bake the pudding in a water bath in a preheated 350° F. [180° C.] oven for about 45 minutes, or until the pudding is firm to the touch. Cool the pudding for about 15 minutes before unmolding it.

MICHEL BARBEROUSSE
CUISINE NORMANDE

## Baked Apple Pudding

*Gebackene Apfelspeise*

To serve 8 to 10

| 10 | cooking apples (about 2½ lb. [1¼ kg.]), peeled, cored and diced | 10 |
|---|---|---|
| 1 | lemon, the peel grated and the juice strained | 1 |
| ½ cup | sugar | 125 ml. |
| | ground cinnamon | |
| 10 tbsp. | butter, softened | 150 ml. |
| 3 | eggs, the yolks separated from the whites | 3 |
| 1 cup | dried currants, soaked in warm water for 15 minutes and drained | 100 g. |
| 2 tbsp. | bread crumbs | 30 ml. |

Sprinkle the apples with the lemon juice, about 2 tablespoons [30 ml.] of the sugar and some cinnamon, and put them aside for one hour.

Beat the butter until creamy. Gradually incorporate the remaining sugar, the egg yolks, lemon peel and currants. Stir in the apples. Beat the egg whites until they are stiff, and add them to the mixture.

Butter a 2-quart [2-liter] ovenproof dish and sprinkle it with the bread crumbs. Fill the dish with the apple mixture and bake for one hour in a preheated 350° F. [180° C.] oven, or until apples are completely soft.

DOROTHEE V. HELLERMANN
DAS KOCHBUCH AUS HAMBURG

## Brown Betty Pudding

*Pouding à la Mulâtresse*

To serve 4

| | | |
|---|---|---|
| 2 cups | chopped, peeled, cored apples | ½ liter |
| 1 cup | stale bread crumbs | ¼ liter |
| 1 cup | sugar | ¼ liter |
| 2 tbsp. | butter, cut into small bits | 30 ml. |
| | ground cinnamon | |
| | ground allspice | |
| | grated nutmeg | |
| | hard sauce *(recipe, page 163)* | |

Butter the bottom of a 1-quart [1-liter] baking pan, and put in a layer of the apples, which you will have stewed nicely with a little water. Put over this a layer of bread crumbs, and sprinkle with sugar and dot with butter. Sprinkle nicely with the spices. Continue this until you have used up all of the apples. Put a layer of bread crumbs on top. Place in a preheated 350° F. [180° C.] oven, and bake to a nice brown. Serve hot, with hard sauce.

THE ORIGINAL PICAYUNE CREOLE COOK BOOK

## Apple and Apricot Brown Betty

To serve 6 to 8

| | | |
|---|---|---|
| 7 or 8 | medium-sized cooking apples, peeled, cored and chopped (about 5 cups [1¼ liters]) | 7 or 8 |
| ¾ cup | dried apricots (about 4 oz. [125 g.]), soaked in water overnight, drained and chopped | 175 ml. |
| 3 cups | coarse, fresh white bread crumbs | ¾ liter |
| 5 tbsp. | melted butter | 75 ml. |
| 1 cup | blanched almonds | ¼ liter |
| 1 tbsp. | orange peel, grated fine | 15 ml. |
| ⅔ to 1 cup | brown sugar | 150 ml. to ¼ liter |
| 2 tbsp. | butter, cut into small pieces | 30 ml. |

Toss the bread crumbs in the melted butter until they have absorbed it evenly. Spread a thin layer of the crumbs in the bottom of a 1½-quart [1½-liter] soufflé dish. Cover with a mixture of the apples, the apricots and the almonds. Sprinkle with a little orange peel and some of the sugar. Repeat the layers until the dish is full, finishing with a layer of crumbs. Dot with the butter pieces and sprinkle with any

remaining sugar. Bake in a preheated 375° F. [190° C.] oven for 30 to 40 minutes, or until golden and crisp. Serve very hot, with cream; whipped cream is especially good.

MARGARET COSTA
MARGARET COSTA'S FOUR SEASONS COOKERY BOOK

## Apple Dumpling

*Steaming puddings is demonstrated on pages 40-41.*
This is a fine old Scottish dish, much relished by children.

To serve 8

| | | |
|---|---|---|
| 4 | large cooking apples, peeled, cored and sliced | 4 |
| 6 oz. | beef suet | 175 g. |
| 4 cups | flour | 1 liter |
| 1 cup | hot water | ¼ liter |
| | salt | |
| ½ tsp. | ground cloves or cinnamon | 2 ml. |
| ⅓ to ½ cup | sugar | 75 to 125 ml. |

Cut the suet into very small pieces, and soften it in hot water. When that is done, strain the suet and allow it to cool, then press out any of the water that may remain. Work the suet in a bowl with a wooden spoon until it is something like a batter. Sift the flour with a pinch of salt and add it to the suet. Work the suet into the flour with your fingertips until the flour is thoroughly absorbed, then gradually work in enough hot water to form a stiff paste.

Mix the apples with the cloves or cinnamon and the sugar. Roll out the paste and place the apples in it. Gather the paste neatly over the lot, tie the bundle in a cloth and cook in a pan of boiling water for at least two hours.

Alternatively, line a buttered 1½-quart [1½-liter] pudding basin with the paste, leaving an overhanging flap; fill the basin with the apple mixture, and turn up the paste over the top. Seal the paste, or pinch a lid of paste in place; tie the basin in a cloth, and boil for about two and one quarter hours. Serve with cream.

JENNY WREN
MODERN DOMESTIC COOKERY

## Date Pudding

*To serve 8*

| | | |
|---|---|---|
| 1 cup | chopped dates | ¼ liter |
| 1 cup | sugar | ¼ liter |
| 2½ tbsp. | flour | 37 ml. |
| 1 tsp. | baking powder | 5 ml. |
| 1 cup | coarsely broken nuts | ¼ liter |
| 2 tbsp. | sour cream | 30 ml. |
| 2 | eggs, the yolks separated from the whites, the yolks lightly beaten and the whites beaten until stiff | 2 |
| | heavy cream, whipped and sweetened | |

Mix the ingredients together, adding the egg yolks last. Pour the mixture into a glass pie plate; set the pie plate in a shallow pan partly filled with water and bake in a preheated 400° F. [200° C.] oven for 40 minutes, or until the pudding begins to pull away from the edge. Serve the pudding with sweetened whipped cream.

SARA B. B. STAMM (EDITOR)
FAVORITE NEW ENGLAND RECIPES

## Algerian Date Pudding

*Gâteau Algérien*

*To serve 6 to 8*

| | | |
|---|---|---|
| ½ lb. | dates (about 2 cups [½ liter]), pitted and finely chopped | ¼ kg. |
| 1 cup | sugar | ¼ liter |
| 1 cup | chopped blanched almonds | ¼ liter |
| 1 cup | unsalted, roasted, shelled peanuts, finely chopped | ¼ liter |
| 4 | egg whites, stiffly beaten | 4 |

Mix together the dates, sugar, almonds and peanuts. Fold this mixture into the egg whites and place in a well-buttered baking dish. Cook in a preheated 325° F. [170° C.] oven for 35 to 40 minutes, or until a straw inserted in the center comes out clean. Serve hot, tepid or cool.

70 MÉDECINS DE FRANCE
LE TRÉSOR DE LA CUISINE DU BASSIN MÉDITERRANÉEN

## Fig Pudding with Lime Sauce

*The original version of this recipe called for coloring the pudding with cochineal, a red powder made from the shells of a desert insect, which is not generally acceptable in the United States for use in food.*

*To serve 6 to 8*

| | | |
|---|---|---|
| 1 cup | dried figs, cut into little pieces | ¼ liter |
| 3 cups | fresh bread crumbs | ¾ liter |
| 2 cups | beef suet, very finely chopped | ½ liter |
| 5 | eggs, well beaten | 5 |
| ½ cup | sugar | 125 ml. |
| 2 | limes, the peel grated and the juice strained | 2 |
| | grated nutmeg | |
| ⅔ cup | rum | 150 ml. |
| | salt | |
| 1 tbsp. | butter | 15 ml. |
| **Lime sauce** | | |
| 2 | limes, the peel pared very thin, the juice strained | 2 |
| ¼ cup | sugar | 50 ml. |
| 1 cup | water | ¼ liter |
| 2 or 3 tbsp. | rum | 30 or 45 ml. |
| 1 or 2 drops | vegetable-based red food coloring (optional) | 1 or 2 drops |

Take the bread crumbs, suet and dried figs, and mix them together well with the beaten eggs, sugar, grated peel and the juice of the limes. Finally, mix in a pinch each of grated nutmeg and salt, and the rum. Put the mixture into a well-buttered 5-cup [1¼-liter] mold, press the mixture down tightly, cover it with buttered wax paper, tie the mold up in a cheesecloth and boil the pudding for no less than four hours, adding more water from time to time, as needed.

To make the lime sauce, put the sugar into a saucepan with the water and the very thin lime peels. Bring to a boil and simmer until a thin syrup is produced, then skim and add the juice of the limes and the rum. A drop or two of food coloring will improve the color of the sauce.

Unmold the pudding and serve it with the lime sauce. If liked, the pudding may be served "on fire" like a Christmas pudding by pouring brandy over it and flaming it.

A. KENNEY HERBERT ("WYVERN")
SWEET DISHES

## Grape Cream

### *Grozdov Krem*

*In Bulgaria this dish is made with petmez, a thick syrup made from fresh grape juice. This recipe produces a similar result, but the cream lacks the slightly caramelized flavor imparted by a petmez.*

To serve 4 to 6

| | | |
|---|---|---|
| 1 quart | unsweetened red or white grape juice | 1 liter |
| ¼ cup | cornstarch | 50 ml. |
| ⅓ cup | superfine sugar | 75 ml. |
| ⅔ cup | walnuts, chopped fine | 150 ml. |
| 1 tsp. | ground cinnamon | 5 ml. |
| ⅓ cup | ground walnuts | 75 ml. |

In an enameled or stainless-steel saucepan, reduce the grape juice to 3 cups [¾ liter] by boiling it gently, uncovered. Mix the cornstarch with a little water and add it to the boiling juice. Stir until the mixture thickens, then add the sugar and the finely chopped walnuts. Continue to cook, stirring, until the sugar dissolves. Let the grape cream cool a little, then pour it into individual dessert bowls or glasses. When the cream is quite cool, sprinkle it with the cinnamon and the ground walnuts.

L. PETROV, N. DJELEPOV, E. IORDANOV AND S. UZUNOVA
BULGARSKA NAZIONALNA KUCHNIYA

## Lemon Dainty

To serve 4

| | | |
|---|---|---|
| 1 | lemon, the peel grated and the juice strained | 1 |
| 3 tbsp. | butter | 45 ml. |
| ⅛ tsp. | salt | ½ ml. |
| ¾ cup | sugar | 175 ml. |
| 2 tbsp. | flour | 30 ml. |
| 2 | eggs, the yolks separated from the whites, the yolks lightly beaten and the whites beaten stiff | 2 |
| 1 cup | milk | ¼ liter |

Combine the butter, salt, sugar and flour, and mix well. Add the egg yolks, milk, lemon juice and lemon peel. Beat the mixture with an egg beater until smooth. Fold in the beaten egg whites. Pour the mixture into a buttered 4-cup [1-liter] baking dish, set the dish in a shallow pan partly filled with boiling water and bake in a preheated 350° F. [180° C.] oven for 45 minutes, or until golden brown. There will be cake on top, pudding in the bottom. Serve the dessert warm or at room temperature.

THE FINE ARTS COOKBOOK

## Alison's Orange Caramel Custard

### *Pudín de Naranjas*

*The technique of caramelizing sugar is demonstrated on pages 8-9. To flame the custard, heat the brandy or rum in a small pot or ladle, pour over the custard and ignite.*

To serve 6 to 8

| | | |
|---|---|---|
| 1¼ cups | strained fresh orange juice | 300 ml. |
| 1¼ cups | sugar | 300 ml. |
| 2 tbsp. | butter | 30 ml. |
| ¼ cup | flour | 50 ml. |
| 6 | eggs, the yolks separated from the whites | 6 |
| | brandy or rum (optional) | |

Caramelize ½ cup [125 ml.] of the sugar in a heavy pan. Pour the caramel into a 3-cup [¾-liter] round ovenproof glass dish, and tip the dish so that the bottom and sides are evenly coated with the caramel.

Cream the butter with the remaining ¾ cup [175 ml.] of sugar. Add the flour and mix well. Beat the egg yolks very well and add them to the butter mixture, then add the orange juice. Beat the egg whites until they are stiff and fold them into the mixture. Pour it into the caramel-lined dish, set the dish in a pan of hot water and bake in a preheated 350° F. [180° C.] oven for one hour.

Turn the dessert onto a serving dish so that the caramel glaze is uppermost. Serve hot and, if you prefer, flaming with brandy or rum.

HELEN BROWN
HELEN BROWN'S WEST COAST COOK BOOK

## Papaya and Egg Yolk Pudding

### *Ovos Moles de Papaia*

*If desired, this dessert from Mozambique may be refrigerated for two hours or more and served chilled.*

To serve 4

| | | |
|---|---|---|
| 1 | medium-sized ripe papaya (1 to 1½ lb. [½ to ¾ kg.]), peeled, seeded and coarsely chopped | 1 |
| 5 | egg yolks | 5 |
| ¼ cup | strained fresh lime or lemon juice | 50 ml. |
| ¼ cup | water | 50 ml. |
| 2 cups | sugar | ½ liter |
| 3-inch | stick cinnamon | 8-cm. |
| 4 | whole cloves | 4 |

Combine the papaya, the lime or lemon juice and the water in a blender. Set it at a high speed for about 30 seconds. Turn off the machine, scrape down the sides of the beaker with a rubber spatula and blend again until the mixture is a smooth purée. With the back of a spoon, rub the purée through a fine nylon sieve into a 2- to 3-quart [2- to 3-liter] enameled or stainless-steel saucepan.

Mix in the sugar, the cinnamon stick and the cloves and, stirring constantly, bring to a boil over high heat. Stirring occasionally, cook briskly until the syrup reaches a temperature of 230° F. [110° C.] on a candy thermometer, or until a few drops spooned into cold water immediately form coarse threads. Remove the pan from the heat and, with a slotted spoon, remove and discard the cinnamon and the cloves.

In a deep bowl, beat the egg yolks with a wire whisk or a rotary or electric beater for about one minute, or until the egg yolks thicken slightly. Beating constantly, pour the hot syrup in a thin stream into the yolks and beat until the mixture is smooth and thick, and is a bright, deep yellow.

Divide the mixture among four small heatproof dessert dishes and cool to room temperature. The dessert will thicken further as it cools.

FOODS OF THE WORLD/AFRICAN COOKING

## Summer Pudding

To serve 4 to 6

| | | |
|---|---|---|
| ¾ cup | raspberries | 175 ml. |
| ¾ cup | red currants | 175 ml. |
| ¾ cup | loganberries | 175 ml. |
| 1½ cups | black currants | 375 ml. |
| ¾ cup | superfine sugar | 175 ml. |
| 8 | fairly thick slices white bread, crusts removed | 8 |
| | cream (optional) | |

Remove the stems from the fruit. Wash the fruit, if necessary, and put it with the sugar in a pan. Cover and cook gently for five to 10 minutes, or until the currants are tender. Drain off the juice, reserving one third of a cup [75 ml.]. Line a 1-quart [1-liter] pudding basin with some of the bread slices, cutting the slices to fit the basin exactly. Spoon in the fruit, packing it in well. Pour in the reserved juice. Place the remaining bread on top of the fruit. Cover with a plate small enough to rest on the pudding itself, and put the heaviest weight from your kitchen scales, or water in a covered plastic container, on the plate. Leave the pudding overnight in the refrigerator or other very cold place. Serve with cream if desired.

SUSAN KING
SUSAN KING'S COOK BOOK

## Loaf of Turin

*Turinois*

To serve 6

| | | |
|---|---|---|
| 1 lb. | chestnuts | ½ kg. |
| 8 tbsp. | unsalted butter | 120 ml. |
| 2 oz. | semisweet baking chocolate, grated | 75 g. |
| ½ cup | sugar | 125 ml. |
| 1 tsp. | vanilla extract | 5 ml. |
| | heavy cream, whipped | |

With a sharp knife, slit the shells of the chestnuts on the convex side. Put them in a saucepan with water to cover, bring to a boil and simmer for five minutes. Remove the pan from the heat and, without draining, take one chestnut at a time from the pan. Remove the shell and inner skin while the nut is still hot. Cook the peeled nuts in boiling water for about 20 minutes, or until tender. Drain, and press them through a fine sieve.

Mix the chestnut purée while still hot with the butter, grated chocolate, sugar and vanilla. Press the mixture firmly into a buttered, paper-lined loaf pan and chill it overnight.

Unmold the loaf onto a serving plate, cut it into thin slices and serve it with whipped cream.

ANN SERANNE
DELECTABLE DESSERTS

## Chestnut Compote

*Instructions on how to roast and peel chestnuts appear on pages 70-71. The technique of making sugar syrup is explained on pages 8-9.*

To serve 6 to 8

| | | |
|---|---|---|
| 2 to 2½ lb. | chestnuts, shells slit, roasted, peeled, and flattened a little with your hands | 1 kg. |
| 2 cups | medium sugar syrup, cooled, made from 1 cup [¼ liter] sugar and 1½ cups [375 ml.] water | ½ liter |
| 1 tbsp. | strained fresh lemon juice | 15 ml. |
| 2 tsp. | finely julienned fresh lemon peel | 10 ml. |
| ¼ cup | confectioners' sugar | 50 ml. |

In a saucepan, put the chestnuts in the cold syrup and warm over low heat, without bringing to a boil, so that the syrup may penetrate the chestnuts. Add the lemon juice and lemon peel, and put the chestnuts and syrup in heatproof serving dishes. Sprinkle the chestnuts with confectioners' sugar, and glaze the sugar with a heated metal skewer or salamander, or beneath the broiler.

G. A. JARRIN
THE ITALIAN CONFECTIONER

## Chestnut Mont Blanc

### Le Mont Blanc aux Marrons

*The techniques of preparing and puréeing chestnuts are demonstrated on pages 70-71.*

*To serve 6*

| | | |
|---|---|---|
| 2 to 2½ lb. | chestnuts, shells slit | 1 kg. |
| | salt | |
| about 2 cups | milk | about ½ liter |
| ⅓ cup | granulated sugar | 75 ml. |
| 1 | vanilla bean | 1 |
| 2 tbsp. | butter | 30 ml. |
| 2 | egg yolks, lightly beaten | 2 |
| 1 cup | heavy cream, whipped | ¼ liter |
| ¼ cup | confectioners' sugar | 50 ml. |

Boil the chestnuts for 10 minutes in salted water. Cool them slightly. Peel them, removing both the outer shells and the inner skins. Put the chestnuts in a saucepan, cover with the milk and add the granulated sugar and vanilla bean. Simmer for about one hour, or until the chestnuts are tender. Remove the vanilla bean.

Drain the chestnuts, reserving the milk, and purée them through a sieve into a bowl using a pestle. Add a little of the hot milk to give the purée a good consistency. Stir in the butter and egg yolks. Form the purée into a mound on a serving plate and refrigerate for at least three hours.

Whip the cream with the confectioners' sugar. Serve the dessert very cold, covered with the whipped cream.

ÉDOUARD DE POMIANE
LE CODE DE LA BONNE CHÈRE

## Candied-Chestnut Pudding

### Gâteau de Marrons

*Instructions for lining a mold with caramel are on page 24.*

*To serve 8*

| | | |
|---|---|---|
| 1 lb. | chestnuts | ½ kg. |
| 2½ cups | milk | ½ liter |
| 1¼ cups | sugar | 300 ml. |
| 1 tbsp. | water | 15 ml. |
| 1 tsp. | vanilla extract | 5 ml. |
| 3 | egg whites | 3 |

With a sharp, pointed knife make a cross on the flat side of each chestnut. Plunge the chestnuts into rapidly boiling water and boil them for 10 minutes. Remove them from the water and, while they are still hot, remove the shells. Scald the milk. Add 1 cup [¼ liter] of the sugar and cook the chestnuts in the sweetened milk for 40 minutes. Force the milk and chestnuts through a food mill or strainer. Add the vanilla extract and allow to cool.

Put the remaining ¼ cup [50 ml.] of sugar into a 1-quart [1-liter] plain or decorative fireproof mold. Melt the sugar and let it brown. Add the water at once and move the mold around until the caramel reaches every part of the inside.

Beat the egg whites stiff and fold them into the chestnut mixture. Pour into the mold. Place the mold in a pan partly filled with hot water, and cook for 40 minutes in a preheated 325° F. [170° C.] oven. Unmold the pudding onto a dish and serve it plain or with sweetened whipped cream.

CHARLOTTE TURGEON
TANTE MARIE'S FRENCH KITCHEN

## Coconut-Lemon Pudding

### Dulce de Coco

*To serve 4*

| | | |
|---|---|---|
| 1 | fresh coconut, the flesh grated and the liquid mixed with enough cold water to make 1 cup [¼ liter] | 1 |
| 2 tbsp. | strained fresh lemon juice | 30 ml. |
| 1½ cups | sugar | 375 ml. |
| 5 | whole cloves | 5 |
| 2 | egg yolks | 2 |
| ⅓ cup | raisins, soaked in warm water for 15 minutes and drained | 75 ml. |

In a 2- to 3-quart [2- to 3-liter] enameled or stainless-steel saucepan, combine the coconut-liquid mixture, sugar and cloves, and bring it to a boil over high heat, stirring only until the sugar dissolves. Reduce the heat to medium and cook, uncovered and undisturbed, until this syrup reaches a temperature of 230° F. [110° C.] on a candy thermometer, or a few drops added to ice water form a thread. Stir the grated coconut into the syrup, reduce the heat and simmer for 15 minutes, stirring occasionally.

Beat the egg yolks with a fork, whisk or rotary beater for a minute or two, until they thicken. Beat into them 2 or 3 tablespoons [30 or 45 ml.] of the simmering coconut mixture, then slowly pour the eggs into the pan, stirring all the while. Still stirring, simmer the mixture for five minutes—but under no circumstances allow it to come to a boil. Remove the pan from the heat, pick out the cloves and add the raisins and lemon juice. Transfer the pudding to a bowl and let it cool to room temperature. Then refrigerate until fully chilled.

Serve the pudding either from the bowl or in individual dessert dishes.

FOODS OF THE WORLD/LATIN AMERICAN COOKING

# Almond and Pistachio Loaf

*Pain des Houris*

Served directly from the oven, this is a soufflé. Served tepid, much of the body of the dessert is lost—though the savors may more easily be appreciated. Cold, the loaf is moist and compact, heavy but delicious.

| | To serve 4 | |
|---|---|---|
| ⅔ cup | almonds (about 4 oz. [125 g.]), parboiled for 2 minutes, rubbed between towels and skinned | 150 ml. |
| ⅓ cup | pistachio nuts (about 2 oz. [75 g.]), parboiled for 2 minutes, rubbed between towels and skinned | 75 ml. |
| 1 tbsp. | julienned orange peel, parboiled for a few seconds and drained | 15 ml. |
| 1 tbsp. | julienned lemon peel, parboiled for a few seconds and drained | 15 ml. |
| 9 tbsp. | sugar | 135 ml. |
| 6 tbsp. | water | 90 ml. |
| ¼ cup | white wine | 50 ml. |
| 3 | eggs, the yolks separated from the whites | 3 |
| | salt | |

In a saucepan, combine the strips of orange and lemon peel with the water and 1 tablespoon [15 ml.] of the sugar. Bring to a boil, and simmer until the liquid is almost entirely reduced and the peel is coated with a thick syrup. Remove from the heat before the sugar begins to caramelize.

Pound the almonds and pistachios together in a large mortar until well crushed into a coarse purée. Add the peel and syrup and a little of the remaining sugar. Continue pounding, adding sugar from time to time, until the mixture becomes too stiff to work easily. Continue pounding, alternating additions of white wine and sugar, until the wine is used up and only 1 tablespoon of the sugar remains. Add the egg yolks and work vigorously, pounding and stirring the mixture with the pestle.

Beat the egg whites with a small pinch of salt until they stand firmly in peaks. Fold a healthy spoonful of the egg whites into the mixture in the mortar, then scrape the contents of the mortar into the bowl containing the remaining egg whites, and fold the two gently together.

Pour into a buttered loaf-shaped oven dish and immerse the dish halfway in a larger pan containing hot water. Bake in a preheated 375° F. [190° C.] oven for about 25 minutes, or until the center of the pudding is firm to the touch. Sprinkle the surface with the remaining sugar before serving.

The ingredients (except for the final incorporation of the beaten egg whites) may be added progressively to a food processor with extremely rapid and satisfactory results.

RICHARD OLNEY
SIMPLE FRENCH FOOD

# Almond Pudding from Puerto Rico

*Pudín de Almendras*

| | To serve 6 | |
|---|---|---|
| 1 cup | finely ground blanched almonds | ¼ liter |
| 1 cup | sugar | ¼ liter |
| 2 | eggs, lightly beaten | 2 |
| 1 cup | milk | ¼ liter |
| 1 cup | heavy cream | ¼ liter |
| 1 cup | soft bread crumbs | ¼ liter |
| 2 tsp. | ground cinnamon | 10 ml. |
| 1 tsp. | grated nutmeg | 5 ml. |
| ½ cup | seedless raisins, soaked in ½ cup [125 ml.] white wine for 15 minutes and drained | 125 ml. |
| | whipped cream (optional) | |

Add the sugar to the eggs, beating well. Add the milk and cream and mix well. Add the bread crumbs, almonds, cinnamon, nutmeg and raisins and mix well. Preheat the oven to 350° F. [180° C.]. Butter six individual custard cups or other individual ovenproof dishes. Pour the mixture into them. Place the dishes in a shallow pan partly filled with boiling water. Bake in the oven for 25 minutes, or until the pudding is delicately browned on top and moderately firm. Serve hot or cold. Whipped cream may be placed on each portion.

MYRA WALDO
THE COMPLETE ROUND-THE-WORLD COOKBOOK

# Tapioca Custard

*Flan au Tapioca*

| | To serve 6 | |
|---|---|---|
| ½ cup | tapioca (not the quick-cooking kind) | 125 ml. |
| 2 cups | water | ½ liter |
| 1 cup | currant or strawberry jelly | ¼ liter |
| ½ cup | sugar | 125 ml. |
| 4 | egg whites | 4 |
| | pouring custard (recipe, page 165), chilled | |

Wash the tapioca well several times, and then soak it in the water for two hours. Put the tapioca and water in a saucepan and add the jelly, mixing thoroughly; then add the sugar and mix again. Cook uncovered over low heat until the tapioca is very clear—about one hour. Beat the egg whites to a very stiff froth and add them to the tapioca. Turn the mixture into a buttered 6-cup [1½-liter] mold and set away in a cool place to harden. Unmold and serve cold with the custard.

THE ORIGINAL PICAYUNE CREOLE COOK BOOK

## Rice Pudding with White Wine

### Sutlach Sharapli

*To serve 6*

| | | |
|---|---|---|
| ½ cup | raw unprocessed rice, washed and drained | 125 g. |
| | boiling water | |
| 1¼ cups | milk | 300 ml. |
| 1¼ cups | light cream | 300 ml. |
| 2 tbsp. | butter | 30 ml. |
| ¾ cup | seedless raisins | 175 ml. |
| 3 tbsp. | superfine sugar | 45 ml. |
| | salt | |
| 2 | eggs, lightly beaten | 2 |
| ¾ cup | ground blanched almonds | 175 ml. |
| ¾ cup | granulated sugar | 175 ml. |
| ⅔ cup | dry white wine | 150 ml. |
| 1 cup | heavy cream, whipped | ¼ liter |

Boil the rice in plenty of water until it is very soft. Strain off any surplus water and add the milk, light cream, butter, raisins, superfine sugar and a pinch of salt. Cook over medium heat until the mixture is quite thick, stirring frequently to prevent burning. Remove the pan from the heat and allow the mixture to cool. Add the beaten eggs and ground almonds and stir thoroughly. Pour the pudding mixture into a well-buttered shallow baking dish and cook in a moderate oven, preheated to 350° F. [180° C.], for about 30 minutes, or until the top of the pudding is golden brown. Remove the pudding from the oven and let it rest for a few minutes. With a very sharp knife cut the pudding into triangular shapes in the baking dish and allow it to cool completely.

Meanwhile, put the granulated sugar and the wine into a heavy saucepan and boil uncovered, stirring until the sugar is dissolved and a thickish syrup is obtained. This should take about 10 minutes. Pour this syrup over the rice shapes in the dish and leave it to be absorbed. Serve the dish cold with the whipped cream.

IRFAN ORGA
COOKING THE MIDDLE EAST WAY

## Rice Pudding

### Riz au Lait

*The author suggests the following variation: When the rice is cooked, stir in three, four, five or six beaten eggs and sweeten with sugar to taste. Pour the rice mixture into a buttered mold, and cook in a shallow pan partly filled with boiling water in a preheated 350° F. [180° C.] oven for 20 minutes.*

*Allow the pudding to stand for a few minutes before unmolding. Serve hot or cold.*

*To serve 4 to 6*

| | | |
|---|---|---|
| ⅓ cup | raw, unprocessed long-grain rice, thoroughly washed and drained | 75 ml |
| 3 cups | milk | ¾ liter |
| | salt | |
| ½ | vanilla bean, or 1 tsp. [5 ml.] finely chopped orange or lemon peel | ½ |
| 2 tbsp. | butter | 30 ml |
| about ¼ cup | superfine sugar | about 50 ml |

Blanch the rice in lightly salted boiling water for five to six minutes. Drain the rice, rinse it in tepid water and then drain it again.

In a heavy casserole, bring the milk to a boil with the vanilla bean half or, if you prefer, the orange or lemon peel. Remove the vanilla bean, if used, then add the butter and sugar to the milk and stir until the sugar is dissolved. Allow the milk to cool slightly, then pour in the rice. Bring to a boil, cover and cook in a preheated 325° F. [160° C.] oven for 30 minutes, without stirring. Transfer the rice to a compotier or serving bowl, and serve hot or cold.

ADRIEN-JEAN BOBINET
GASTRONOMIE

## Milk-and-Rice Pudding with Cardamom and Nuts

### Khir

*To serve 10 to 12*

| | | |
|---|---|---|
| 2 quarts | milk | 2 liters |
| ⅓ cup | raw unprocessed long-grain rice, washed and drained | 75 ml. |
| 1 cup | sugar | ¼ liter |
| ½ cup | blanched almonds, finely chopped | 125 ml |
| ¼ tsp. | cardamom seeds, coarsely crushed with a mortar and pestle or in a food processor | 1 ml |
| 1 tsp. | rose water | 5 ml |
| ¼ cup | slivered, blanched almonds, lightly toasted | 50 ml |

In a heavy 5- to 6-quart [5- to 6-liter] saucepan, bring the milk to a boil over high heat, stirring constantly to prevent kin from forming on the surface. Reduce the heat to medium and, stirring occasionally, cook for 30 minutes. Add the ice and continue cooking and stirring for an additional 30 minutes, or until the rice is so soft that the grains have almost disintegrated.

Add the sugar and the finely chopped almonds and stir for 15 minutes over low heat until the pudding is thick enough to coat the spoon heavily. Remove the pan from the heat, stir in the cardamom seeds and rose water, and pour the pudding into a shallow 7-by-12-inch [18-by-30-cm.] baking dish. With a rubber spatula, spread it out evenly and smooth the top. Then sprinkle with the toasted almonds. Refrigerate the *khir* for at least four hours, or until it is thoroughly chilled and somewhat firm to the touch.

FOODS OF THE WORLD
THE COOKING OF INDIA

## Apple Rice Pudding

*Apfelreis*

To serve 6

| | | |
|---|---|---|
| 6 to 8 | cooking apples (about 2 lb. [1 kg.]), peeled, cored and sliced | 6 to 8 |
| ½ cup | raw unprocessed rice | 125 ml. |
| 1¼ cups | milk | 300 ml. |
| ½ tsp. | freshly grated lemon peel | 2 ml. |
| ½ cup | granulated sugar | 125 ml. |
| ½ tsp. | salt | 2 ml. |
| 2 tbsp. | butter | 30 ml. |
| ½ cup | sweet cider or apple juice | 125 ml. |
| 2 | egg whites | 2 |
| 2 tbsp. | confectioners' sugar | 30 ml. |

Cook the rice in the milk with the lemon peel, granulated sugar and salt for about 25 minutes, or until the rice is soft. Place a layer of rice in a buttered, deep, 1½-quart [1½-liter] baking dish. Add half of the apples, dot with half of the butter, add the remaining rice and top with the rest of the apples. Dot with the remaining butter. Pour the cider or apple juice over all.

Bake for 45 minutes in a preheated 350° F. [180° C.] oven. Beat the egg whites until they are stiff and blend in the confectioners' sugar. Spread the meringue topping over the apples and bake for about 20 minutes, or until the meringue is golden. Serve warm.

BETTY WASON
THE ART OF GERMAN COOKING

## Natural Rice Pudding, English-Style

This rice pudding is made without eggs. It may be served alone or with fruit sauce or poached fruit such as plums, apples or rhubarb. If the pudding is flavored with cinnamon, ground cinnamon can be sprinkled on just before serving. Or you can add ¼ cup [50 ml.] raisins or currants to the pudding with the honey.

To serve 4

| | | |
|---|---|---|
| ½ cup | short-grain brown rice | 125 ml. |
| 2½ cups | milk | 625 ml. |
| 2 tbsp. | honey | 30 ml. |
| ½ | vanilla bean, or two 2-inch [5-cm.] orange peel strips, or one 3-inch [8-cm.] cinnamon stick | ½ |

Put the rice into a heavy 2- to 3-quart [2- to 3-liter] pan with the milk and flavoring. Bring to a simmer, stir, then cover and cook over a very low heat for one hour. Stir in the honey and cook, covered, for 15 minutes longer. The rice will be slightly chewy. Add a little more milk if the rice seems dry. Serve the pudding warm or cold.

ELIZABETH ALSTON
THE BEST OF NATURAL EATING AROUND THE WORLD

## Russian Semolina Pudding

*Kasha Gureva Sladkaya Mannaya*

To serve 6 to 8

| | | |
|---|---|---|
| 1 cup | semolina | ¼ liter |
| 5 cups | light or half-and-half cream | 1¼ liters |
| 1-inch | piece vanilla bean, pulverized in a mortar or blender | 2-cm. |
| 1 cup | ground, blanched almonds | ¼ liter |
| 1 cup | superfine sugar | ¼ liter |
| ¼ cup | water | 50 ml. |
| | toasted bread crumbs | |

Put the cream and pulverized vanilla bean in a saucepan and bring to a boil. Sprinkle in the semolina, stirring constantly, then simmer for 10 minutes, or until the mixture thickens. Add the almonds, sugar and water, and return to a boil.

Remove the pan from the heat and pour the mixture into a buttered ovenproof dish. Sprinkle with bread crumbs and bake in a preheated 375° F. [190° C.] oven for 30 minutes.

ELENA MOLOKHOVETS
PODAROK MOLODȲM KHOZYAĬKAM

## Semolina Pudding

*Flamri*

*To serve 8*

| | | |
|---|---|---|
| 1 cup | semolina | ¼ liter |
| 2 cups | dry white wine | ½ liter |
| 2 cups | water | ½ liter |
| 1¼ cups | sugar | 300 ml. |
| 2 | eggs | 2 |
| | salt | |
| 6 | egg whites, beaten stiff | 6 |
| 2 cups | puréed raspberries, strawberries, red currants or other soft fruit, sweetened with sugar to taste | ½ liter |

Put the wine and water in a saucepan and bring to a boil. Gradually pour in the semolina, stirring constantly. Cover and simmer gently over low heat, stirring occasionally, for 25 minutes or until the semolina is thick and smooth. Remove the pan from the heat and, to this "porridge," add the sugar, the whole eggs and a pinch of salt. Fold in the beaten egg whites. Pour this mixture into a plain buttered mold.

Place the mold in a pan partly filled with boiling water, cover the mold and poach the pudding over low heat, or in a preheated 325° F. [170° C.] oven, for 25 to 40 minutes, or until it is firm to the touch. Remove the mold from the pan and let the pudding cool. Turn the pudding onto a serving dish, pour the fruit purée over it and serve.

PROSPER MONTAGNÉ
THE NEW LAROUSSE GASTRONOMIQUE

## Cream Mousse Molds

*Les Crémets d'Angers*

*To serve 4*

| | | |
|---|---|---|
| 3 cups | heavy cream | ¾ liter |
| 4 | egg whites, beaten stiff | 4 |
| 4 tbsp. | confectioners' sugar, vanilla-flavored if possible | 60 ml. |

Whip 2¼ cups [½ liter] of the cream until stiff. Gently fold in the egg whites with a whisk and pour the mixture into little perforated molds lined with cheesecloth. Set the molds on a tray and refrigerate them for five or six hours to let the mousses exude excess liquid and become firm.

Unmold the mousses onto a serving dish, coat them with the remaining—and unwhipped—cream and sprinkle them with the sugar.

AUSTIN DE CROZE
LES PLATS RÉGIONAUX DE FRANCE

## Macaroni Pudding with Pears

*Mahal*

*To serve 6*

| | | |
|---|---|---|
| ¼ lb. | macaroni, broken into very small pieces (about 1 cup [¼ liter]) | 250 ml. |
| 6 | ripe pears, peeled, halved and cored | 6 |
| | salt | |
| 2½ cups | milk | 625 ml. |
| 1¼ cups | light cream | 300 ml. |
| ½ cup | brown sugar | 125 ml. |
| 4 tbsp. | butter | 60 ml. |
| 1 tbsp. | freshly grated lemon peel | 15 ml. |
| ¾ cup | ground almonds | 175 ml. |
| 2 | eggs, the yolks separated from the whites, and the yolks thoroughly beaten with a whisk | 2 |

Cook the macaroni in boiling salted water for 10 minutes. Drain the macaroni, put it into a saucepan with the milk and cream, and simmer it for 20 minutes. Remove the pan from the heat and let the mixture cool a little.

Add the sugar and stir until dissolved. Add the butter, lemon peel, ground almonds and the beaten egg yolks. Whip the egg whites and fold them in carefully.

Pour half of the mixture into a buttered baking dish large enough to hold the pears in one layer. Arrange the pears on top and finish with a layer of macaroni mixture. Cook in a preheated 350° F. [180° C.] oven for 30 minutes. Serve hot.

IRFAN ORGA
COOKING THE MIDDLE EAST WAY

## Ozark Pudding

*To serve 6 to 8*

| | | |
|---|---|---|
| 1 | egg | 1 |
| ¾ cup | sugar | 175 ml. |
| 2 tbsp. | flour | 30 ml. |
| 1½ tsp. | baking powder | 7 ml. |
| ⅛ tsp. | salt | ½ ml. |
| ½ cup | nuts, broken | 125 ml. |
| 1 | apple, peeled, cored and diced | 1 |
| 1 tsp. | vanilla extract | 5 ml. |
| 1 cup | heavy cream, whipped with 1 tbsp. [15 ml.] Cointreau | ¼ liter |

Beat the egg and sugar together until smooth. Add the flour, baking powder and salt and continue stirring. Incorporate the nuts, apple and vanilla into the mixture. Bake in a buttered 8-inch [20-cm.] piepan in a preheated 350° F. [180° C.] oven for 35 minutes, or until a small knife plunged into the center comes out clean. Serve with flavored whipped cream.

THE JUNIOR LEAGUE OF BATON ROUGE
RIVER ROAD RECIPES

# Durgin-Park's Indian Pudding

*To serve 6*

| | | |
|---|---|---|
| ½ cup | dark molasses | 125 ml. |
| 1 cup | yellow cornmeal | ¼ liter |
| 2 | eggs | 2 |
| 6 cups | milk | 1½ liters |
| ¼ cup | sugar | 50 ml. |
| ¼ tsp. | baking soda | 1 ml. |
| ¼ tsp. | salt | 1 ml. |
| 4 tbsp. | butter, cut into ½-inch [1-cm.] bits | 60 ml. |
| | heavy cream, whipped, or vanilla ice cream (optional) | |

Preheat the oven to 350° F. [180° C.]. Butter a 2-quart [2-liter] soufflé or baking dish and set it aside.

In a heavy 4- to 5-quart [4- to 5-liter] saucepan, beat the eggs with a wire whisk until they are well mixed. Stirring constantly with the whisk, gradually add 4 cups [1 liter] of the milk, the molasses, sugar, baking soda and salt. Then bring to a simmer over medium heat, stirring until the molasses and sugar dissolve.

Pour in the cornmeal very slowly, making sure the simmering continues, and stirring constantly to keep the mixture smooth. Cook uncovered, stirring from time to time, until the pudding is thick enough to hold its shape solidly in a spoon. Beat in the butter bits and remove the pan from the heat. Then pour in the remaining 2 cups [½ liter] of milk in a thin stream, beating constantly.

Pour the pudding into the buttered dish and bake in the middle of the oven for one hour. Reduce the oven temperature to 300° F. [150° C.] and continue baking for four hours longer, or until the pudding is very firm when prodded gently with a finger.

Serve the pudding at once, directly from the baking dish, or let it cool and serve at room temperature. Indian pudding may be accompanied by unsweetened whipped cream or vanilla ice cream, if you like.

FOODS OF THE WORLD/AMERICAN COOKING: NEW ENGLAND

# Pumpkin Custard

## Millet au Potiron

*Crème fraîche is a slightly sour raw cream, naturally matured from unpasteurized cream and available in France. To make your own crème fraîche, combine 1 cup [¼ liter] of heavy cream—not the ultra-pasteurized variety—with 1 teaspoon [5 ml.] of buttermilk. Cover the mixture and let stand at room temperature, 72° F. [22° C.], for 14 to 18 hours, or until the cream thickens and acquires a slightly acid and nutty flavor. Refrigerate.*

*To serve 6*

| | | |
|---|---|---|
| 1½ lb. | fresh pumpkin, peeled, seeded, cut into chunks, boiled in salted water for 10 minutes and drained | ¾ kg. |
| 1½ tbsp. | butter | 22 ml. |
| 5 tbsp. | flour | 75 ml. |
| 3½ tbsp. | sugar | 52 ml. |
| 3 | eggs | 3 |
| 1 cup | milk | ¼ liter |
| 3 tbsp. | *crème fraîche* or heavy cream | 45 ml. |
| 3 tbsp. | dark raisins, soaked in cold water for 15 minutes and drained | 45 ml. |
| | grated nutmeg | |
| | ground white pepper | |
| 1 tsp. | grated or finely chopped lemon peel | 5 ml. |

Melt the butter in a large sauté pan and add the pumpkin. Stirring frequently, cook for about 30 minutes, or until all of the liquid from the pumpkin has evaporated and the pumpkin has become a purée.

In a large mixing bowl, combine the flour, sugar, eggs, milk and the *crème fraîche* or cream. Mix briefly with a wire whisk, then incorporate the pumpkin purée. Add the raisins to the mixture with a sprinkling of freshly grated nutmeg, a pinch of white pepper and the lemon peel.

Spoon the pumpkin mixture into a 6-by-9-inch [15-by-23-cm.] shallow baking dish with sides about 2½ inches [6 cm.] high. Place the baking dish in a larger pan of hot water and bake 45 minutes in a preheated 350° F. [180° C.] oven.

Cool the pudding and chill it in the refrigerator for two to three hours. When ready to serve, mound it in individual dessert dishes as you would an ice cream or mousse.

JEAN AND PIERRE TROISGROS
THE NOUVELLE CUISINE OF JEAN & PIERRE TROISGROS

# Grandmother's Pudding

## *Pwdin Mamgu*

*This pudding comes from the Gower Peninsula, South Wales.*

| | To serve 6 to 8 | |
|---|---|---|
| 2½ cups | stale bread crumbs | 625 ml. |
| 1¼ cups | milk | 300 ml. |
| 2 oz. | finely chopped beef suet (about ½ cup [125 ml.]) | 75 g. |
| 2½ cups | blackberries | 625 ml. |
| 3 | medium-sized apples (about ¾ lb. [⅓ kg.]), peeled, cored and sliced | 3 |
| ⅓ cup | sugar | 75 ml. |

Soak the bread crumbs in the milk, add the suet and mix well. Place a layer of the bread-crumb mixture on the bottom of a well-buttered 5-cup [1¼-liter] pie dish or shallow baking dish, and cover with a layer of blackberries, apples and sugar. Continue to fill the dish with alternate layers of the bread-crumb mixture and of the fruit and sugar, finishing with a thick layer of the bread-crumb mixture. Bake in a preheated 375° F. [190° C.] oven for approximately one hour, or until the pudding is golden brown.

S. MINWEL TIBBOTT
WELSH FARE

# Paradise Pudding

| | To serve 4 to 6 | |
|---|---|---|
| ¾ cup | butter | 175 ml. |
| ¾ cup | sugar | 175 ml. |
| 3 | eggs | 3 |
| 1½ cups | flour | 375 ml. |
| 2 tbsp. | brandy | 30 ml. |
| 1¼ cups | light cream | 300 ml. |
| | superfine sugar | |
| | glacéed cherries, halved | |
| | angelica, cut into leaf shapes | |
| | pouring custard (recipe, page 165) | |

With a wooden spoon, beat the butter and the sugar together to a cream. Add the eggs, one at a time, and beat for five minutes after the addition of each egg. Lightly mix in the flour, then the brandy and the cream.

Butter the inside of a 1-quart [1-liter] mold, dredge it with superfine sugar, and decorate the bottom with the glacéed cherries and the angelica. Pour in the pudding mixture and tie a cloth over the top of the mold. Put it into a pan filled with enough boiling water so that the water will come half-

way up the sides of the mold; take care that the water does not get into the pudding. Boil the pudding for one hour. Unmold it and serve with pouring custard.

MAY BYRON
MAY BYRON'S PUDDINGS, PASTRIES AND SWEET DISHES

# Christmas Pudding

*The quantities given here may be multiplied and several puddings prepared at the same time. If well stored, the puddings will keep for up to two years. The techniques of covering the pudding with a cloth for cooking and of creating an airtight seal for long-term storage are demonstrated on page 41.*

| | To serve 8 to 10 | |
|---|---|---|
| 1½ cups | dried currants | 375 ml. |
| 1½ cups | raisins | 375 ml. |
| 1½ cups | golden seedless raisins | 375 ml. |
| ½ cup | mixed candied citrus peel (about 1 oz. [50 g.]), chopped | 125 ml. |
| 1 cup | glacéed cherries (about 4 oz. [125 g.]), halved | 250 ml. |
| 2 tsp. | finely grated fresh lemon peel | 10 ml. |
| ⅔ cup | coarsely chopped blanched almonds | 150 ml. |
| 5 oz. | beef suet | 150 g. |
| 1¼ cups | bread crumbs, made from stale, firm, whole bread with the crusts removed | 300 ml. |
| ¾ cup | soft brown sugar | 175 ml. |
| 3 | large eggs | 3 |
| 3 tbsp. | Scotch whisky | 60 ml. |

Pick over the dried fruits; remove any woody stems. Then wash the currants and raisins in cold water. Put them in a colander or a strainer and leave them to drain. Lay a clean dish towel over wire cake racks. Spread the fruits over the dish towel and leave them in a warm place to dry. Then chop the raisins in coarse pieces.

Thoroughly grease a 2-quart [2-liter] pudding basin with vegetable oil. Cut rounds of wax or parchment paper the same size as the top and the bottom of the basin; brush the paper well with vegetable oil. It is very important to do all this, otherwise the pudding will stick.

Remove the transparent tissue from the suet, then grate the suet on a fine or medium grater into a large mixing bowl. Put all of the fruit and nuts into the bowl with the suet. Add the bread crumbs and sugar, and mix all of the ingredients together well. Then mix in the eggs and the whisky. Put the fitted round of oiled paper in the bottom of the basin and spoon in the mixture. Place the other round of paper on top of the mixture. Cover the basin with a piece of foil, and put a foil sling around the basin or, alternatively, cover the basin with a floured cloth pleated and secured with string. Make a handle by tying together the four corners of the floured cloth.

Put a trivet in the bottom of a large saucepan; this will ensure that the bottom of the pudding is not too near the heat. Lower the pudding by the string handle into the saucepan. Fill the saucepan with water to about halfway up the sides of the pudding basin. Cover the saucepan with a tightly fitting lid. Bring the water to a boil, then reduce the heat. Boil the pudding gently for nine hours. Replenish the water in the saucepan at intervals with boiling water.

Remove the pudding from the saucepan by the string handle. Wipe the pan well, and remove the foil or cloth and the top round of oiled paper. Brush a fresh round of wax or parchment paper with vegetable oil and cover the pudding with it. Cover the basin with fresh foil, tied securely around the top with string. Wrap the pudding in a clean dish towel and store it in a cool place until Christmas Day. Before serving, boil the pudding for a further two hours. Turn the pudding out onto a plate, and serve with whipped cream.

SUSAN KING
WOMAN'S REALM

# Steamed Chocolate Pudding
## *Mohr im Hemd*

### To serve 6

| | | |
|---|---|---|
| 3½ oz. | semisweet baking chocolate, broken into pieces | 100 g. |
| 7 tbsp. | butter | 105 ml. |
| 4 | large eggs, the yolks separated from the whites | 4 |
| ½ cup | superfine sugar | 125 ml. |
| ½ cup | flour, sifted | 125 ml. |
| ¾ cup | ground almonds or hazelnuts | 175 ml. |
| ¾ cup | crumbled stale spongecake, ladyfingers or bread | 175 ml. |
| ⅔ cup | heavy cream | 150 ml. |

### Chocolate sauce

| | | |
|---|---|---|
| 2 oz. | semisweet baking chocolate, broken into pieces | 75 g. |
| ¼ cup | sugar | 50 ml. |
| ⅔ cup | water | 150 ml. |

Butter a 5-cup [1¼-liter] pudding basin and dust it with either superfine sugar or ground almonds.

Put the chocolate into a preheated 275° F. [140° C.] oven to melt it. Cream the butter. Beat in the melted chocolate, the egg yolks and half of the sugar. Continue beating with a wooden spoon until smooth. Whisk the egg whites as stiff as you can, adding the remaining sugar toward the end. Fold the egg whites into the butter mixture, simultaneously working in the flour, ground almonds or hazelnuts, and cake

crumbs. Put the mixture into the prepared pudding basin at once, leaving about 1 inch [2½ cm.] at the top for the pudding to rise. Steam it for 30 to 45 minutes in a covered water bath, or bake in a bain-marie in a 350° F. [180° C.] oven.

To make the chocolate sauce, put the chocolate into a saucepan with the sugar and water, and boil gently for a few minutes, stirring continuously.

Test the pudding for doneness with a skewer; when this comes out clean, the pudding is ready. Invert a heated plate onto the pudding basin and, with one gentle shake, unmold the pudding. Pour the chocolate sauce over and around it. Top with the whipped cream. Serve at once.

ROSL PHILPOT
VIENNESE COOKERY

# Holyrood Pudding

### To serve 4 to 6

| | | |
|---|---|---|
| 2½ cups | milk | ½ liter |
| ⅓ cup | semolina | 75 ml. |
| ⅓ cup | sugar | 75 ml. |
| ⅓ cup | crushed almond macaroons (recipe, page 167) | 75 ml. |
| 2 tbsp. | butter | 30 ml. |
| 3 | eggs, the yolks separated from the whites | 3 |
| 2 tsp. | orange marmalade | 10 ml. |

### Almond sauce

| | | |
|---|---|---|
| 1 | egg | 1 |
| 2 tbsp. | superfine sugar | 30 ml. |
| ⅔ cup | milk | 150 ml. |
| ¼ cup | ground almonds | 50 ml. |
| 1 tbsp. | orange-flower water | 15 ml. |

Bring the milk to a boil and stir in the semolina with the sugar, macaroons and butter. Let the mixture boil for about five minutes, stirring it all the time. Pour it into a bowl and allow it to cool. Meanwhile, beat the egg whites to a stiff froth and butter a 1½-quart [1½-liter] pudding mold.

One at a time, beat the egg yolks into the semolina mixture. Add the marmalade and fold in the beaten egg whites. Mix gently, pour into the buttered mold. Place the mold in a bain-marie and steam on top of the stove for 1¼ hours.

Meanwhile, make the almond sauce. Mix together in a small saucepan the egg, sugar, milk, ground almonds and orange-flower water. Over low heat, stir the mixture with a whisk until it is as thick as cream; do not let it boil.

Unmold the pudding; serve the almond sauce separately.

F. MARIAN MC NEILL
THE SCOTS KITCHEN

# Crepes, Omelets and Fried Desserts

*The basic recipe for crepes appears in Standard Preparations, page 166.*

## Crepes with Orange Sauce

### *Crêpes Suzette*

With this method for making *Crêpes Suzette*, the sauce melts right into the crepes and is the essence of all that is subtle and delicate. The recipe works as well with tangerines.

|        | To serve 4                 |          |
|--------|----------------------------|----------|
| 16     | crepes (recipe, page 166)  | 16       |
| 4 tbsp.| unsalted butter            | 60 ml.   |
| 3 tbsp.| sugar                      | 45 ml.   |
| 1      | orange                     | 1        |
| 3 tbsp.| orange liqueur             | 45 ml.   |
| 2 cups | boiling water              | ½ liter  |

The sauce can be prepared by hand or in a blender or—best of all—in a food processor, using the plastic blade. Cream the butter well, gradually add the sugar and keep beating.

Peel the zest from the orange and reserve it. Halve the orange, squeeze one half of it and strain the juice into the butter-sugar mixture. (You will have to force the juice into the butter by adding only 1 or 2 teaspoons [5 to 10 ml.] at a time. The sauce will nevertheless not be completely smooth; but no matter, since no one ever will see it.) Add the liqueur gradually and, if the butter will hold more juice, squeeze in the juice from the other half of the orange.

Cut the zest of the orange into fine, thin strips and blanch them in the boiling water for three minutes. Drain the strips and set them aside.

Butter a serving dish that can go into the oven. Spread a heaping teaspoonful of the sauce on each crepe. Fold the crepe in half, and then in half again, to form a triangle. Place the folded crepe on the buttered serving dish and repeat the process with the rest, placing each crepe so that the rounded bottom of one slightly overlaps the point of the preceding crepe. If there is sauce left over, dot it on top of the crepes. Scatter the blanched orange strips over the crepes.

Sprinkle the crepes with powdered sugar and just the lightest sprinkling of orange liqueur. Put the crepes in a preheated 350° F. [180° C.] oven for about five minutes and serve them hot.

THE GREAT COOKS' GUIDE TO CREPES AND SOUFFLÉS

## Ricotta-and-Strawberry Crepes

|         | To serve 8                            |          |
|---------|---------------------------------------|----------|
| ⅔ lb.   | ricotta cheese                        | 150 g.   |
| 2 cups  | fresh strawberries, hulled and crushed| ½ liter  |
| 2       | eggs                                  | 2        |
| 2       | egg yolks                             | 2        |
| ½ cup   | flour, sifted before measuring        | 125 ml.  |
| 2 cups  | milk                                  | ½ liter  |
| 5 tbsp. | granulated sugar                      | 75 ml.   |
|         | salt                                  |          |
| 2 tbsp. | butter, melted                        | 30 ml.   |
| 1 tsp.  | vanilla extract                       | 5 ml.    |
|         | confectioners' sugar                  |          |

Beat the eggs and yolks lightly, then add the flour, milk, 1 tablespoon [15 ml.] of the granulated sugar and a pinch of salt, and blend well.

Brush a 6-inch [15-cm.] crepe pan with the melted butter. Pour in about 3 tablespoons [45 ml.] of the batter and spread it over the entire pan. Cook the crepes on both sides, stacking them as they are cooked. Cover them with wax paper until you are ready to fill them.

Cream the ricotta with the remaining granulated sugar and the vanilla. Add the strawberries and mix gently. Spoon the mixture down the center of each crepe and roll it up. Serve sprinkled with confectioners' sugar.

GIOVANNA D'AGOSTINO
MAMA D'S HOMESTYLE ITALIAN COOKBOOK

## Apricot Pancakes

### *Palacsinták Barackízzel*

|            | To make about 14 pancakes          |             |
|------------|-------------------------------------|-------------|
| 3          | eggs                                | 3           |
| 1 cup      | milk                                | ¼ liter     |
| ⅓ cup      | club soda, freshly opened           | 75 ml.      |
| 1 cup      | flour, sifted before measuring      | ¼ liter     |
| 3 tbsp.    | granulated sugar                    | 45 ml.      |
| ¼ tsp.     | salt                                | 1 ml.       |
| 1 tsp.     | vanilla extract                     | 5 ml.       |
| 4 to 6 tbsp.| butter                             | 60 to 90 ml.|
| ¾ cup      | apricot jam                         | 175 ml.     |
| 1 cup      | ground walnuts or hazelnuts         | ¼ liter     |
|            | confectioners' sugar                |             |

Beat the eggs lightly with the milk in a small bowl. Combine with the club soda in a large mixing bowl. With a wooden spoon stir in the flour and granulated sugar, then add the salt and vanilla. Continue to stir until the batter is smooth.

Melt 1 teaspoon [5 ml.] of butter in an 8-inch [20-cm.] crepe pan. When the foam subsides, ladle in enough batter to cover the bottom of the skillet thinly and tilt the skillet from side to side to spread it evenly. Cook for two to three minutes, or until slightly browned on one side, then turn and brown lightly on the other side. When a pancake is done, spread 2 teaspoons [10 ml.] of jam over it, roll it loosely into a cylinder, then place it in a baking dish in a 200° F. [100° C.] oven to keep warm. Add butter to the pan as needed.

Serve the pancakes warm as a dessert, sprinkled with nuts and confectioners' sugar.

FOODS OF THE WORLD/THE COOKING OF VIENNA'S EMPIRE

---

# Crepes with Wild Strawberries

### Crêpes Richelieu

To serve 4 to 6

| | | |
|---|---|---|
| 12 | crepes (recipe, page 166) | 12 |
| ½ lb. | wild strawberries | ¼ kg. |
| ¼ cup | superfine sugar, mixed with ¼ cup [50 ml.] kirsch | 50 ml. |
| | **Pastry cream** | |
| 2 tbsp. | superfine sugar | 30 ml. |
| 2 tbsp. | flour | 30 ml. |
| ½ cup | milk | 125 ml. |
| | salt | |
| ½ tsp. | vanilla extract | 2 ml. |
| 1 | egg yolk, lightly beaten | 1 |

Macerate the strawberries in the sugar and kirsch for 30 minutes. Meanwhile, prepare the crepes.

To make a pastry cream, mix together in a heavy saucepan the sugar, flour and milk along with a pinch of salt and the vanilla extract. Bring to a boil, stirring constantly. Remove from the heat and whisk in the egg yolk. Allow the pastry cream to cool completely, then gently incorporate the strawberries, taking care not to crush them.

Place a little of the strawberry-cream filling in each crepe, roll up and serve.

PAUL BOUILLARD
LA CUISINE AU COIN DU FEU

# Pancakes with Cheese Filling

### Blinchiki s Tvorogom

*This Russian recipe is taken from the best-selling cookbook of the Stalin era.*

To serve 6

| | | |
|---|---|---|
| 1 | egg | 1 |
| 3 tbsp. | sugar | 45 ml. |
| ½ tsp. | salt | 2 ml. |
| 3 cups | milk | ¾ liter |
| 2 cups | flour, sifted | ½ liter |
| 4 tbsp. | butter | 60 ml. |
| ¾ to 1 cup | sour cream | 175 to 250 ml. |
| | **Cheese filling** | |
| 1 lb. | pot cheese, or substitute soft ricotta | ½ kg. |
| 1 | egg, the yolk separated from the white, and the white lightly beaten | 1 |
| ¾ cup | sugar | 175 ml. |
| ½ tsp. | salt | 2 ml. |
| 2 tsp. | freshly grated lemon or orange peel | 10 ml. |
| 1 tbsp. | butter, melted | 15 ml. |
| ¼ cup | raisins, soaked in warm water for 15 minutes and drained (optional) | 50 ml. |

First prepare the pancakes. Break the egg into a bowl and beat it with a wooden spoon. Add 1 tablespoon [15 ml.] of the sugar, the salt and 1 cup [¼ liter] of the milk, and stir well. Add a little flour and some more milk, stirring continuously. Add more flour and milk until all are incorporated into the batter. Melt a little butter in a 5-inch [13-cm.] crepe pan over medium heat. Pour in enough batter to cover the base of the pan with a thin layer. As soon as the pancake is cooked on one side, remove it to a side dish. Continue to make pancakes in this fashion until the batter is used up; if the batter becomes too thick, thin it with a little more milk.

To make the filling, first rub the pot cheese through a sieve into a bowl. Mix into it the egg yolk, sugar, salt, grated lemon or orange peel, melted butter and, if desired, the raisins. Place 1 tablespoon of filling on the fried surface of each pancake and roll up the pancake, folding in the sides when it is partly rolled. To keep the pancake from coming apart while it is frying, smear the last edge with beaten egg white before folding down this flap.

Fry the pancakes in butter on both sides, starting with the flap side down and turning once, until the pancakes are nicely browned. Serve the pancakes hot, sprinkled with the remaining sugar, with a bowl of sour cream on the side.

O. P. MOLCHANOVA
KNIGA O VKUSNOÏ I ZDOROVOÏ PISHCHE

# Rolled Pancakes Filled with Cottage Cheese

## *Blintzes*

*To make 10 rolled pancakes*

| | | |
|---|---|---|
| 3 | eggs | 3 |
| ½ cup | water | 125 ml. |
| ¾ cup | flour, sifted before measuring | 175 ml. |
| ¼ tsp. | salt | 1 ml. |
| 2 tbsp. | butter, melted and cooled | 30 ml. |
| 4 tbsp. | melted butter, combined with 1 tbsp. [15 ml.] flavorless vegetable oil | 60 ml. |
| 1 cup | sour cream | ¼ liter |
| | **Cottage cheese filling** | |
| 1 lb. | dry cottage cheese or creamed cottage cheese, wrapped in cheesecloth and squeezed dry | ½ kg. |
| 2 tbsp. | sour cream | 30 ml. |
| 1 | egg yolk | 1 |
| 2 tbsp. | sugar | 30 ml. |
| ½ tsp. | vanilla extract | 2 ml. |
| ¼ tsp. | salt | 1 ml. |

First prepare the filling by using the back of a large wooden spoon to force the cottage cheese through a fine sieve into a deep bowl, or put the cheese through a food mill set over a bowl. Add the sour cream, egg yolk, sugar, vanilla and salt. Stirring and mashing vigorously, beat with a large spoon until all of the ingredients are well blended and the filling mixture is smooth. Set it aside.

To make the blintzes, first combine the eggs, water, flour, salt and cooled melted butter in the jar of an electric blender, and blend them at high speed for a few seconds. Turn off the machine, scrape down the sides of the jar with a rubber spatula and blend again for 40 seconds. The batter should have the consistency of heavy cream; dilute it if necessary by beating in cold water, a teaspoon [5 ml.] at a time.

Heat a 6-inch [15-cm.] crepe pan or skillet over high heat. With a pastry brush or crumpled paper towels, lightly grease the bottom and sides of the pan with a little of the combined oil and butter.

Pour about 3 tablespoons [45 ml.] of batter into the pan and tip the pan so that the batter quickly covers the bottom.

Cook the blintze for a minute or so, until a rim of brown shows around the edge. Then, without turning it over, slide the blintze onto a plate. Grease the skillet again and proceed with the rest of the blintzes. As they are cooked, stack the blintzes one on top of the other.

When all the blintzes have been browned on one side, fill and roll each of them in the following fashion: Place about 3 tablespoons [45 ml.] of filling on the cooked side of the blintze an inch or so from the top edge. Smooth the filling into a strip about 3 inches [8 cm.] long and 1 inch [2½ cm.] deep. Fold the sides of the blintze toward the center, covering the ends of the filling. Then turn the top edge over the filling and roll the blintze into a cylinder about 3 inches [8 cm.] long and 1 inch [2½ cm.] wide.

Pour the remaining butter-and-oil mixture into a heavy 10- to 12-inch [25- to 30-cm.] skillet and set over moderate heat. Place four or five blintzes, seam side down, in the pan and fry them for three to five minutes on each side, turning them with a metal spatula and regulating the heat so they color quickly and evenly without burning. As they are browned, transfer them to a heated serving platter.

Serve the blintzes hot, accompanied by the sour cream, presented separately in a bowl.

FOODS OF THE WORLD/AMERICAN COOKING: THE MELTING POT

# Souffléed Crepes with Champagne Sabayon Sauce

## *Crêpes Soufflées au Sabayon*

*This recipe is from Le Taillevent restaurant in Paris.*

*To serve 4*

| | | |
|---|---|---|
| 12 | small crepes (recipe, page 166) | 12 |
| 4 | eggs, the yolks separated from the whites | 4 |
| ⅓ cup | superfine sugar | 75 ml. |
| ¼ cup | flour | 50 ml. |
| 1 cup | milk, heated to the boiling point | ¼ liter |
| ⅓ cup | Grand Marnier | 75 ml. |
| ¼ cup | confectioners' sugar | 50 ml. |
| | **Champagne sabayon sauce** | |
| 4 | egg yolks | 4 |
| ¼ cup | superfine sugar | 50 ml. |
| ⅔ cup | Champagne | 150 ml. |

First prepare the crepes, and set them aside.

To make the soufflé mixture, whisk the egg yolks with the superfine sugar for one minute in an enameled saucepan. Add the flour, stirring, then gradually stir in the boiling milk. Stirring constantly, bring to a boil, reduce the heat to low and cook for two minutes. Remove from the heat and add the Grand Marnier. Beat the egg whites until they stand in stiff peaks, then fold them into the mixture.

Butter a large, ovenproof dish. Fill the prepared crepes by placing a generous spoonful of the soufflé mixture on one half of each crepe, then folding the other half loosely over the top. As the crepes are filled, arrange them side by side in the dish. Bake the crepes in a preheated 425° F. [220° C.] oven for seven minutes. Halfway through the baking, sprinkle the crepes with the confectioners' sugar to glaze them.

Serve the crepes accompanied by the Champagne sabayon sauce, prepared as follows: Put the egg yolks, superfine sugar and Champagne into a copper bowl. Place the bowl in a water bath over moderate heat and whisk the mixture constantly until it has a creamy, frothy consistency.

LES PRINCES DE LA GASTRONOMIE

# Souffléed Crepes

*Crêpes Soufflées*

To serve 4

| | | |
|---|---|---|
| 10 | crepes (recipe, page 166) | 10 |
| 3 tbsp. | superfine sugar | 45 ml. |
| 5 | eggs, the yolks separated from the whites | 5 |
| | vanilla extract | |

To prepare the soufflé mixture, first put the sugar, egg yolks and a drop or two of vanilla extract into a bowl. Mix with a wooden spoon, stirring until the mixture becomes thoroughly amalgamated. Beat the egg whites until stiff and fold them into the yolk mixture.

Lightly butter a gratin dish. Stack the crepes one on top of the other, spreading a generous spoonful of the soufflé mixture on each crepe. Cover the stack completely with the remaining soufflé mixture and bake in a preheated 400° F. [200° C.] oven for 20 minutes. Serve immediately.

LES PETITS PLATS ET LES GRANDS

# Basic Dessert Omelet

To serve 2

| | | |
|---|---|---|
| 3 | eggs, the yolks separated from the whites | 3 |
| 2 tsp. | superfine sugar | 10 ml. |
| 1/8 tsp. | salt | 1 ml. |
| 1 tbsp. | butter | 15 ml. |
| | fresh or cooked fruit (optional) | |
| | confectioners' sugar (optional) | |

Put the egg yolks, superfine sugar and salt in a bowl and beat with a small wire whisk until the yolks are light and fluffy. In a copper bowl use a large wire whisk, or an electric mixer or rotary beater, to whip the egg whites until they hold soft peaks. With a rubber spatula, carefully fold the yolk mixture into the beaten whites.

Heat an omelet pan slowly over low to medium heat, gradually raising the heat until a speck of butter dropped in the pan instantly turns brown, but not black. If the pan is too hot and the butter turns black, the pan must be cooled a little and retested. Heat the broiler.

Wipe the test butter from the omelet pan. Put 1 tablespoon [15 ml.] of butter into the pan and spread it around with a wad of paper towels. Immediately put the egg-and-sugar mixture into the pan and spread it with a fork to cover the bottom of the pan completely. Stir the eggs with the back of the fork, being careful to stir only the surface of the egg mixture. Do not let the fork touch the bottom of the pan.

When the edges of the omelet appear firm, run the tines of the fork around the edges of the omelet. When the bottom of the omelet appears golden brown, put the omelet—still in its pan—under the broiler for a minute or two to set the top.

If fruit is to be included as a filling, place it down the center of the omelet. Fold the omelet, using the fork, and slide it onto a hot, flat, metal serving platter. To serve an unfilled omelet, dust the top heavily with confectioners' sugar. Heat a metal skewer until it is red hot, then use it to make a large X on the sugar-sprinkled omelet.

Use a large serving fork and spatula to divide the omelet into two servings.

DIONE LUCAS AND MARION GORMAN
THE DIONE LUCAS BOOK OF FRENCH COOKING

# Marbled Eggs

## Oeufs Marbrez

*To prepare the green coloring for the eggs, parboil the chard or spinach for two or three minutes, then drain it and purée it through a sieve. For the red coloring, first broil the pepper until its skin blackens on all sides, then peel, halve and seed the pepper before puréeing it.*

### To serve 8 to 10

| | | |
|---|---|---|
| 24 | eggs | 24 |
| 1 | red pepper, puréed | 1 |
| ½ lb. | chard or spinach, puréed | ¼ kg. |
| ¼ tsp. | powdered saffron, dissolved in 1 tsp. [5 ml.] boiling water | 1 ml. |
| | salt | |
| 1 tsp. | ground cinnamon | 5 ml. |
| 1 cup | sugar | ¼ liter |
| 2 tbsp. | butter | 30 ml. |
| | orange-flower water | |
| | pomegranate seeds | |

Break the eggs into four bowls, six eggs in each. Color the eggs by adding the red-pepper purée to one bowl, the chard or spinach purée to another and the dissolved saffron to a third. Leave the eggs in the fourth bowl uncolored. Season the eggs in all four bowls to taste with salt, cinnamon and sugar, and beat the eggs in each bowl thoroughly.

Melt the butter over low heat in a fireproof 1½-quart [1½-liter] oven dish. When the butter is melted, pour in a layer of the red egg mixture. When the red layer is barely firm, pour in a layer of the yellow saffron mixture. Subsequent layers, with the exception of the top layer, may be barely set by passing the dish beneath a broiler until just firm enough to pour in an additional layer. Continue making layers of the four colors in rotation, until all of the eggs are used. Put the dish into a preheated 325° F. [170° C.] oven for 30 minutes.

Serve the dessert cut into slices, sprinkled with orange-flower water and decorated with pomegranate seeds.

PIERRE DE LUNE
LE NOUVEAU CUISINIER

# Omelets Normandy-Style

## Omelettes Normandes

### To serve 6

| | | |
|---|---|---|
| 8 | medium-sized eggs | 8 |
| 5 or 6 | medium-sized tart apples | 5 or 6 |
| 2 to 3 tbsp. | fresh lemon juice | 30 to 45 ml. |
| 12 tbsp. | unsalted butter | 180 ml. |
| 1¼ cups | sugar | 300 ml. |
| ⅓ cup | Calvados or dark rum | 75 ml. |
| ⅓ cup | heavy cream | 75 ml. |

Peel and core the apples, sprinkling them with lemon juice to keep them white. Slice them about ¼ inch [6 mm.] thick, measure out about 3 cups [¾ liter] and set aside.

In a large, heavy omelet pan or skillet, heat 3 tablespoons [45 ml.] of the butter until it is brown and foaming. Add only as many apples as will fit in one layer, and sauté them over high heat for seven to 10 minutes, stirring occasionally to keep them from burning. Remove the cooked apples, add more butter and repeat until all of the apples are cooked.

Return all the apples to the pan, sprinkle them with ¾ cup [175 ml.] of the sugar and stir for a couple of minutes until the sugar caramelizes. Then pour in half of the Calvados or rum, set aflame and shake the pan until the flame goes out. Remove from the heat, wait for the bubbling to subside and stir in the cream. Put the apple mixture into a bowl. The recipe can be made two hours in advance to this point.

Ten minutes before serving, warm a large oval serving platter. Separate three of the eggs. Beat the three egg whites with a pinch of salt until firm; add 2 tablespoons [30 ml.] of sugar and continue to beat until stiff. Beat the whole eggs, 2 tablespoons of sugar and the egg yolks lightly with a fork. Fold the beaten eggs into the stiffly beaten whites.

Separate the omelet mixture into two batches, to make two omelets. Set the omelet pan over high heat, and melt 2 tablespoons of the butter until it is nut brown and foaming. When the foam subsides, pour in one batch of the eggs. Let the eggs cook just long enough to set the exterior—less than half a minute. (Resist the temptation to let them cook longer.) Remove the pan from the heat, and put half of the apples in the center of the omelet. Then fold the omelet: First slide it down to the edge of the pan, grasping the handle of the pan from underneath. In one motion invert the pan over the middle of the serving dish, so that the bottom of the omelet will be on top. Make the other omelet exactly the same way and put it on the serving dish.

Sprinkle each omelet with the remaining sugar. Heat the remaining Calvados or rum and pour it over the omelets. Bring them to the table and set them aflame. As the Calvados or rum runs to the bottom of the dish, spoon it over the omelets to caramelize them.

SIMONE BECK
SIMCA'S CUISINE

## A Sweet Puffed Omelet

Before folding the omelet, you may spread the top with jam or jelly. Or you may spread the bottom with slices of fruit.

| | To serve 1 or 2 | |
|---|---|---|
| 2 | large eggs, the yolks separated from the whites | 2 |
| 1 tsp. | superfine sugar | 5 ml. |
| ¼ tsp. | vanilla extract | 1 ml. |
| 2 tbsp. | butter | 30 ml. |
| | confectioners' sugar | |

With a whisk or beater, beat the egg whites until they are stiff enough to cling to the beater. Immediately add the sugar and vanilla to the yolks and beat them with the unwashed beater until they thicken, after about a minute.

With a rubber spatula, scrape the whites over the yolks and fold the two together until well combined. A few streaks of white showing in the mixture is desirable.

Over a high heat, melt the butter in a nonstick 10-inch [25-cm.] frying pan with sloping sides. When the butter browns lightly, pour in the egg mixture, filling the pan evenly. Reduce the heat to medium and cook until the edges turn light brown. To make sure the omelet is not cooking too quickly, lift the edge slightly with the spatula and peek under it. When the bottom is golden brown, and the top of the omelet has puffed somewhat, remove the pan from the heat. Tilting the pan an inch [2½ cm.] or so above, and at the edge of a heated plate, allow the omelet to slide out of the pan onto the plate. When it is about halfway out, use the edge of the pan to help you fold the half remaining in the pan over the omelet half already lying on the plate. Sprinkle the omelet generously with confectioners' sugar and serve at once.

MICHAEL FIELD
ALL MANNER OF FOOD

## Souffléed Fritters
### Les Pets-de-Nonne ou Beignets Soufflés

| | To serve 10 | |
|---|---|---|
| 2¼ cups | water | 550 ml. |
| 7 tbsp. | butter | 105 ml. |
| ¼ tsp. | salt | 1 ml. |
| ¼ cup | superfine sugar | 50 ml. |
| 2¾ cups | flour, sifted | 675 ml. |
| 6 | eggs | 6 |
| | oil for deep frying | |
| | confectioners' sugar (optional) | |

In a saucepan combine the water, butter, salt and sugar. Bring to a boil, then remove the pan from the heat. Pour in the flour all at once, stirring rapidly. Place the saucepan over medium heat and stir vigorously for a few minutes until the mixture comes away from the sides of the saucepan. Off the heat, add the eggs, mixing in each one thoroughly before adding the next.

In a deep skillet, heat the oil to 350° F. [180° C.]. Use a teaspoon to form each fritter, and with your finger carefully push each spoonful of the mixture into the hot oil. As soon as there are several fritters in the oil, increase the heat to keep the oil at 350° F. When the fritters are golden, remove them with a wire skimmer or a slotted spoon and drain them on paper towels. Adjusting the heat as necessary, fry the remaining batches in the same way.

Serve the fritters hot or cold, sprinkled with confectioners' sugar if desired.

JOSÉPHINE BESSON
LA MÈRE BESSON "MA CUISINE PROVENÇALE"

## Magnolia Petal Fritters
### Pétales de Magnolia

Other perfumed flowers, such as locust flowers and orange blossoms, can be prepared in the same way.

| | To serve 4 | |
|---|---|---|
| 12 | magnolia petals | 12 |
| | oil for deep frying | |
| | confectioners' sugar, sifted | |
| | **Egg-white batter** | |
| 6 | egg whites | 6 |
| ¼ tsp. | salt | 1 ml. |
| 2 tbsp. | superfine sugar | 30 ml. |
| ¼ cup | flour, sifted | 60 ml. |

To make the batter, mix the unbeaten egg whites with the salt, superfine sugar and flour until smooth. Dip the flower petals one at a time into the batter and drop them into hot oil. The petals will swell up considerably. When the fritters are golden, drain them well, sprinkle them with confectioners' sugar and serve immediately.

H. LECOURT
LA CUISINE CHINOISE

# Fried Custard

## *Crème Frite*

*The technique of frying custards is shown on pages 50-51.*

|  | To serve 12 |  |
|---|---|---|
| 2¼ cups | sifted flour | 550 ml. |
| ½ cup | superfine sugar | 125 ml. |
| 12 | egg yolks | 12 |
| 5 | eggs, 1 beaten | 5 |
|  | salt |  |
| 1 quart | milk, scalded with a vanilla bean and the bean removed | 1 liter |
| 4 tbsp. | butter | 60 ml. |
|  | bread crumbs |  |
|  | confectioners' sugar |  |
|  | fat or oil for deep frying |  |

Put the sifted flour in a pan and gradually stir in the superfine sugar, the 12 egg yolks, four of the whole eggs and a pinch of salt. Moisten with the milk. Add the butter. Mix well and put the pan over medium heat. Stirring constantly to prevent sticking, bring the custard mixture to a boil and let it boil for a few minutes.

Spread the custard on a buttered baking sheet in an even layer about ¼ inch [6 mm.] thick, and leave it to cool. Cut the custard into pieces and dip each one first in the beaten egg and then in the bread crumbs.

Deep fry the coated custards in fat or oil. Drain the pieces on a cloth and sprinkle them with confectioners' sugar.

PROSPER MONTAGNÉ
THE NEW LAROUSSE GASTRONOMIQUE

# Fried Custard, Chinese-Style

## *Chih Ma Kuo Cha*

|  | To serve 6 |  |
|---|---|---|
| ¼ cup | sesame seeds | 50 ml. |
| ½ cup | sugar | 125 ml. |
| ½ cup | flour | 125 ml. |
| ⅔ cup | cornstarch | 150 ml. |
| ⅔ cup | cold water | 150 ml. |
| 1 | large egg, lightly beaten | 1 |
| 1½ cups | warm water | 375 ml. |
| 2 cups | peanut or corn oil | ½ liter |

Toast the sesame seeds in a skillet until golden brown. Let cool on a piece of wax paper, then crush them fine with a rolling pin. Mix the crushed sesame seeds with the sugar. Set the mixture aside.

In a large mixing bowl, combine the flour, 2 tablespoons [30 ml.] of the cornstarch and cold water, and mix well until smooth. Add the beaten egg and mix some more; there should not be any lumps.

Heat a wok, add the warm water and bring it to a boil. Slowly pour the batter into the boiling water, using a wire whisk while stirring in one direction. Stir until the custard mixture has an elastic consistency. Pour the entire contents of the wok into a greased 5- to 6-inch [13- to 15-cm.] square cake pan; the custard will fill the pan to a depth of about ¾ inch [2 cm.]. Let cool, then place the custard in the refrigerator until firmly set.

Cut the custard into sticks about 2 inches [5 cm.] long and ¾ inch [2 cm.] wide. You should have about 24 sticks. Lightly roll the sticks in the remaining cornstarch. Heat a wok, add the oil and heat it to about 375° F. [190° C.]. Deep fry the coated custard for three to four minutes, or until a light-brown crust forms and the sticks are very crisp. Drain, and set the fried custard on a dish. Sprinkle the sesame seed and sugar mixture over the custard and serve hot.

FLORENCE LIN
FLORENCE LIN'S CHINESE VEGETARIAN COOKBOOK

# Fried Ricotta Balls

## *Ricotta Fritta*

Ricotta—sweetened and orange flavored, then formed into little balls held together with a few egg yolks before being deep fried—makes an unusual, imaginative and very good dessert. The balls are not difficult to make if you are sure to squeeze out the excess water from the ricotta so that the balls don't fall apart.

|  | To serve 8 |  |
|---|---|---|
| 1 lb. | soft ricotta cheese | ½ kg. |
| 3 | egg yolks | 3 |
| about 2 cups | flour | about ½ liter |
| 2 to 3 tbsp. | freshly grated orange peel | 30 to 45 ml. |
| 2 | eggs | 2 |
|  | salt |  |
| 2 cups | solid vegetable shortening | ½ liter |
| about 1 cup | granulated sugar | about ¼ liter |

Drain the ricotta very well by wrapping it in cheesecloth and squeezing tightly to remove all of the excess water. Place the drained ricotta in a bowl, along with the egg yolks and 3 tablespoons [45 ml.] of the flour. Sprinkle in the orange peel and mix all of the ingredients well with a wooden spoon.

Spread the remaining flour on a sheet of aluminum foil. On the floured foil, roll the ricotta mixture into balls 1 inch

[2½ cm.] in diameter: this lightly coats the balls with flour.

In a second bowl, beat the eggs with a pinch of salt. Prepare a serving dish by lining it with paper towels.

Heat the shortening in a deep fryer. When the shortening is hot, quickly dip a few balls at a time into the beaten eggs and then drop them into the fryer. Cook the balls until they are light golden brown all over—about two minutes—then remove them from the fryer with a strainer-skimmer and place them on the prepared serving dish. When all of the balls are cooked and on the serving dish, remove the paper towels and sprinkle the balls with sugar. Serve hot.

GIULIANO BUGIALLI
THE FINE ART OF ITALIAN COOKING

## Sweet Cheese Fritters

### Baignets de Plusieurs Façons

*The custard mixture may be cooked and cut up ahead of time, but it must be fried immediately before serving.*

These fritters may be flavored according to taste with ¼ cup [50 ml.] of ground almonds or ground pistachio nuts, or with the grated peel of one lemon. The flavoring should be added with the main ingredients.

To serve 4 to 6

| | | |
|---|---|---|
| ½ lb. | cream cheese, soft ricotta or pot cheese | ¼ kg. |
| 5 | eggs | 5 |
| | salt | |
| ¼ cup | sugar | 50 ml. |
| ⅔ cup | flour | 150 ml. |
| 2¼ cups | heavy cream | 550 ml. |
| | oil for deep frying | |
| | confectioners' sugar | |

In a mixing bowl, mash the cheese until smooth and beat in the eggs. Incorporate a pinch of salt, the sugar and the flour. Whisk in the cream, a little at a time, until the mixture is a smooth, fluid custard.

Transfer the mixture to a saucepan and cook over medium heat, stirring continuously, until it thickens. Pour the mixture onto a lightly floured surface, spreading it to a thickness of about ½ inch [1 cm.]. Lightly dust the top with flour and let the mixture cool.

Cut the cool fritter mixture into 1-inch [2½-cm.] squares or diamond shapes. Heat the oil and deep fry the fritters, a few at a time, until golden brown—about one or two minutes on each side. Drain the fritters well, sprinkle them with confectioners' sugar while still hot and pass them under a hot broiler for a few seconds to glaze them before serving.

MENON
LES SOUPERS DE LA COUR

## White Cheese Croquettes

### Cyrniki ou Croquettes de Fromage Blanc

*The original version of this recipe called for tvorog, a firm, white, slightly tart cheese. A little lemon juice may be added to the ricotta or pot cheese to approximate the taste of tvorog.*

To serve 4

| | | |
|---|---|---|
| 1 lb. | pot cheese or ricotta | ½ kg. |
| 3 or 4 | eggs, lightly beaten | 3 or 4 |
| 3 tbsp. | granulated sugar | 45 ml. |
| | salt | |
| 1¼ cups | flour | 300 ml. |
| 1 to 1¼ cups | heavy cream | 250 to 300 ml. |
| 7 tbsp. | butter | 105 ml. |
| | vanilla extract (optional) | |
| 2 tbsp. | superfine sugar | 30 ml. |

Press the cheese through a fine strainer into a bowl. Add the eggs, the sugar, a pinch of salt, the flour and 1 to 2 tablespoons [15 to 30 ml.] of the cream. When these are mixed together thoroughly, form the mixture into oval or round croquettes a finger-width thick. Cook the croquettes in hot butter until golden on all sides. Drain and serve with the remaining cream, lightly whipped and—if you wish—flavored with vanilla and the superfine sugar.

H. WITWICKA AND S. SOSKINE
LA CUISINE RUSSE CLASSIQUE

## Poor Knights of Windsor

English cookery books are full of recipes for this—strips of crustless bread, dipped in sweetened milk and egg, fried in butter and served with warm jam or maple syrup. Here is a Spanish variation.

| | To serve 4 | |
|---|---|---|
| 8 | slices white bread with the crusts removed, cut into strips | 8 |
| 2 | egg yolks | 2 |
| ½ cup | sweet sherry | 125 ml. |
| | oil | |
| | confectioners' sugar | |
| | ground cinnamon | |

Beat the egg yolks and sherry together and dip the bread strips into this mixture. Heat the oil in a pan and fry the bread quickly so that the strips are golden brown and crisp. Dust with the confectioners' sugar and the cinnamon, and serve immediately.

MARGARET COSTA
MARGARET COSTA'S FOUR SEASONS COOKERY BOOK

## Fried Cake Slices with Wine Custard

### Croûte à la Belle Aurore

*Either spongecake or poundcake may be used for this recipe, and crumbled sugar cookies or vanilla wafers can be substituted for the cracker crumbs.*

| | To serve 6 | |
|---|---|---|
| 1 cup | thick applesauce | ¼ liter |
| 1 lb. | stale cake, cut into slices ½ inch [1 cm.] thick | ½ kg. |
| ⅓ cup | rum | 75 ml. |
| 1 tbsp. | heavy cream | 15 ml. |
| 3 tbsp. | chopped, mixed glacéed fruits | 45 ml. |
| 2 | eggs, beaten | 2 |
| 1 cup | rolled, sifted cracker crumbs | ¼ liter |
| | butter for frying | |
| | hot wine custard (recipe, page 165) | |

Sprinkle the slices of cake generously with the rum. Mix the cream and glacéed fruits into the applesauce and spread this mixture over half of the cake slices. Place the other slices of cake on the prepared ones, pressing them together. Dip these cake sandwiches in the beaten egg, cover with the cracker crumbs and fry them in butter over medium heat. Serve the sauce separately in a warmed bowl or sauceboat.

ALICE B. TOKLAS
THE ALICE B. TOKLAS COOK BOOK

# Frozen Desserts

*Recipes for basic ice creams appear in Standard Preparations, page 166.*

## Rhubarb Granita

*The technique of freezing granita is shown on pages 54-55.*

| | To serve 6 to 8 | |
|---|---|---|
| 1½ lb. | tender rhubarb, cut into 1-inch [2½-cm.] pieces | ¾ kg. |
| 1 cup | sugar | ¼ liter |
| 1 cup | water | ¼ liter |
| 3 to 4 tbsp. | strained fresh lemon juice | 45 to 60 ml. |
| 2 cups | small strawberries | ½ liter |

Make a sugar syrup by simmering the sugar and water together in a saucepan for five minutes. Add the rhubarb and stew until tender. Add the lemon juice and a few strawberries for color, then pass the entire lot through a sieve. Cool and taste for sweetness; add more sugar if necessary.

Freeze for three to four hours, or until needed. This granita is a particularly lush shade of rose and deserves to be viewed through a transparent dish. Garnish with the remaining unstemmed strawberries.

JUDITH OLNEY
SUMMER FOOD

## Blackberry Water Ice

If sweet-scented geranium leaves are unavailable, a tablespoon or two of rose water makes a fair substitute.

| | To serve 4 to 6 | |
|---|---|---|
| 3½ cups | blackberries, puréed through a sieve | 875 ml. |
| ½ cup | sugar | 125 ml. |
| ⅔ cup | water | 150 ml. |
| 3 | sweet-scented geranium leaves | 3 |

Make a syrup by boiling the sugar and water together for five to six minutes with two of the geranium leaves. When cool, remove the geranium leaves, add the syrup to the sieved blackberries and put into a freezing tray with the remaining geranium leaf on the top. Cover with foil and freeze, at the normal temperature for ice making, for two and one half hours.

ELIZABETH DAVID
SUMMER COOKING

## Italian Coffee Ice

*Espresso Granita*

To serve 4

| 2 cups | hot, freshly made espresso coffee | ½ liter |
|---|---|---|
| 2 tsp. | unsweetened cocoa | 10 ml. |
| ¼ cup | sugar | 50 ml. |
| ½ tsp. | vanilla extract | 2 ml. |

Combine the espresso, cocoa and sugar, and stir well. Let the mixture cool. Add the vanilla. Pour the mixture into an ice-cube tray without dividers. Freeze until the mixture is frozen about ½ inch [1 cm.] in from the edge of the tray; how much time this takes will depend on your freezer—probably an hour or two.

Take the tray out of the freezer and chop the contents with a wooden spoon, breaking them up until they are mushy. Put the tray back in the freezer. When the mixture is completely frozen—allow another hour—chop it once more.

Twenty minutes before you plan to serve it, move the coffee ice from the freezer to a refrigerator shelf. Just before serving, chop it in the tray again, breaking up any big clumps. It should be slightly soft but still icy.

ELEANOR GRAVES
GREAT DINNERS FROM LIFE

## Claret Granita

*Granité au Vin de Saint-Émilion*

This dessert must be made a day in advance because the mixture of syrup, wine and fruit juice takes a long time to set and crystallize into flakes. If desired, the orange juice can be replaced by mandarin-orange or tangerine juice.

You can dress up this granita with well-ripened fresh peaches prepared in the following manner: Plunge the peaches in boiling water for 15 seconds to make them easier to peel. Peel them and cook for 15 minutes in 1 quart [1 liter] of boiling water to which 2¼ cups [550 ml.] of superfine sugar and a split vanilla bean have been added. Cool the peaches. Place a whole peach on top of each serving of granita and arrange two mint leaves under the peach to make it look as if it were growing.

To serve 6

| 3 cups | dry red wine, preferably Saint-Émilion | ¾ liter |
|---|---|---|
| 1 cup | water | ¼ liter |
| 1 cup | superfine sugar | ¼ liter |
| ½ cup | strained fresh orange juice | 125 ml. |
| ¼ cup | strained fresh lemon juice | 50 ml. |
| | fresh mint leaves (optional) | |

Boil the water and the sugar together for one minute in a medium-sized saucepan. Pour the syrup thus obtained into a

bowl and allow to cool. When the syrup is quite cold, add the wine, orange juice and lemon juice, and mix together with a small whisk. Pour the mixture into a long, shallow dish or tray and put it into the freezer; the shallow depth of the liquid allows it to set more rapidly. During the course of the day, regularly stir the solidifying liquid with a fork, scraping the crystals from the edges of the dish into the still-liquid central part. Continue until the whole is set into a mass of small, light crystals.

To serve, fill six chilled claret glasses with the granita, forming it into domes with a spoon. Arrange a few mint leaves prettily on top of each serving.

MICHEL GUÉRARD
MICHEL GUÉRARD'S CUISINE GOURMANDE

## Lemon Sorbet

*Any shallow, metal, cake or baking pan with a total capacity of about 2 quarts [2 liters] may be substituted for the metal ice-cube trays called for in this recipe.*

Sorbets are half-frozen water ices, generally orange or lemon, though sometimes flavored with rum or liqueur. In Victorian and Edwardian days, they were often served at large dinner parties to provide a welcome pause between the roast and the entrée.

To serve 8

| 1¼ cups | strained fresh lemon juice (from about 8 lemons) | 300 ml. |
|---|---|---|
| 5 tbsp. | lemon peel, grated fine | 75 ml. |
| ¾ cup | strained fresh orange juice | 175 ml. |
| 1 cup | granulated sugar | 250 ml. |
| 1 quart | water | 1 liter |
| 2 | egg whites | 2 |
| ¼ cup | superfine sugar | 50 ml. |

In a saucepan, boil the granulated sugar and the water for five minutes, skimming off any scum or froth on the surface. Add the lemon peel, lemon juice and orange juice. Bring to a boil again, then strain and cool to room temperature.

Pour the cooled sorbet mixture into metal ice trays and place in the freezing compartment of the refrigerator until the mixture is half-frozen—about one hour.

Whisk the egg whites until they stand in peaks. Transfer the half-frozen sorbet to a bowl and beat in the egg whites and the superfine sugar. Return the mixture to the ice trays and freeze until the consistency is as you like it.

ELISABETH AYRTON
THE COOKERY OF ENGLAND

# Melon-and-Champagne Ice

### Granité de Melon au Champagne

*The technique of making a sugar syrup is shown on pages 8-9.*
Buy more melons than you need, and taste them before using them: flavorless melons will make a flavorless ice.

| | To serve 4 to 6 | |
|---|---|---|
| 2 or 3 | Ogen melons or small cantaloupes | 2 or 3 |
| 1 cup | iced Champagne | ¼ liter |
| ¼ cup | sugar | 50 ml. |
| ½ cup | water | 125 ml. |
| 2 tbsp. | fresh lemon juice | 30 ml. |
| ¼ cup | Cognac | 50 ml. |

Halve the melons, discard the seeds and scoop out the flesh. Purée the melon flesh through a sieve or food mill into a bowl to produce 2 cups [½ liter] of purée. If you have a freezer, freeze the melon shells, otherwise chill them thoroughly.

Boil the sugar and water together to make a syrup, and leave to cool before mixing with the melon purée, lemon juice and Champagne. Freeze in ice trays, loosening the mixture from the sides and stirring occasionally as it freezes. It is best to start the ice several hours before it is needed.

Just before serving, turn the ice into a chilled bowl, working it a bit with a fork if it is too firm: it should be just slightly mushy. Rinse out the frozen or chilled melon shells with the Cognac, pour it into the frozen mixture, mix, and then fill the melon shells with the ice.

RICHARD OLNEY
SIMPLE FRENCH FOOD

# Strawberry Sorbet

| | To serve 8 | |
|---|---|---|
| 6 cups | fresh strawberries, hulled | 1½ liters |
| 2 cups | sugar | ½ liter |
| 1½ cups | strained, fresh orange juice | 375 ml. |
| ¾ cup | strained, fresh lemon juice | 175 ml. |
| ⅓ cup | Grand Marnier or other orange-flavored liqueur | 75 ml. |

In a bowl combine the strawberries, sugar, orange juice and lemon juice, and let stand at room temperature for two to three hours. Put the mixture through a sieve or food mill, or purée it in an electric blender. Stir in the Grand Marnier and pour the mixture into two large ice-cube trays. Freeze until about 1 inch [2½ cm.] of the mixture is frozen on all sides of the trays. Remove and beat the mixture until mushy. Return the mixture to the trays and freeze until firm. For a more

delicate sorbet, beat the mixture twice, freezing slightly in between. You may also freeze it in an ice-cream freezer.

JAMES BEARD AND SAM AARON
HOW TO EAT BETTER FOR LESS MONEY

# Margarita Sherbet

| | To serve 4 | |
|---|---|---|
| ⅓ cup | tequila | 75 ml. |
| 1½ cups | sugar | 375 ml. |
| 3 cups | water | ¾ liter |
| ½ tsp. | freshly grated lime peel | 2 ml. |
| ½ cup | strained fresh lime juice | 125 ml. |
| 1 | egg white | 1 |
| ¼ tsp. | salt | 1 ml. |

Stir together the sugar and water and boil for five minutes to make a syrup. During the last minute of cooking time, add the lime peel. Remove the syrup from the heat and stir in the lime juice, then pour the mixture into an ice-cube tray and place it in the freezer.

When the syrup mixture is frozen to a thick mush, after about 45 minutes, transfer it to a blender. Add the remaining ingredients and blend thoroughly. Spread the sherbet evenly in the ice-cube tray and freeze it. If it becomes too hard or forms ice crystals, whirl the sherbet in a blender before serving.

PATRICIA GINS (EDITOR)
GREAT SOUTH WEST COOKING CLASSIC

# Bitter Chocolate Sherbet with Coffee Granita

### Granité de Chocolat Amer

| | To serve 6 | |
|---|---|---|
| 3½ oz. | semisweet baking chocolate, broken into small pieces | 100 g. |
| 2¼ cups | milk | 300 ml. |
| ⅓ cup | superfine sugar | 75 ml. |
| 1 cup | unsweetened cocoa | ¼ liter |
| 1 cup | heavy cream, whipped | ¼ liter |
| **Coffee crystals** | | |
| 2 tbsp. | instant coffee | 30 ml. |
| 1 cup | water | ¼ liter |
| 2 tbsp. | superfine sugar | 30 ml. |

Prepare the coffee crystals one day ahead of serving: Bring the water and the sugar to a boil in a medium-sized saucepan. Remove from the heat and thoroughly whisk in the instant coffee. Transfer the mixture to an ice-cube tray and put it in the freezing compartment or freezer, stirring from time to time with a fork until the mixture sets and turns into small, light crystals.

Next day, put the milk and sugar into a saucepan and bring to a boil over medium heat. Beat in the chocolate with a small wire whisk. Put the cocoa into a small bowl. Take 4 tablespoons [60 ml.] of the sweetened milk and beat it into the cocoa, little by little, avoiding lumps. Then pour the diluted cocoa into the milk in the saucepan and whisk thoroughly over low heat. When everything is thoroughly blended and melted, strain the mixture into a large bowl. Then carefully fold in the heavy cream.

Put the chocolate mixture into an ice-cream maker and work it for about 20 minutes, or until the mixture has set and thickened. With a fork mix half of the coffee crystals delicately into the chocolate ice.

Fill six chilled champagne flutes with the granita; use a spoon to form each into a dome shape. Sprinkle the tops with the rest of the coffee crystals.

MICHEL GUÉRARD<br>MICHEL GUÉRARD'S CUISINE GOURMANDE

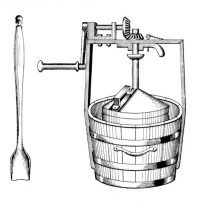

## Frozen Ginger-Peach Yogurt

*To make about 1 quart [1 liter] frozen yogurt*

| | | |
|---|---|---|
| 2 tbsp. | finely chopped preserved ginger, plus 2 tbsp. [30 ml.] of the syrup | 30 ml. |
| 3 | medium-sized ripe peaches, unpeeled, but halved, pitted and coarsely chopped (about ¾ lb. [⅓ kg.]) | 3 |
| 2 cups | unflavored yogurt | ½ liter |
| ⅓ cup | pale honey | 75 ml. |
| 1 tbsp. | strained fresh lemon juice | 15 ml. |
| 1 | egg, the yolk separated from the white | 1 |
| ⅛ tsp. | salt | ½ ml. |
| ⅛ tsp. | cream of tartar | ½ ml. |
| 2 tbsp. | superfine sugar | 30 ml. |

In an enameled saucepan, combine the peaches, honey, lemon juice, ginger and ginger syrup and bring to a boil. Boil

gently over medium heat, stirring often, for 10 minutes or until the fruit is soft.

In a medium-sized bowl, beat the egg yolk for a moment, then add the peach mixture bit by bit, stirring vigorously.

In a small bowl, beat the egg white with the salt and cream of tartar until soft peaks form. Beat in the superfine sugar, ½ tablespoon [7 ml.] at a time, until stiff peaks form.

Stir the yogurt into the fruit mixture, then fold in the egg white. Turn the mixture into the canister of a 1-quart [1-liter] ice-cream maker and freeze.

THE GREAT COOKS' GUIDE TO ICE CREAM & OTHER FROZEN DESSERTS

## Frozen Raspberry Yogurt

To make frozen banana yogurt, substitute three coarsely mashed ripe bananas for the raspberries, combining the bananas in the saucepan with 6 tablespoons [90 ml.] of sugar and 2 tablespoons [30 ml.] of honey rather than the ½ cup [125 ml.] of sugar. Also, increase the amount of lemon juice to 2 teaspoons [10 ml.] and that of the vanilla extract to 1½ teaspoons [7 ml.].

*To make about 1 quart [1 liter] frozen yogurt*

| | | |
|---|---|---|
| 1 cup | ripe raspberries | ¼ liter |
| 2 cups | unflavored yogurt | ½ liter |
| ½ cup | sugar | 125 ml. |
| 1 tsp. | strained fresh lemon juice | 5 ml. |
| 1 tsp. | vanilla extract | 5 ml. |
| 1 | egg, the yolk separated from the white | 1 |
| | salt | |
| | cream of tartar | |

In a large enameled or stainless-steel saucepan, combine the raspberries and all but 1 tablespoon [15 ml.] of the sugar. Bring to a boil over high heat, stirring constantly. Reduce the heat to medium and cook, stirring and crushing the berries, for about two minutes, or until they soften. Remove from the heat and purée the berries through a sieve to remove the seeds. Stir in the lemon juice and vanilla extract.

In a small mixing bowl, lightly beat the egg yolk. Stir in 2 tablespoons [30 ml.] of the hot raspberry purée. Then add the egg-yolk mixture to the purée, stirring constantly. Cool to room temperature.

In a large mixing bowl beat the egg white, a pinch of salt and a little cream of tartar until soft peaks form. Beat in the remaining tablespoon of sugar until stiff peaks form.

In a large bowl beat the yogurt with a wire whisk until smooth. Fold the raspberry mixture into the yogurt until thoroughly blended. Then, carefully fold in the beaten egg white. Freeze in a 1-quart [1-liter] or larger hand-cranked or electric ice-cream maker.

SONIA UVEZIAN<br>THE BOOK OF YOGURT

## Vanilla Yogurt Ice Cream

*To make 1 quart ice cream*

| ¾ cup | unflavored yogurt | 175 ml. |
|---|---|---|
| 1½ tsp. | vanilla extract | 7 ml. |
| 1 | egg, lightly beaten | 1 |
| ⅓ cup | sugar | 75 ml. |
| ¼ cup | light corn syrup | 50 ml. |
| ¾ cup | heavy cream | 175 ml. |
| ¼ tsp. | salt | 1 ml. |

Place all of the ingredients in a medium-sized bowl and mix thoroughly. Refrigerate for two hours, or until well chilled. Freeze in a 1-quart [1-liter], or larger, hand-cranked or electric ice-cream maker.

SONIA UVEZIAN
THE BOOK OF YOGURT

## Almond Crunch Spumone

*To serve 8*

| 1 cup | sugar | ¼ liter |
|---|---|---|
| ⅓ cup | water | 75 ml. |
| 6 | egg yolks | 6 |
| 2 cups | heavy cream | ½ liter |
| ½ tsp. | almond extract | 2 ml. |
| 3 tbsp. | kirsch | 45 ml. |
| 1 cup | strawberries or raspberries | ¼ liter |
| | **Nut crunch** | |
| ½ cup | chopped almonds or filberts | 125 ml. |
| 2 tsp. | butter | 10 ml. |
| 2 tbsp. | sugar | 30 ml. |

To make the nut crunch, heat the butter and sugar in a skillet. Add the nuts and sauté them, stirring until the sugar melts and caramelizes, and the nuts are lightly toasted. Turn the mixture out of the pan onto a sheet of buttered foil and let the nut crunch cool.

In a saucepan combine the sugar and water and bring to a boil. Keep boiling until the temperature reaches 238° F. [114° C.] on a candy thermometer. Meanwhile, beat the egg yolks until thick and pale yellow. Continue beating the yolks and immediately pour the hot syrup over them in a fine stream. Beat until the mixture cools to room temperature, about seven minutes. Refrigerate the mixture until cold.

Crumble the nut crunch into small pieces. Whip the cream until stiff and flavor it with the almond extract and kirsch. Fold the cream and two thirds of the nut crunch into the yolks. Pour into a 2-quart [2-liter] mold, cover and freeze until firm—at least eight hours.

Unmold by dipping the mold briefly into warm water. Turn onto a platter and sprinkle with the remaining nut crunch. Decorate with strawberries or raspberries.

LOU SEIBERT PAPPAS
EGG COOKERY

## Rum-flavored Frozen Cream

*Biscuit Tortoni*

A popular Italian-American restaurant dessert, biscuit tortoni was introduced in Paris in 1798 by a Neapolitan restaurateur named Tortoni.

*To serve 12*

| ¼ cup | dark rum | 50 ml. |
|---|---|---|
| 2½ cups | heavy cream, chilled | 625 ml. |
| 5 to 8 | stale almond macaroons (recipe, page 167), crushed in a blender or wrapped in a towel and crushed with a rolling pin (1 cup [¼ liter] crumbs) | 5 to 8 |
| ½ cup | confectioners' sugar | 125 ml. |
| | salt | |
| 1½ tsp. | vanilla extract | 7 ml. |
| ¼ cup | sliced toasted almonds | 50 ml. |
| 6 | candied cherries, halved (optional) | 6 |

Place a ready-made, pleated paper cupcake liner in each of twelve 2- to 2½-inch [5- to 6-cm.] muffin-tin cups and set aside. In a bowl, combine 1¼ cups [300 ml.] of the heavy cream, the macaroons, sugar and a pinch of salt, and chill the mixture for 30 minutes.

In a large chilled mixing bowl, beat the remaining heavy cream until it thickens and forms soft peaks. With a rubber spatula, fold in the macaroon mixture, the rum and the vanilla extract. Fill the paper liners with the cream mixture. Sprinkle the tops evenly with the sliced almonds and, if you like, top each portion with a candied cherry half. Freeze for at least two hours before serving.

FOODS OF THE WORLD/AMERICAN COOKING: THE MELTING POT

## Mango Parfait

*Instead of beating the yolks with confectioners' sugar, you can sweeten this mousse by gradually adding to them 1 cup [¼ liter] of a medium-heavy syrup made by boiling ⅔ cup [150 ml.] sugar with ⅔ cup [150 ml.] water. The technique for making sugar syrup is explained on pages 8-9.*

This recipe, based on egg mousse, is a good way of sharing a delectable but expensive fruit among several people.

| | To serve 5 or 6 | |
|---|---|---|
| 2 | very ripe large mangos, peeled, halved and pitted | 2 |
| 6 | egg yolks | 6 |
| ⅔ cup | confectioners' sugar | 150 ml. |
| | superfine sugar | |
| 3 to 4 tsp. | strained fresh lemon juice | 15 to 20 ml. |
| | salt | |
| 1¼ cups | heavy cream, whipped | 300 ml. |

In a heatproof bowl, beat the egg yolks lightly with the confectioners' sugar; then, still beating, place the bowl carefully over a pan of barely simmering water. When the mixture is just lukewarm, remove the bowl from the pan and go on beating until the mixture is cool.

Sieve the mango, sweeten to taste with superfine sugar, and sharpen it with lemon juice and a pinch of salt. Fold the purée into the egg mixture and fold in the whipped cream. Freeze in a 6-cup [1½-liter] mold. The color is beautiful.

SUSAN CAMPBELL
THE TIMES OF LONDON

---

## Maple Parfait

| | To make about 1 quart [1 liter] parfait | |
|---|---|---|
| ⅔ cup | maple syrup, heated | 150 ml. |
| 4 | eggs, lightly beaten | 4 |
| 2 cups | heavy cream, whipped into stiff peaks | ½ liter |
| ¼ tsp. | salt | 1 ml. |

Pour the hot maple syrup in a fine stream onto the lightly beaten eggs, beating briskly and constantly. Pour the mixture into the top of a double boiler and, stirring constantly, cook over simmering water until the mixture coats the spoon. Cool, then add the whipped heavy cream with the salt. Freeze for about two and one half hours in ice-cube trays or let stand in an ice-cream maker, using equal parts of ice and rock salt, for three to three and one half hours.

LOUIS P. DE GOUY
ICE CREAM AND ICE CREAM DESSERTS

## Butterscotch Rum Parfait

You can make the following variations of this recipe: For the syrup, use granulated sugar instead of brown sugar; flavor the egg yolks with 1 tablespoon [15 ml.] of vanilla extract instead of rum; fold in ½ cup [125 ml.] of melted chocolate, or melted chocolate and a coffee-flavored liqueur, or fresh berries or sliced peaches, along with the whipped cream.

| | To serve 6 | |
|---|---|---|
| ¾ cup | brown sugar | 175 ml. |
| 4 tbsp. | butter | 60 ml. |
| ¾ cup | water | 175 ml. |
| 3 | egg yolks | 3 |
| 1 tbsp. | rum | 15 ml. |
| | salt | |
| 1 cup | heavy cream | ¼ liter |
| 3 tbsp. | crushed, blanched almonds | 45 ml. |

In a small saucepan, make a syrup by bringing the brown sugar, butter and water to a boil, stirring to dissolve the sugar, then boiling hard for three minutes. Set the syrup aside until it cools.

In the small bowl of an electric mixer, beat the egg yolks at medium speed until light and fluffy. Gradually pour in the reserved syrup in a thin stream, beating all the while. Beat in the rum and a pinch of salt, then place the mixture in a heavy saucepan and whisk over high heat until the mixture is as thick as heavy cream.

Return the mixture to the bowl, set over ice and whisk for about 10 minutes, or until cold. Whip the cream until it is the same consistency as the parfait base, then fold it in. Pour the mixture into parfait glasses and set the glasses in a freezer for at least one hour. (The longer the parfait stays in the freezer, the more solid it becomes. I like to make it the day before I plan to serve it.)

Three hours before serving, remove the parfaits from the freezer and place them in the refrigerator so that the parfaits are the consistency of frozen custard when served. Before serving, sprinkle the tops with the almonds.

JULIE DANNENBAUM
JULIE DANNENBAUM'S CREATIVE COOKING SCHOOL

## Pumpkin Ice Cream

*To make about 2 quarts [2 liters] ice cream*

| 2 cups | puréed, cooked pumpkin | ½ liter |
|---|---|---|
| 2 cups | milk | ½ liter |
| 4 | egg yolks | 4 |
| ⅔ cup | sugar | 150 ml. |
| ⅛ tsp. | salt | ½ ml. |
| 2 tsp. | ground cinnamon | 10 ml. |
| 1 tsp. | grated nutmeg | 5 ml. |
| ½ tsp. | ground allspice | 2 ml. |
| ¼ tsp. | ground ginger | 1 ml. |
| 1 cup | heavy cream | ¼ liter |
| ½ tsp. | vanilla extract | 2 ml. |

Scald the milk in the top of a double boiler. In a bowl, beat the egg yolks well; beat in the sugar. Add the salt, pumpkin and spices. Incorporate the mixture with the milk and cook over hot water, stirring constantly for about four minutes, or until the mixture is smooth and thick enough to coat the spoon. Cool and stir in the cream and vanilla.

Pour into a 1-gallon [4-liter] ice-cream maker and freeze.

ELISE W. MANNING (EDITOR)
HOMEMADE ICE CREAM AND CAKE

---

## White Ice with Coffee Sauce

*To serve 8 to 10*

| 5 cups | heavy cream | 1¼ liters |
|---|---|---|
| ½ cup | sugar | 125 ml. |
| 1 | vanilla bean, pulverized in a mortar or food processor | 1 |
| 4 oz. | semisweet baking chocolate, broken into very small pieces, but not grated | 125 g. |
| | **Coffee sauce** | |
| 2½ cups | freshly made very strong black coffee | 625 ml. |
| ¼ cup | sugar | 50 ml. |

Beat the cream with the sugar and the vanilla until it just begins to thicken. Mix in the chocolate pieces. Pour into a 1½-quart [1½-liter] mold, cover and freeze for two and one half to three hours.

For the coffee sauce, sweeten the coffee with the sugar and serve it hot or cold in a sauceboat with the white ice.

RUTH LOWINSKY
MORE LOVELY FOOD

---

## Nougat Ice Cream

*Orange-flower water is a flavoring liquid made from orange blossoms. It is obtainable from pharmacies and shops specializing in Middle Eastern foods. The technique of blanching pistachio nuts is demonstrated on page 12.*

*To serve 6 to 8*

| ¾ cup | unsalted pistachio nuts, blanched | 175 ml. |
|---|---|---|
| ½ cup | blanched, split almonds | 125 ml. |
| 3 cups | light cream | ¾ liter |
| 6 | egg yolks | 6 |
| 1 cup | honey, preferably orange-flower honey | ¼ liter |
| 2 tbsp. | orange-flower water | 30 ml. |
| ¾ cup | heavy cream, whipped | 175 ml. |
| 3 | egg whites, beaten stiff | 3 |

Heat the light cream in a saucepan over low heat. Stir the egg yolks in another saucepan and add the hot cream. Put over the lowest possible heat and stir until the mixture coats the back of a spoon. Remove from the heat and, stirring continuously, pour the mixture slowly into the honey in a bowl. Add 1 tablespoon [15 ml.] of the orange-flower water. Strain the mixture and leave it to cool.

Incorporate the whipped cream into the cooled honey mixture, then fold in the beaten egg whites and the pistachio nuts and almonds. Flavor with the remaining orange-flower water and freeze.

ALICE B. TOKLAS
THE ALICE B. TOKLAS COOK BOOK

---

## Ginger Ice Cream

*For the ginger syrup called for in this recipe, use the syrup at the bottom of a jar of preserved ginger. The technique of cooking the custard is demonstrated on pages 20-21.*

*To serve 6 to 8*

| 3 to 4 oz. | preserved ginger, chopped | 100 to 125 g. |
|---|---|---|
| ¼ cup | ginger syrup | 50 ml. |
| 1 cup | milk | ¼ liter |
| 2 | egg yolks | 2 |
| 1 | egg | 1 |
| 1 cup | heavy cream, whipped | ¼ liter |
| 2 tbsp. | confectioners' or soft brown sugar | 30 ml. |

Bring the milk to a boil in a saucepan over high heat and pour it into the yolks and the egg very gradually, beating the whole thing together (small wire whisks are the best for this kind of operation). Pour the mixture back into the saucepan and cook slowly over low heat until the custard thickens; it must not boil or the egg will curdle.

As soon as the thickness seems right, dip the base of the pan into a bowl of very cold water; this prevents the custard from continuing to cook. Add the ginger syrup immediately after this to further hurry the cooling process.

When the custard is cool, place the pan in the freezing compartment of the refrigerator, which should be set at the coldest possible temperature. When the custard has set around the edges, remove it to a bowl, stir it up well and quickly incorporate the ginger pieces and the whipped cream. Taste and add sugar gradually; ice creams should not be too sickly sweet, mainly on account of the flavor, but also because an oversweetened mixture freezes less well.

Return the mixture to the freezer and leave it until it is hard. If the custard was frozen to the right degree before the ginger and the cream were added, it should not be necessary to stir it at all during the second freezing process. If there was any doubt about this, stir it up gently after an hour so that the ginger pieces do not sink to the bottom.

JANE GRIGSON
ENGLISH FOOD

## Tea and Rum Ice Cream

### *Glace au Thé et Rhum*

To serve 4 to 6

| | | |
|---|---|---|
| ⅔ cup | freshly made strong black tea | 150 ml. |
| ¼ cup | rum | 50 ml. |
| 1 quart | milk | 1 liter |
| 1¼ cups | sugar | 300 ml. |
| 10 | egg yolks | 10 |

Bring the milk and sugar to a boil in a saucepan, then add the rum and tea. Whisk the egg yolks in a bowl and gradually add the hot milk mixture, whisking all the time. Return the mixture to the saucepan and, over very low heat, stir constantly until it thickens—but without letting it boil, which would make the mixture curdle. Remove from the heat and strain into a bowl through a strainer lined with a double layer of dampened cheesecloth or through a fine sieve. Stir constantly with a wooden spoon until the mixture is quite cold. Freeze in an ice-cream maker until firm. Transfer the mixture to a bombe mold and place it in a freezer for at least two hours.

To serve, dip the mold in hot water for a second, and unmold onto a napkin-covered serving dish.

LÉON ISNARD
LA CUISINE FRANÇAISE ET AFRICAINE

## Coffee Ice Cream

To serve 6 to 8

| | | |
|---|---|---|
| ¼ lb. | whole roasted mocha coffee beans | 125 g. |
| 7 or 8 | egg yolks, lightly beaten | 7 or 8 |
| 2½ cups | heavy cream | 625 ml. |
| 1 | lemon, the zest thinly peeled | 1 |
| 1 | slice lemon | 1 |
| ¾ cup | sugar | 175 ml. |

Pour the egg yolks into a tin-lined copper pan, add the cream and mix together gently. Add the lemon peel and lemon slice to the cream and egg yolks. Put the pan over medium heat and stir constantly with a wooden spoon; you must not let the cream boil, as it would then curdle and be spoilt.

When it gets thick and refuses to obey the motion of stirring, remove the mixture from the heat, for it is done. Put it in a jug or pot. Add the coffee beans to the cream mixture, cover tightly and let it stand for a short time (about 30 minutes) in a warm place. When the cream has become tinctured with the coffee, strain it through a sieve. Sweeten to taste with the sugar.

When quite cold, put the coffee cream into an ice-cream maker and freeze it until it has the consistency of, and is as smooth as, butter.

WILLIAM JEANES
GUNTER'S MODERN CONFECTIONER

## Caledonian Ice

### *Iced Stapag*

Whole-wheat bread crumbs toasted in a 325° F. [160° C.] oven for 10 minutes can be substituted for the oatmeal.

To serve 4 to 6

| | | |
|---|---|---|
| 5 cups | heavy cream, whipped until stiff | 1¼ liters |
| ½ cup | superfine sugar | 125 ml. |
| 2 tsp. | vanilla extract | 10 ml. |
| ⅔ cup | coarse, toasted Scottish oatmeal, well dried in the oven without being browned | 150 ml. |

Sweeten the whipped cream with the sugar and flavor it with the vanilla extract. Set it to freeze. When nearly frozen, stir in the oatmeal. Serve the ice in a glass bowl or in glasses.

F. MARIAN MCNEILL
THE SCOTS KITCHEN

## Avocado Ice Cream

*Using an ice-cream maker is demonstrated on pages 56-57.*

| | To serve 6 | |
|---|---|---|
| 2 | ripe avocados, mashed smooth | 2 |
| 2 | egg yolks | 2 |
| ¾ cup | sugar | 175 ml. |
| 2 cups | light cream | ½ liter |
| ½ tsp. | salt | 2 ml. |
| ½ tsp. | vanilla extract | 2 ml. |
| ½ tsp. | almond extract | 2 ml. |
| 1 tsp. | strained fresh lemon juice | 5 ml. |

Beat the egg yolks. Add ¼ cup [50 ml.] of the sugar and all of the cream, a little at a time. Cook over low heat until slightly thickened. Add the salt and vanilla; chill.

Add the remaining sugar to the avocado pulp and flavor with the almond extract and lemon juice. Add the custard mixture and freeze in an ice-cream maker, using 1 part rock salt to 8 parts crushed ice.

EDITORS OF HOUSE & GARDEN
HOUSE & GARDEN'S NEW COOK BOOK

## Avocado Whip

### *Eskrim Pokat*

| | To serve 4 | |
|---|---|---|
| 1 | avocado, halved lengthwise, pit removed | 1 |
| 2 to 3 tbsp. | strained fresh lemon juice | 30 to 45 ml. |
| 2 tbsp. | sugar | 30 ml. |
| 1 cup | vanilla ice cream *(recipe, page 166)* | ¼ liter |

Peel the avocado, mash the flesh and put it through a sieve. Add the lemon juice and sugar. Combine the avocado mixture and the ice cream, and beat until smooth. Place in a freezer to chill for about one and one half hours, but do not freeze hard.

YOHANNI JOHNS
DISHES FROM INDONESIA

## New York Ice Cream

*The original version of this early-20th Century English recipe calls for freezing the bombe by submerging it in a tub of ice for one and a half hours. A modern freezer is more convenient to use, but requires four hours to complete the process.*

| | To serve 8 to 10 | |
|---|---|---|
| | **Almond ice cream** | |
| ¼ cup | blanched almonds | 50 ml. |
| 2 cups | milk | ½ liter |
| ⅔ cup | heavy cream | 150 ml. |
| 3 | egg yolks | 3 |
| ½ cup | superfine sugar | 125 ml. |
| 1 tsp. | kirsch | 5 ml. |
| | **Candied chestnut filling** | |
| 4 oz. | marrons glacés (about ¾ cup [175 ml.]) | 125 g. |
| ½ cup | superfine sugar | 125 ml. |
| 5 | egg yolks | 5 |
| ½ tsp. | vanilla extract | 2 ml. |
| 2 tbsp. | Curaçao or Benedictine | 30 ml. |
| 1¼ cups | whipped cream | 300 ml. |
| 1¼ cups | fresh raspberries | 300 ml. |
| 1 tbsp. | kirsch | 15 ml. |
| | **Decoration** | |
| 1-inch square | angelica, cut into strips | 2½-cm. square |
| | glacéed cherries, halved | |
| 2 to 3 tbsp. | pistachio nuts, chopped | 30 to 45 ml. |

First make the almond ice cream. Place the almonds in a mortar and pound them to a paste; add the milk and the cream. Mix thoroughly together, then transfer the mixture to a small saucepan, place on the heat and bring to a boil. Remove the almond milk from the heat. Place the egg yolks and the sugar in a bowl, and add the kirsch. Mix well for five minutes, then gradually add the almond milk, mixing well with a wooden spoon.

Pour the mixture into the saucepan and place it over low heat. Stirring continuously, heat it for five minutes without letting it boil. Then allow it to cool. Strain through a sieve into an ice-cream maker and freeze until the ice cream is thoroughly firm.

Meanwhile, prepare the filling. Press the marrons glacés through a sieve into a heatproof bowl. Add all but 1 tablespoon [15 ml.] of the sugar, then add the egg yolks. Set the bowl in a water bath over low heat and whisk for 10 minutes. Place the bowl on ice and stir the mixture with a spatula until thoroughly cold. Add the vanilla extract and Curaçao or Benedictine. Mix well. Add the whipped cream and gently mix until well amalgamated.

Line the bottom of a 1½-quart [1½-liter] mold with a sheet of white paper cut to fit it, then line the bottom and the sides of the mold with three quarters of the almond ice cream. Place the raspberries in a bowl with the remaining tablespoon of sugar and the kirsch. Mix thoroughly, then arrange three quarters of the raspberries evenly over the almond ice cream lining the bottom and sides of the mold. Pour in the marron glacé filling. Place the remaining raspberries on top and fill the mold with the remaining almond ice cream. Cover with a sheet of paper, place the lid on the mold and freeze for four hours.

To unmold, remove the lid and the paper, and turn the dessert onto a cold dish. Place the strips of angelica on the center of the dessert. Arrange glacéed cherry halves all around the surface and decorate the base with whipped cream; sprinkle with chopped pistachio nuts and serve.

MAY BYRON
PUDDINGS, PASTRIES AND SWEET DISHES

---

# Black Forest Bombe

*The chocolate ice cream may be prepared in advance.*

To serve 8

### Chocolate ice cream

| | | |
|---|---|---|
| 2½ oz. | semisweet or unsweetened chocolate, broken into small pieces | 75 g. |
| 1 cup | light cream | ¼ liter |
| 3 | egg yolks | 3 |
| ⅓ cup | sugar | 75 ml. |
| 1 cup | heavy cream | ¼ liter |

### Cherry bombe mousse

| | | |
|---|---|---|
| about 1 cup | pitted black cherries preserved in syrup, drained and coarsely chopped | about 250 ml. |
| ¼ cup | water | 50 ml. |
| ⅓ cup | sugar | 75 ml. |
| 3 | egg yolks | 3 |
| 2 tbsp. | kirsch | 30 ml. |
| ⅔ cup | heavy cream | 150 ml. |
| ½ cup | finely grated stale pumpernickel | 125 ml. |
| 1 | egg white | 1 |

To prepare the chocolate ice cream, rinse out a saucepan with cold water and in it heat the chocolate in the light cream, stirring from time to time, until the chocolate has melted and the mixture is hot but not boiling. In a heatproof bowl or the top of a double boiler, beat the yolks and the sugar until they are thick and creamy; slowly add the chocolate mixture, stirring well. Place over a pan of simmering water and stir or gently beat the mixture until it begins to thicken. Cool. Whip the heavy cream lightly and fold it into the chocolate mixture. Freeze in an ice-cream freezer.

If the ice cream has been prepared in advance, transfer it from the freezer to the refrigerator one hour before use to allow the ice cream to soften. Line a chilled 1-quart [1-liter] bombe mold with the softened ice cream, cover the mold and freeze the ice cream.

To prepare the bombe mousse, boil the water and sugar until a thick syrup forms, but do not allow the syrup to change color; the time this takes depends on the quantity of syrup in relation to the size of the saucepan, but three minutes' steady boiling should be about right. In a heatproof bowl or double-boiler top, whisk the egg yolks until they are pale and fluffy, and still whisking pour in the hot but not boiling syrup in a thin stream. Place the bowl over a pan of simmering water, and continue to beat until the mixture has thickened and doubled in volume.

Remove the bowl from the heat, place it in a larger bowl partly filled with ice water and continue to beat until the mousse mixture has cooled. Blend in the kirsch. Whip the cream lightly and fold it in, together with the pumpernickel and the cherries. Beat the egg whites until stiff, and fold them into the mixture.

Fill the center of the bombe with the mousse mixture, cover the mold and freeze for about four hours. Remove the bombe from the freezer about 45 minutes before serving. Turn it onto a plate and place it in the refrigerator until ready to serve.

HELGA RUBINSTEIN AND SHEILA BUSH
ICES GALORE

## Apricot-and-Chablis Bombe

### *Bombe Marquise*

*The technique for making sugar syrup is on pages 8-9.*

To serve 8

### Apricot ice

| | | |
|---|---|---|
| 2 lb. | fresh apricots, pitted | 1 kg. |
| 1 cup | water | ¼ liter |
| 1¼ cups | sugar | 300 ml. |
| ¼ tsp. | ground cinnamon | 1 ml. |
| 1 | lemon, the peel finely grated and the juice strained | 1 |

### Chablis ice

| | | |
|---|---|---|
| ¾ cup | Chablis wine | 175 ml. |
| 3 cups | medium-heavy sugar syrup, made from 1¾ cups [400 ml.] sugar and 1¾ cups water | ¾ liter |
| ½ | vanilla bean | ½ |
| 1 | lemon or orange, thinly peeled | 1 |
| ⅓ cup | strained fresh lemon juice | 75 ml. |

First prepare the apricot ice. In a saucepan cook the apricots, water, sugar, cinnamon and lemon peel over medium heat until the mixture thickens like jam. Rub through a fine sieve and add the lemon juice. Reheat the mixture until it holds together in a soft mass on the spoon. Let cool, then freeze in an ice-cream maker or in the freezer.

Now prepare the Chablis ice. In a saucepan gently simmer the sugar syrup with the vanilla bean and lemon or orange peel for 15 minutes. Let this flavored syrup cool, remove the vanilla bean and the peel, and add the wine and lemon juice. Freeze as above.

To assemble the bombe, line a 2-quart [2-liter] bombe mold with apricot ice and fill the inside with Chablis ice. Refreeze the ices for at least one hour before unmolding and serving the bombe.

JOSEPH FAVRE
DICTIONNAIRE UNIVERSEL DE CUISINE PRATIQUE

## Chocolate Chestnut Bombe

*The chocolate ice cream in this recipe can be frozen in an ice-cream maker if you prefer that method. The technique of making a chestnut purée is shown on pages 70-71.*

To serve 8

### Chocolate ice cream

| | | |
|---|---|---|
| 4½ oz. | semisweet chocolate, broken into small pieces | 140 g. |
| 3 | egg yolks | 3 |
| ⅓ cup | superfine sugar | 75 ml. |
| | salt | |
| 1¼ cups | light cream | 300 ml. |
| 5 to 6 tbsp. | milk | 75 to 90 ml. |
| ¾ cup | heavy cream, whipped | 175 ml. |

### Chestnut filling

| | | |
|---|---|---|
| 1 lb. | sweetened chestnut purée | ½ kg. |
| 1 | egg white | 1 |
| 1¼ cups | heavy cream | 300 ml. |

### Decoration

| | | |
|---|---|---|
| 1 | egg white | 1 |
| ⅔ cup | heavy cream | 150 ml. |
| about 1 tbsp. | confectioners' sugar | about 15 ml. |
| ¼ tsp. | vanilla extract | 1 ml. |
| | marrons glacés, crystallized violets, and angelica cut into diamond-shaped leaves | |

To prepare the chocolate ice cream, first beat the egg yolks with the sugar and a pinch of salt until light and lemon-colored. Scald the light cream and add it to the egg mixture, beating vigorously until well blended. Pour the mixture into the top of a double boiler and cook over hot water for about 10 minutes, stirring, until the mixture coats the back of the spoon. Melt the chocolate in the milk and add it to the custard. Mix well; strain and cool. When the chocolate custard is cool, fold in the whipped heavy cream. Pour the mixture into an ice-cube tray and freeze until firm, two to three hours.

Thoroughly chill a 1½-quart [1½-liter] bombe mold in the freezer. Soften the chocolate ice cream slightly and, with a spatula, spread it smoothly over the base and sides of the mold to make an even layer about 1 inch [2½ cm.] thick. Refreeze the mold until the ice cream is firm again.

Meanwhile, turn the chestnut purée into a bowl. If necessary, beat it with a spoon or spatula to eliminate lumpiness. Beat the egg white until stiff but not dry. Whip the heavy cream until it just leaves a trail on the surface when the beaters are lifted. Fold the chestnut purée gently into the whipped cream until the mixture is no longer streaky. Fold in the beaten egg white. Pour the chestnut mixture into the mold. Cover the mold with a lid or a sheet of foil. Freeze until firm, preferably overnight.

About one hour before you intend to serve it, transfer the bombe to the main compartment of the refrigerator. To unmold, remove the lid or foil and invert the mold onto a serving dish. Wrap a cloth that has been wrung out in hot water around it for about 30 seconds; when the cloth cools, redip it in hot water, wring it out again and wrap again. If the ice-cream surface of the bombe melts slightly as you unmold it, smooth it over with a knife and return the bombe to the freezer for 15 to 30 minutes.

Just before serving, make a decorative *crème Chantilly* as follows: Beat the egg white until stiff but not dry. Whip the cream into stiff peaks, adding a little confectioners' sugar and a few drops of vanilla extract to taste—the cream should be only faintly sweet. Fold enough beaten egg white into the cream to lighten its texture without making it flow. Pipe the *crème Chantilly* decoratively over and around the bombe, and finish decorating with a few marrons glacés, crystallized violets and angelica leaves.

ROBERT CARRIER
THE ROBERT CARRIER COOKERY COURSE

## Frozen Pistachio Soufflé

*The technique of blanching nuts is demonstrated on page 12. The technique of fastening a paper collar around a soufflé dish appears on page 33.*

To serve 4

| | | |
|---|---|---|
| ⅓ cup | green pistachio nuts, blanched and very finely chopped | 75 ml. |
| 12 | egg yolks | 12 |
| 4 | egg whites | 4 |
| ⅓ cup | superfine sugar | 75 ml. |
| 1 tsp. | vanilla extract | 5 ml. |
| 1 tbsp. | orange-flower water | 15 ml. |
| ⅛ tsp. | green food coloring | ½ ml. |
| 1¼ cups | heavy cream, stiffly whipped with 1 tbsp. [15 ml.] sugar | 300 ml. |

Put into a heatproof bowl the egg yolks, egg whites, sugar, vanilla extract, orange-flower water, a few drops of food coloring and the pistachio nuts. Whisk this over boiling wa-

ter until the mixture is warm, then take it off the heat and continue to whisk it until cold and thick.

Add to the pistachio mixture the slightly sweetened, stiffly whipped cream, folding it in carefully. Then pour the whole into a 1-quart [1-liter] soufflé dish around which a band of wax or parchment paper has been folded and fastened, standing 4 to 5 inches [10 to 13 cm.] above the top of the dish. Freeze for three and one half to four hours. When sufficiently frozen, remove the paper. Place the soufflé dish on a napkin-covered plate and serve.

MRS. A. B. MARSHALL
FANCY ICES

## Frozen Macaroon Soufflé

*Soufflé all'Amaretto*

*The technique of fastening a collar around a soufflé dish is demonstrated on page 33.*

As a variation, if you wish, dip some additional macaroons in sherry and put them in the bottom of the dish before pouring in the soufflé mixture.

To serve 6

| | | |
|---|---|---|
| 6 | almond macaroons (recipe, page 167), coarsely crumbled | 6 |
| 3 | eggs, the yolks separated from the whites, and the whites stiffly beaten with a pinch of salt | 3 |
| ¼ cup | superfine sugar | 50 ml. |
| ⅓ cup | sweet sherry | 75 ml. |
| 1½ cups | heavy cream, whipped | 375 ml. |

Beat the egg yolks with the sugar until pale and creamy; the yolk mixture should form a slowly dissolving ribbon when the whisk is lifted from the bowl. Add the crumbled macaroons and the sherry, and mix well. Fold in the whipped cream, then gently fold in the beaten egg whites.

Surround a 5-cup [1¼-liter] soufflé dish with a collar of aluminum foil, cut to stand about 1 inch [2½ cm.] above the rim of the soufflé dish. Pour the soufflé mixture into the dish and place in the freezer for about four hours. Remove the aluminum-foil collar at the last minute before serving.

ELENA SPAGNOL
I GELATI FATTI IN CASA CON O SENZA MACCHINA

# Rainbow Iced Soufflé

## Soufflé Glacé Arc-en-Ciel

*This recipe is from La Réserve restaurant in Beaulieu-sur-Mer. The technique for making chocolate rolls is on page 11.*

Rainbow iced soufflé is composed of layers of four different colors and flavors: pistachio, vanilla with roasted hazelnuts and almonds, raspberry and coffee.

*To serve 10 to 12*

| | | |
|---|---|---|
| 8 | egg yolks | 8 |
| 1 cup | vanilla-flavored sugar | ¼ liter |
| 3 cups | heavy cream, whipped | ¾ liter |
| 3½ cups | fresh raspberries (3 cups [¾ liter] puréed through a nylon sieve and sweetened to taste, ½ cup [125 ml.] left whole) | 875 ml. |
| ½ cup | freshly made strong black coffee, cooled | 125 ml. |
| 1 tsp. | vanilla extract | 5 ml. |
| 3 to 4 tbsp. | finely chopped toasted hazelnuts | 45 to 60 ml. |
| 3 to 4 tbsp. | finely chopped toasted almonds | 45 to 60 ml. |
| about ⅓ cup | green pistachio nuts, pounded to a paste with 3 tbsp. [45 ml.] light sugar syrup and 2 tbsp. [30 ml.] boiling water | about 75 ml. |
| 1 oz. | semisweet baking chocolate, melted and shaved into rolls | 50 g. |
| | confectioners' sugar | |

Mix the egg yolks and the vanilla-flavored sugar in a copper bowl and place over very low heat, or over hot water in a water bath, and whisk until the mixture reaches the consistency of a lightly beaten cream. Take the bowl off the heat, set over ice and continue to whisk the mixture until it is cool; then fold in the whipped cream, incorporating it thoroughly.

Divide the mixture into four parts. Flavor one part with all but 2 or 3 tablespoons [30 or 45 ml.] of the raspberry purée, one with the coffee, one with the vanilla extract and chopped nuts, and one with the pistachio paste.

Fasten a wax-paper collar three times the height of the dish around a soufflé dish 7 inches [18 cm.] in diameter. Make a layer of about half of the raspberry-flavored mixture in the dish. Put the dish in the freezer until the mixture is firm. Add a layer of about half of the coffee-flavored mixture, then freeze; repeat the process with a vanilla-and-nut layer, then a pistachio layer. Continue layering in this way, then put the dessert in the freezer for three to six hours.

Remove the paper collar, spoon the reserved raspberry purée on top and decorate with the whole raspberries, the chocolate shavings and a sprinkling of confectioners' sugar.

LES PRINCES DE LA GASTRONOMIE

# Iced Plum Pudding

*The original version of this recipe called for 24 sweet and six bitter almonds. Bitter almonds contain traces of poisonous prussic acid, and are no longer available in the United States. To give sweet almonds a slightly bitter flavor, you can add ¼ teaspoon [1 ml.] of almond extract to the paste. The preserved apricots, peaches and limes called for were canned at home, probably in sugar syrup. You can use commercially canned apricots and peaches, and substitute 1 cup of lime marmalade or six limes boiled in medium syrup for 30 minutes.*

*To serve 10 to 12*

| | | |
|---|---|---|
| 30 | blanched almonds | 30 |
| | rose water or strained fresh lemon juice | |
| 1 cup | raisins, soaked in warm water for 15 minutes and drained | ¼ liter |
| 1 cup | dried currants, soaked in warm water for 15 minutes and drained | ¼ liter |
| ½ cup | candied citron or candied citrus peel (about 3 ounces [100 g.]), chopped | 125 ml. |
| ¼ cup | flour | 50 ml. |
| 1 cup | half-and-half cream | ¼ liter |
| 1 | vanilla bean, split and cut into 2-inch [5-cm.] pieces | 1 |
| 1 quart | heavy cream | 1 liter |
| 1 cup | sugar | ¼ liter |
| 1 tsp. | grated nutmeg | 5 ml. |
| ¾ cup | maraschino, noyau, Curaçao or brandy | 175 ml. |
| 8 | egg yolks | 8 |
| ¾ cup | strawberry or raspberry preserves | 175 ml. |
| 6 | preserved apricots or peaches | 6 |
| 6 | preserved limes | 6 |

Pound the almonds one at a time in a mortar till they become a smooth paste free of the smallest lumps; add frequently a few drops of rose water or lemon juice to make them light and prevent "oiling." Mix the raisins, currants and citron, and dredge well with flour.

Put the half-and-half cream in a pan with the pieces of vanilla bean and boil it till the flavor of the vanilla is well extracted, then strain the pieces out and mix the vanilla cream with half of the heavy cream. Gradually stir in the sugar and grated nutmeg. Then add the pounded almonds and the liqueur or brandy.

In a shallow bowl, beat the egg yolks till very pale, thick and smooth, and stir them gradually into the cream mixture. Simmer over medium heat (stirring all the time), but take the mixture off the heat just before it boils, otherwise it will curdle. At once stir in the dried fruit, and set the pudding mixture to cool. Then add the preserves and gently stir in the preserved fruit.

Whip the remaining heavy cream and add it lightly to the pudding mixture. Put the whole into a large 7-cup [1¾-liter] melon-shaped mold that opens in the middle and freeze for four hours. Turn out and serve in a glass dish.

OHIO HOUSEWIVES COMPANION

---

## Christmas Ice Pudding

*The authors suggest that the fruit mixture for this pudding may include any combination of raisins, dried currants, candied orange peel, glacéed cherries and marrons glacés.*

*This dessert is strictly for adults, and is no less rich than the traditional Christmas pudding.*

To serve 4 to 6

| | | |
|---|---|---|
| 1 cup | roughly chopped mixed, dried, glacéed fruits | ¼ liter |
| ¼ cup | rum | 50 ml. |
| 1¼ cups | light cream | 300 ml. |
| 5 | egg yolks, lightly beaten | 5 |
| ⅔ cup | superfine sugar | 150 ml. |
| ¾ cup | unsweetened chestnut purée | 175 ml. |
| 4 oz. | unsweetened baking chocolate | 125 g. |
| 1¼ cups | heavy cream, whipped | 300 ml. |

Soak the mixed chopped fruits in the rum. In a saucepan, heat the light cream over medium heat to near the boiling point, then pour it onto the egg yolks mixed with the sugar and return this custard to the pan. Stir over low heat until the custard thickens, but do not allow it to boil; you may find it easier to do this in a double boiler. When the custard has thickened, add the chestnut purée and the chocolate, and stir well until they have dissolved and the custard is quite smooth. Remove the pan from the heat, taste the custard for sweetness and let it cool. Mix in the rum-soaked fruits and finally fold in the whipped cream.

Line a 1-quart [1-liter] pudding basin with foil or plastic wrap. Pour in the mixture, wrap the basin and freeze the pudding. If you cannot spare the basin until the pudding is eaten, lift it out of the basin after 24 hours, wrap the pudding in foil or plastic wrap and replace the pudding in the freezer.

Remove the pudding from the freezer about one hour before serving it. Unwrap the pudding and place it in the refrigerator until you are ready to eat it.

HELGE RUBINSTEIN AND SHEILA BUSH
A PENGUIN FREEZER COOKBOOK

---

# Jellies

*The recipe for calf's-foot jelly appears in Standard Preparations, page 164.*

---

## Orange Jelly

*Gelée à l'Orange*

*To prepare this jelly in a 5-cup [1¼-liter] mold, increase the quantity of gelatin to 4 tablespoons [60 ml.] and use 1¾ cups [400 ml.] of superfine sugar. Refrigerate for about two hours before and after adding the orange segments.*

To serve 12

| | | |
|---|---|---|
| 1 or 2 | oranges, peeled and cut into segments, pith and membrane removed | 1 or 2 |
| 1 | sugar lump, rubbed on orange peel | 1 |
| ⅔ cup | strained fresh orange juice | 150 ml. |
| 2 to 3 tbsp. | strained fresh lemon juice | 30 to 45 ml. |
| 2 tbsp. | unflavored powdered gelatin | 30 ml. |
| 1¼ cups | granulated sugar | 300 ml. |
| 2¼ cups | cold water | 550 ml. |
| 2 | egg whites, stiffly beaten | 2 |

Put the gelatin, granulated sugar, water and beaten egg whites into a tin-lined copper saucepan; stir and beat over gentle heat until the sugar and gelatin have dissolved. As soon as the mixture comes to a boil, remove it from the heat and strain it through a sieve lined with dampened muslin or a double layer of cheesecloth to ensure that the liquid comes out really clear.

Dissolve the sugar lump in the orange and lemon juices, and strain the juice. Mix the juice with the gelatin mixture.

Half-fill little glass bowls or wine glasses with the jelly and let it set in the refrigerator for about two hours. Put an orange segment in each bowl or glass, pour in enough jelly to cover it, chill again, then fill each bowl or glass with the remaining jelly. Leave to set in the refrigerator for about two hours, or until required.

ÉMILE DUMONT
LA BONNE CUISINE

# Striped Jelly

*Gelée Rubanée*

To serve 6 to 8

| | | |
|---|---|---|
| 2 tbsp. | unflavored powdered gelatin, softened in ¼ cup [50 ml.] water | 30 ml. |
| 2 cups | sugar | ½ liter |
| 2 cups | cold water | ½ liter |
| ⅓ cup | puréed red currants or puréed, mixed red currants, raspberries and strawberries | 75 ml. |
| ⅓ cup | kirsch, light rum or anisette | 75 ml. |

Put the gelatin, sugar and water into a saucepan; stir, then whisk over gentle heat until the sugar and gelatin have dissolved. Remove the mixture from the heat as soon as it reaches the boiling point.

Immediately add half of this gelatin mixture to the red fruit purée and add the remainder to the white liqueur or rum. Pour half of the red mixture into a 5-cup [1¼-liter] jelly mold, and leave to set in a cool place or in the refrigerator. When set, pour half of the white mixture on top, and let this set. Add the rest of the red mixture, and when this is set, the remainder of the white mixture. Let the jelly set firmly in the refrigerator; when ready to serve, dip the mold in hot water so that the jelly will slip out easily.

ÉMILE DUMONT
LA BONNE CUISINE

# Champagne Jelly with Raspberries

To serve 4

| | | |
|---|---|---|
| ¾ cup | Champagne | 175 ml. |
| 2 tbsp. | unflavored powdered gelatin, softened in ¼ cup [50 ml.] of water | 30 ml. |
| | fresh raspberries | |
| 1½ cups | water | 375 ml. |
| ¾ cup | sugar | 175 ml. |
| 1 | lemon, the zest cut into wide strips and the juice extracted | 1 |
| 1 | egg white and shell, crushed | 1 |
| ½ cup | dry white wine | 125 ml. |

Heat the water in a saucepan, add the gelatin and stir until dissolved. Add the sugar, the lemon juice and the zest. Heat until the liquid is about to break into a boil. Remove the pan from the heat, cover and steep for 20 minutes.

Whisk together the egg white, eggshell and white wine until lightly foamy. Whisk the mixture into the gelatin syrup and place the pan over low heat. Continue a lazy whisk-

ing action. As the liquid heats, the egg-white albumen will gradually rise to the top, bringing with it specks of impurities that might otherwise cloud the jelly. As soon as a frothy scum forms and the liquid starts to simmer, remove the scum, stop stirring and cook slowly for 10 minutes. Cover, remove from the heat and let stand for five minutes.

Rinse a clean kitchen towel in cool water. Wring it out and use it to line a sieve. Place the sieve over a large bowl, making sure there is plenty of space under the sieve. Carefully pour in the syrup and let it drip through of its own accord. Do not allow the clear jelly to touch the bottom of the sieve or it may become cloudy again.

Let the jelly cool. As soon as it turns cold and just before it sets, stir in the Champagne. Pour into four Champagne or balloon wine glasses. Leave to set until thoroughly cold. Serve with raspberries, sprinkled with sugar if desired.

JUDITH OLNEY
SUMMER FOOD

# Wine Jelly

To serve 10 to 12

| | | |
|---|---|---|
| 2 cups | Rhine wine or other medium-dry white wine | ½ liter |
| ⅓ cup | port wine | 75 ml. |
| ½ lb. | grapes | ¼ kg. |
| 1 cup | sugar | ¼ liter |
| 3 cups | water | ¾ liter |
| 4 | egg whites, lightly beaten | 4 |
| 4 tbsp. | unflavored powdered gelatin, softened in ½ cup [125 ml.] water | 60 ml. |
| 1 cup | strained fresh lemon juice, squeezed from about 6 lemons | ¼ liter |

Set aside one small bunch of grapes. Remove the rest of the grapes from their stems, then peel and seed them.

Dissolve the sugar in 2½ cups [625 ml.] of the water over medium heat. Stir in the egg whites and bring to a boil, stirring constantly. Stir in the softened gelatin. Let the liquid boil again, then add half of the remaining cold water. Bring to a boil again and add the rest of the cold water. Remove the pan from the heat and add the lemon juice and Rhine wine. Let this jelly mixture stand for about 20 minutes and then filter it three times through muslin or a cloth napkin. Add the port to the jelly. Embed a glass dish in a bowl of crushed ice and pour half of the jelly into the dish. When this jelly has set, lay grapes around the border of the dish and place the small bunch you have reserved in the center. Pour in about ½ inch [1 cm.] of jelly and let it set to hold the grapes in place. Then pour in the rest of the jelly. Refrigerate until the wine jelly sets firmly. Unmold to serve.

J. M. ERICH WEBER
THEORY AND PRACTICE OF THE CONFECTIONER

## Boiled Cider Jelly

| | To serve 6 | |
|---|---|---|
| 2 cups | boiled cider, made by boiling down 2 quarts [2 liters] fresh apple cider | ½ liter |
| 2 tbsp. | unflavored powdered gelatin, softened in ½ cup [125 ml.] cold water | 30 ml. |
| 1 cup | boiling water | ¼ liter |
| 1 tsp. | strained fresh lemon juice | 5 ml. |
| | sugar | |
| | heavy cream | |

Add boiling water to the softened gelatin to dissolve it. Strain if necessary, then cool. Add the lemon juice and boiled cider. The mixture will be sweet, but extra sugar may be added to taste. Turn into a 4-cup [1-liter] mold and chill. Serve with heavy cream.

AMY B. W. MILLER AND PERSIS W. FULLER (EDITORS)
THE BEST OF SHAKER COOKING

## Black-Coffee Jelly

| | To serve 4 | |
|---|---|---|
| 2½ cups | freshly made strong black coffee | 625 ml. |
| ½ cup | sugar | 125 ml. |
| 6 tbsp. | water | 90 ml. |
| 1 tbsp. | unflavored powdered gelatin, softened in 2 or 3 tbsp. [30 or 45 ml.] water | 15 ml. |
| | heavy cream, whipped | |

Make a syrup by boiling the sugar and water together for one or two minutes. Add the freshly made coffee to the syrup and stir in the gelatin, dissolving it completely. Pour the mixture into a 1-quart [1-liter] mold, and allow it to cool. Then refrigerate the jelly until it is set. Serve with whipped cream.

RUTH LOWINSKY
MORE LOVELY FOOD

# Assemblies

## Rice Meringue

### Riz Meringue

| | To serve 12 | |
|---|---|---|
| 1¼ cups | raw unprocessed long-grain rice, washed and drained | 300 ml. |
| | long, thin strip of orange peel | |
| 4 cups | milk | 1 liter |
| | salt | |
| 1¼ cups | granulated sugar | 300 ml. |
| 2 tbsp. | butter | 30 ml. |
| 6 | egg yolks | 6 |
| 3 tbsp. | water | 45 ml. |
| 4 | almond macaroons, crushed (recipe, page 167) | 4 |
| 4 | egg whites, beaten stiff | 4 |
| ¼ cup | confectioners' sugar | 50 ml. |

Place the rice in a large pot. Place the orange peel in another pot with the milk. Add the salt, ½ cup [125 ml.] of the granulated sugar and the butter. Bring to a boil. Pour this mixture over the rice. Cover and simmer for 35 minutes. Remove from the heat, and stir in the egg yolks. Pour into a buttered 6-cup [1½-liter] mold (any shape you like). Bake in a preheated 375° F. [190° C.] oven for 35 minutes.

Turn out the rice pudding from its mold onto an ovenproof dish. Sprinkle the macaroons over the pudding and use a spatula to spread the egg whites over its surface. Sprinkle the pudding with the confectioners' sugar. Bake in a preheated 425° F. [220° C.] oven for five minutes.

Dissolve the remaining ¾ cup [175 ml.] of granulated sugar in the water in a saucepan over low heat. Swirl occasionally to keep the sugar from burning. Cook until this caramel mixture is light gold, but not brown.

To serve, pour the caramel over the meringue as soon as the pudding is taken from the oven, being careful not to cover it entirely with caramel. (The caramel should run down the sides.) Serve immediately.

CÉLINE VENCE AND ROBERT COURTINE
THE GRAND MASTERS OF FRENCH CUISINE

## Frozen Meringues Sandwiched with Ice Cream

### Le Vacherin Glacé

*To make the strawberry or raspberry ice cream called for in this recipe, purée 1 cup [¼ liter] of strawberries or raspberries through a nylon sieve and sweeten the purée to taste with about ¼ cup [50 ml.] superfine or confectioners' sugar. Whip ⅔ cup [150 ml.] of heavy cream until it forms soft peaks, fold the cream into the puréed fruit and freeze for at least two hours.*

*In order to assemble the vacherin—a dessert typical of Alsace—the ice creams should be soft enough to handle. But the vacherin must be returned to the freezer whenever the ice creams begin to melt. The technique of making meringue rounds is shown on page 84.*

*To serve 6 to 8*

| | | |
|---|---|---|
| 2 | meringue rounds, each 8 inches [20 cm.] in diameter | 2 |
| 2½ cups | vanilla ice cream *(recipe, page 166)* | 625 ml. |
| 2 tbsp. | kirsch | 30 ml. |
| ¼ cup | whole strawberries, poached in 1 cup [¼ liter] sugar and 1 cup water for 2 minutes, and drained | 50 ml. |
| ½ cup | coarsely diced fresh pineapple | 125 ml. |
| 6 | macaroons, crushed | 6 |
| 1¼ cups | strawberry or raspberry ice cream, slightly softened | 300 ml. |
| 1 cup | fresh whole strawberries or raspberries | ¼ liter |
| 1 cup | heavy cream, chilled | ¼ liter |
| 2 tbsp. | vanilla sugar | 30 ml. |

Soften the vanilla ice cream just enough to blend in the kirsch, strawberry preserves, pineapple and macaroons. Sandwich the meringue cases together with this ice-cream mixture and, working quickly, coat the sides of the frozen assembly with the strawberry or raspberry ice cream. Freeze just until firm—no longer than one hour. Decorate the sides with whole berries of the same sort as those in the ice cream.

Whip the cream until it is stiff, adding the vanilla sugar at the last moment. Decorate the top of the *vacherin* with the cream, so that the assembly is pink around the sides, with a white topping.

AUSTIN DE CROZE
LES PLATS RÉGIONAUX DE FRANCE

## Baked Alaska

For the base of the baked Alaska, you may use any other spongecake you like, but this is a very quick, easy recipe.

*To serve 6 to 8*

| | | |
|---|---|---|
| 1 cup | flour, sifted before measuring | ¼ liter |
| ⅔ cup | sugar | 150 ml. |
| 1½ tsp. | baking powder | 7 ml. |
| ½ tsp. | salt | 2 ml. |
| ¼ cup | shortening | 50 ml. |
| ½ cup | milk | 125 ml. |
| 1 | egg | 1 |
| 1 tsp. | vanilla extract | 5 ml. |
| 1 quart | vanilla ice cream *(recipe, page 166)*, frozen in a brick-shaped mold or loaf pan about 4 inches [10 cm.] wide and 8 inches [20 cm.] long | 1 liter |
| **Meringue topping** | | |
| 3 | egg whites | 3 |
| ½ cup | granulated sugar | 125 ml. |

Butter and flour a 9-inch [23-cm.] square cake pan. Sift the flour with the sugar, baking powder and salt into a mixing bowl. Add the shortening and milk. Beat for one and a half minutes with an electric mixer on a slow speed, or with a spoon until well blended and thick. Add the egg and the vanilla. Beat for one and a half minutes more.

Pour the mixture into the cake pan. Bake in a preheated 350° F. [180° C.] oven for 20 to 25 minutes, or until the cake springs back when lightly touched in the center. Cool.

Place the cake on a cutting board. Cut strips 2 inches [5 cm.] wide from two parallel sides of the cake and discard them. Make a meringue by beating the egg whites until they hold soft peaks, then beat in the sugar, a tablespoon [15 ml.] at a time, until the whites are thick and glossy.

Place the ice-cream brick on top of the cake. Completely cover the ice cream and the cake with the meringue. Bake in the oven at 450° F. [230° C.] for five minutes, or until the baked Alaska is delicately brown. Serve at once.

JAMES BEARD
JAMES BEARD'S AMERICAN COOKERY

## Decorated Easter Cheese Mold

### Paskha

A traditional *paskha* is shaped in a four-sided wooden pyramidal mold that has a small opening at the narrow end to
drain off any moisture. Alternatively, a large clay flowerpot
about 7 inches [18 cm.] tall, with an upper diameter of 7½
inches [19 cm.], can be used. The flowerpot should be
smoothly lined with two or three layers of fine cheesecloth or
with muslin, leaving an overhang to fold over the top.

| | To serve 15 to 20 | |
|---|---|---|
| 3 lb. | pot or cottage cheese | 1½ kg. |
| ¾ cup | blanched almonds | 175 ml. |
| ¾ cup | glacéed cherries | 175 ml. |
| 1 cup | raisins, soaked in warm water for 15 minutes and drained | ¼ liter |
| 1 lb. | unsalted butter, softened | ½ kg. |
| 1 tsp. | rose water or vanilla extract | 5 ml. |
| ⅔ | mixed candied citrus peel | 150 ml. |
| 3 | eggs | 3 |
| 1 cup | sugar | ¼ liter |
| ½ cup | sour cream or heavy cream | 125 ml. |

The pot cheese or cottage cheese must be absolutely dry before it is used. Hang it in a cheesecloth bag over a bowl for 12
hours, or place it in a colander under a heavy weight—at
least 3 to 4 pounds [1½ to 2 kg.]. When dry, rub the cheese
through a fine sieve into a bowl. Set aside 3 tablespoons [45
ml.] each of the almonds and glacéed cherries for decoration,
then chop the remainder and mix them with the cheese,
adding the raisins, softened butter, rose water or vanilla
extract, and the mixed peel. Beat the eggs and sugar together and add them to the cheese mixture. Beat thoroughly
until no lumps remain. Then stir in the cream and, using a
wooden spoon, beat the mixture until it is absolutely smooth.

Pour the mixture into a 2- to 2½-quart [2- to 2½-liter]
mold lined with fine cheesecloth or muslin. Fold the ends of
the cloth over the top of the *paskha,* cover with a small plate
to distribute the weight and weigh the plate down with any-
thing heavy—at least 2 to 3 pounds [1 to 1½ kg.]. Stand the
mold small end down in a deep plate or a large bowl, and
refrigerate the *paskha* for another 12 hours.

When the *paskha* is removed from the refrigerator, a lot
of moisture will have drained out into the plate or bowl.
Unfold the cheesecloth or muslin, place a flat serving dish on
top of the mold and turn both of them over; carefully remove
the mold and the cheesecloth. Decorate the *paskha* with the
reserved almonds and glacéed cherries, and serve it, if possible, with *koulitch* (a not too sweet yeast bun).

SOFKA SKIPWITH
EAT RUSSIAN

## Russian Easter Cheese Mold

### Paskha Obiknovennaya

*The original version of this recipe produces a 3½-quart [3½-
liter] mold to serve 20—or more. If the special and perforated
paskha mold called for is not obtainable, you may substitute a
clay flowerpot of equal capacity.*

*Paskha* means Easter in Russian, and it is also the name
given to a traditional Easter dessert. After being decorated
with the Orthodox Cross and the letters *XB*—standing for
*Khristos Voskres,* or "Christ is Risen"—the *paskha* is taken
to the church to be blessed. Later it is taken back home and
consumed on Easter Sunday.

| | To serve 10 to 12 | |
|---|---|---|
| 3 lb. | pot cheese | 1½ kg. |
| ½ cup | sour cream | 125 ml. |
| 7 tbsp. | unsalted butter, brought to room temperature | 105 ml. |
| 1 tsp. | salt | 5 ml. |
| about ¼ cup | superfine sugar | about 50 ml. |

Place the pot cheese in a colander set in a pan or bowl. Cover
the cheese with muslin or cheesecloth, top with a heavy 3- to
4-pound [1½- to 2-kg.] weight, and set the cheese aside in a
cool place or a refrigerator to drain for 24 hours.

Press the drained cheese through a sieve into a large
bowl. Gradually beat in the sour cream, butter, salt and
sugar; mix well so that not one lump remains. More sugar
may be added to taste, if desired.

Transfer the mixture to a 2½-quart [2½-liter] *paskha*
mold, which first should be lined with fine cheesecloth. Cover with a 2- to 3-pound [1- to 1½-kg.] weight, set in a pan or
bowl and chill in the refrigerator for 24 hours. Then carefully turn the *paskha* out onto a dish. Remove the cheesecloth
and decorate the *paskha.*

ELENA MOLOKHOVETS
PODAROK MOLODÝM KHOZYAÍKAM

## Molded Rice Ring with Apricots

### Abricots Condé

*The technique of making sugar syrup is shown on pages 8-9.*

When fresh ripe apricots are not available, use canned apricots in syrup and thicken the reduced syrup with a tablespoon [15 ml.] of apricot jam.

| | To serve 4 to 6 | |
|---|---|---|
| 10 | large ripe apricots | 10 |
| ⅔ cup | sugar | 150 ml. |
| 1¼ cups | water | 300 ml. |
| 1 | vanilla bean | 1 |
| 4 tsp. | kirsch | 20 ml. |
| | **Rice ring** | |
| ⅔ cup | raw unprocessed long-grain rice, well washed, blanched in boiling water for 2 minutes, drained, washed again and thoroughly drained | 150 ml. |
| 2¼ cups | milk | 550 ml. |
| 1 | vanilla bean | 1 |
| 1 | small strip orange or lemon peel | 1 |
| ¼ tsp. | salt | 1 ml. |
| 2 tbsp. | unsalted butter, melted | 30 ml. |
| about ¼ cup | sugar | about 50 ml. |
| 3 | eggs, the yolks separated from the whites, and the yolks beaten lightly and thinned with 1 tbsp. [15 ml.] light cream or boiled milk | 3 |
| about 1 tbsp. | kirsch | about 15 ml. |
| | angelica, candied fruits and peel, and glacéed cherries | |

Prepare a light sugar syrup with the ⅔ cup [150 ml.] of sugar, the water and the vanilla bean. Plunge the apricots for a moment into boiling water, peel them immediately, then halve and pit them. Crack four of the pits, extract the kernels, cut them in half and add them to the syrup, along with the apricots. Bring the syrup slowly to a boil, reduce the heat and poach, simmering, for five to eight minutes, or until just tender, being careful that the apricots do not break or lose their shape. Keep the apricot halves warm in the syrup until time to use.

To prepare the rice mold, bring the milk with the second vanilla bean, the orange or lemon peel and the salt to a boil. Remove the vanilla bean and the peel. Put the rice into a saucepan and add ½ cup [125 ml.] of the boiling milk, along with the melted butter. Cook, covered, over low heat, stir-

ring occasionally with a fork until the milk is absorbed by the rice. Continue to cook, adding about ½ cup of milk at a time, until all of the milk is absorbed. Cool the rice slightly.

Sprinkle about ¼ cup [50 ml.] of sugar over the surface of the rice. Using a fork, and taking care not to break the grains of rice, mix in the egg yolks. Stir in about 1 tablespoon [15 ml.] of kirsch. Beat the egg whites until they form soft peaks, then fold them into the rice. Pour the mixture into a 1-quart [1-liter] buttered ring mold.

Cover the mold with buttered wax paper and cook in a bain-marie in a preheated 350° F. [180° C.] oven for 45 minutes. To test for doneness, insert a trussing needle into the mold. It should come out clean. Let the rice stand for 10 minutes before unmolding it onto a round plate.

Drain the apricot halves, then boil the syrup to reduce it to about ½ cup; remove the kernels and vanilla bean. Place 16 of the apricot halves on the rice, overlapping them around the curved top of the ring. Decorate the apricots with angelica, candied fruits and peel, and glacéed cherries.

Rub the remaining four apricot halves through a fine sieve and mix this purée with the syrup. Flavor this sauce with the 4 teaspoons [20 ml.] of kirsch. Coat the molded rice with the sauce and serve warm.

PAUL BOCUSE
PAUL BOCUSE'S FRENCH COOKING

---

## Molded Rice and Fruit Custard

### Riz à l'Impératrice

| | To serve 6 | |
|---|---|---|
| ⅔ cup | raw unprocessed long-grain rice | 150 ml. |
| ½ cup | sugar | 125 ml. |
| | salt | |
| 2 tbsp. | butter | 30 ml. |
| 1 | vanilla bean, split lengthwise | 1 |
| 2½ cups | milk | 625 ml. |
| 5 to 6 tbsp. | apricot jam | 75 to 90 ml. |
| ½ cup | mixed candied cherries, pineapple and angelica, diced and steeped in 5 tbsp. [75 ml.] kirsch sweetened with 1 tbsp. [15 ml.] sugar | 125 ml. |
| 4 tbsp. | unflavored powdered gelatin, softened in ½ cup [125 ml.] water, warmed for 5 minutes until dissolved | 60 ml. |
| 2½ cups | pouring custard *(recipe, page 165)* | 625 ml. |
| 3 tbsp. | kirsch | 45 ml. |

Blanch the rice in boiling water for five minutes; drain the rice, plunge it into cold water, then drain it again. In a heavy casserole combine the sugar, a pinch of salt, the butter, vanilla bean and milk, and bring the mixture to a boil. Add the rice, cover the casserole tightly and cook the mixture in a preheated 300° F. [150° C.] oven for 30 minutes, or until the rice is tender but the grains remain whole.

Remove the vanilla bean and place the rice in a bowl. Stir in the apricot jam and the diced candied fruits. Add the gelatin to the pouring custard, stir until the gelatin dissolves, and add the custard and the kirsch to the rice. Pour the mixture into an oiled 5-cup [1¼-liter] ring mold.

Chill the custard until set—for two to three hours if embedded in a bowl of crushed ice, or for four to five hours in the refrigerator. To serve, unmold onto a napkin-covered dish.

PHILÉAS GILBERT
LA CUISINE DE TOUS LES MOIS

## Molded Vanilla Bavarian Cream with Rice and Glacéed Fruits

*Riz à l'Impératrice*

To serve 8 to 10

| | | |
|---|---|---|
| ½ cup | raw unprocessed long-grain rice | 125 ml. |
| ½ cup | finely diced mixed, glacéed fruit | 125 ml. |
| ¼ cup | kirsch | 50 ml. |
| 4 tsp. | unflavored powdered gelatin, softened in ¼ cup [50 ml.] water | 20 ml. |
| 2½ cups | milk | 625 ml. |
| 1 cup | sugar | ¼ liter |
| 2 tbsp. | unsalted butter | 30 ml. |
| 1 | vanilla bean | 1 |
| 5 | egg yolks | 5 |
| ¼ cup | apricot jam, rubbed through a fine sieve | 50 ml. |
| 2 cups | heavy cream, whipped | ½ liter |
| | angelica and assorted thinly sliced candied fruits | |

### Raspberry sauce

| | | |
|---|---|---|
| 2 cups | fresh raspberries | ½ liter |
| ¾ cup | sugar | 175 ml. |
| ¼ cup | kirsch | 50 ml. |

Combine the glacéed fruit and the kirsch in a bowl, stir well and marinate at room temperature for at least 45 minutes.

In a heavy 2- to 3-quart [2- to 3-liter] saucepan, bring 1 quart [1 liter] of water to a boil over high heat, drop in the rice and cook briskly for five minutes. Pour the rice into a sieve, rinse it under cold water and drain.

Pour 1 cup [¼ liter] of the milk into the top of a double boiler, add ¼ cup of the sugar, the butter and vanilla bean. Stirring occasionally, cook over moderate heat until the sugar and butter dissolve and small bubbles appear around the edge of the pan. Set the pan above simmering (not boiling) water and stir the rice into the mixture. Cover tightly and cook for 25 to 30 minutes, or until the rice is soft. Drain the rice in a fine sieve; remove and discard the vanilla bean.

In a 2- to 3-quart [2- to 3-liter] enameled or stainless-steel saucepan, heat the remaining 1½ cups [375 ml.] of milk over moderate heat until bubbles form around the edge of the pan. Cover and remove from the heat.

With a wire whisk or a rotary or electric beater, beat the egg yolks and the remaining ¾ cup [175 ml.] of sugar together in a deep bowl for three to four minutes, or until the yolks form a slowly dissolving ribbon when the whisk is lifted from the bowl. Whisking constantly, pour in the milk in a slow, thin stream. When thoroughly blended, return the mixture to the saucepan. Cook over low heat, stirring constantly until the custard is as thick as heavy cream; do not let the custard come near a boil or it will curdle. Mix in the softened gelatin and continue to mix until it is dissolved.

Strain the custard through a fine sieve set over a bowl. Stir in the glacéed fruits, kirsch and the apricot jam, then gently mix in the rice.

Place the bowl of custard in a pot filled with ice cubes and water, and stir for four or five minutes, or until the custard is cool and begins to thicken very slightly. Remove the bowl from the ice and scoop the whipped cream over the custard. With a rubber spatula, fold the custard and cream gently together until no trace of white remains. Ladle the mixture into the mold, cover with foil and refrigerate for six hours, or until it is completely firm.

To make the raspberry sauce, combine the berries, sugar and kirsch in the jar of an electric blender and blend at high speed for 10 seconds. Turn off the machine, scrape down the sides of the jar with a rubber spatula and blend again for a minute. Then rub the purée through a fine sieve set over a small bowl. Cover tightly and refrigerate until ready to use.

To serve, unmold the *riz à l'impératrice* onto a chilled serving platter. Decorate the mold as fancifully as you like with the angelica and candied fruit, pressing the slices gently into place. Refrigerate the *riz à l'impératrice* until ready to serve. Before serving, pour some of the raspberry sauce around the edge of the platter and present the rest in a bowl.

FOODS OF THE WORLD/CLASSIC FRENCH COOKING

# To Make a Trifle

*This 19th Century recipe depends for success on a cream much richer in butterfat than the usual heavy cream. You can use the heavy cream available at some dairy and health food stores, which is not ultra-pasteurized, as is the supermarket variety. Or you can beat ultra-pasteurized heavy cream until stiff, then mix it with the other ingredients for the whip and use it immediately, without draining it, to garnish the trifle.*

The whip to lay over the top of the trifle should be made the day before it is required for table, as the flavor is better, and it is much more solid than when prepared the same day.

| | *To serve 8* | |
|---|---|---|
| 6 | small spongecakes, or slices of spongecake | 6 |
| 12 | almond macaroons *(recipe, page 167)* | 12 |
| 24 | ratafias *(recipe, page 167)* | 24 |
| 1¼ cups | sherry or sweet white wine | 300 ml. |
| 6 tbsp. | brandy | 90 ml. |
| 2 tsp. | finely grated fresh lemon peel | 10 ml. |
| ½ cup | slivered blanched almonds | 125 ml. |
| | raspberry or strawberry jam | |
| 2 cups | pouring custard *(recipe, page 165, but made with 8 egg yolks)*, cooled | ½ liter |

| | **Whip** | |
|---|---|---|
| ⅓ cup | superfine sugar | 75 ml. |
| 2 | egg whites, stiffly beaten | 2 |
| 2 to 3 tbsp. | sherry or sweet white wine | 30 to 45 ml. |
| 2½ cups | heavy cream | 625 ml. |

To make the whip, put into a large bowl the sugar, beaten egg whites, sherry or sweet wine and the cream. Whisk these ingredients well in a cool place. Take off the froth with a skimmer as fast as it rises, and put the froth on a sieve to drain. Continue the whisking till there is sufficient froth, or whip, which must be covered and put away in a cool place to drain overnight.

The next day, place the spongecakes, macaroons and ratafias at the bottom of a 5-cup [1½-liter] dish. Mix the sherry or wine with the brandy and pour over the cakes; should this proportion of wine be found not quite sufficient, add a little more, as the cakes should be well soaked. Over the cakes put the grated lemon peel, the almonds and a layer of raspberry or strawberry jam. Pour the custard over all and heap the whip lightly over the top: this should stand as high as possible. The result may be garnished with bright currant jelly, crystallized fruits or flowers.

MRS. ISABELLA BEETON
THE BOOK OF HOUSEHOLD MANAGEMENT

# Floating Island Trifle

This dessert was very often served as a side dish at feasts and great dinners in the 17th Century and was still made for Victorian dinner parties, though it is scarcely ever seen today. Many variants exist; most recipes build one large island to float in its lake of cream, but some suggest small, individual islands. In either case, the dish used must be large and fairly flat. A pouring custard *(recipe, page 165)* can be used instead of the fruit purée.

| | *To serve 4* | |
|---|---|---|
| 1¾ cups | puréed raspberries or strawberries, made from about 1 quart [1 liter] whole berries | 400 ml. |
| 2½ cups | heavy cream | 625 ml. |
| 1 lb. | round spongecake, sliced horizontally into 3 thin layers | ½ kg. |
| ⅓ cup | apricot jam | 75 ml. |
| ⅔ cup | blanched almonds, finely chopped | 150 ml. |
| 2 tbsp. | sherry | 30 ml. |
| ½ cup | superfine sugar | 125 ml. |
| ½ tsp. | vanilla extract | 2 ml. |

Mix the fruit purée with half of the cream, beat well together or blend, and pour onto a large, rather flat dish. Spread each of the three slices of spongecake with a little apricot jam and sprinkle with almonds. Lay the first layer lightly on the purée, centering it. Put the other layers, always lightly, one above the other. The cake should be floating, supported on the purée. Pour onto the cake a little sherry. Whip the remaining cream with the sugar and vanilla, and pile high on the island cake.

Chill in the refrigerator for an hour, if possible, and serve. If the island does not float the dish is still delicious, but the cake should move freely on the purée.

ELISABETH AYRTON
THE COOKERY OF ENGLAND

## An Excellent Trifle

*If possible, the syllabub called for in this recipe should be made 24 hours in advance. The wine in the trifle may be replaced by 1 cup [¼ liter] of good sherry or Madeira, in which case use only ½ cup [125 ml.] of brandy.*

| | To serve 8 | |
|---|---|---|
| ¾ cup | white wine | 175 ml. |
| ¾ cup | brandy | 175 ml. |
| 8 | ladyfingers *(recipe, page 167)* | 8 |
| 10 to 14 | mixed macaroons and ratafias *(recipes, page 167)* | 10 to 14 |
| 1 cup | heavy cream, flavored with about 2 tbsp. [30 ml.] wine | ¼ liter |

| | **Whipped syllabub** | |
|---|---|---|
| 2 | large lemons | 2 |
| ½ cup | superfine sugar | 125 ml. |
| 1½ cups | sherry | 375 ml. |
| 1½ cups | brandy | 375 ml. |
| 2½ cups | heavy cream | 625 ml. |

| | **Lemon custard** | |
|---|---|---|
| 1 | lemon, peel only, very thinly pared | 1 |
| 1 cup | milk | ¼ liter |
| ½ cup | superfine sugar | 125 ml. |
| 6 | egg yolks, thoroughly beaten | 6 |
| 1 cup | cream | ¼ liter |
| ⅓ cup | brandy (optional) | 75 ml. |
| ¼ cup | slivered blanched almonds (optional) | 50 ml. |

To make the syllabub: Peel the lemons very thin indeed and infuse the peel for some hours in the juice from the lemons. Put the sugar into a bowl with the strained lemon juice, sherry and brandy. When the sugar has dissolved, add the cream and whisk the mixture well. When it has become a solid froth, pour the mixture into a sieve lined with dampened muslin or a double layer of cheesecloth to drain.

To make the custard: Add the lemon peel to the milk and let it infuse for 30 minutes, then simmer them together for a few minutes and add the superfine sugar. Mix the beaten egg yolks with the cream, stir the boiling milk quickly into them, take out the lemon peel and turn the custard into a double boiler. Set this over the heat in a pan of boiling water and keep the custard stirred gently, without ceasing, until it begins to thicken; then move the spoon rather more quickly, making it always touch the bottom of the bowl. Once the mixture is brought to the point of boiling, it must be instantly taken from the heat or it will curdle. Pour the custard into another bowl, and keep stirring until it is nearly cold. Add to

it by degrees the brandy and blanched almonds, or omit these, if you prefer.

To make the trifle: Mix the wine and brandy, and soak the ladyfingers, macaroons and ratafias in this mixture. Cover the bottom of a trifle dish with half of these and pour the custard over them. Lay the remainder of the soaked cookies on the custard and pile over the whole the whipped syllabub, previously well drained. Now whip the wine-flavored cream to the lightest possible froth. Skim it off and heap the froth gently over the trifle.

ELIZABETH RAY (EDITOR)
THE BEST OF ELIZA ACTON

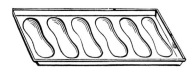

## Cake with Zabaglione Sauce
### *Zuppa Inglese*

*The Italian name for this recipe translates as English soup — probably because the dessert resembles an English trifle.*

| | To serve 4 | |
|---|---|---|
| ½ cup | heavy cream, whipped | 125 ml. |
| 4 | thin slices poundcake | 4 |
| 2 tbsp. | rum | 30 ml. |
| 2 tbsp. | semisweet chocolate pieces, broken or shaved | 30 ml. |

| | **Zabaglione sauce** | |
|---|---|---|
| 8 | egg yolks | 8 |
| ¼ cup | sugar | 50 ml. |
| ¾ cup | Marsala wine | 175 ml. |
| 4 tbsp. | apricot brandy | 60 ml. |
| 1 tbsp. | ice water | 15 ml. |

To make the zabaglione sauce, place the egg yolks and sugar in the top of a double boiler. Beat well with an egg beater or wire whisk. Add the wine and 2 tablespoons [30 ml.] of the brandy and continue beating; add the water and beat some more. Place the pan over simmering water and beat until this custard mixture thickens, but do not let it boil.

Remove the pan from the heat and fold the whipped cream into the custard. Place slices of poundcake on four individual serving dishes. Sprinkle the rum over the slices and then cover them with zabaglione sauce. Scatter the chocolate on top and refrigerate the dessert for an hour. When ready to serve, sprinkle the dessert with the remaining apricot brandy.

GENE LEONE
LEONE'S ITALIAN COOKBOOK

# Gooseberry Trifle

*To serve 6 to 8*

| | | |
|---|---|---|
| 2 to 2½ lb. | gooseberries | 1 kg. |
| ⅔ cup | water | 150 ml. |
| about 2 cups | soft brown sugar | about ½ liter |
| 2½ cups | pouring custard (recipe, page 165) | 625 ml. |
| 1¼ cups | heavy cream, whipped | 300 ml. |
| | preserved or crystallized fruit | |

Boil the gooseberries with the water, and with brown sugar to taste, for 15 to 25 minutes over medium heat. When the gooseberries are soft enough to pulp, put them at the bottom of a glass trifle dish and pour the custard over them. Set the trifle in a cool place. When the custard has set, pile the whipped cream over the trifle. Decorate with rings of preserved or crystallized fruit, and serve.

MARY JEWRY (EDITOR)
WARNE'S MODEL COOKERY AND HOUSEKEEPING BOOK

# Cream-filled Crepe Cake

*Pain de Crêpes à la Crème*

*For instructions on how to prepare crepes, see pages 44-45.*

*To serve 6 to 8*

| | | |
|---|---|---|
| 2 to 3 cups | flour | ½ to ¾ liter |
| 1 tbsp. | sugar | 15 ml. |
| | salt | |
| 4 | eggs, the yolks separated from the whites, and the whites stiffly beaten | 4 |
| 2¼ cups | milk | 550 ml. |
| 4 tbsp. | butter, melted and cooled | 60 ml. |
| | oil | |
| | dry bread crumbs | |
| **Cream filling** | | |
| 1¼ cups | heavy cream | 300 ml. |
| 4 | egg yolks | 4 |
| ⅓ cup | sugar | 75 g. |
| ½ tsp. | vanilla extract and/or 1 tsp. [5 ml.] finely grated lemon peel | 2 ml. |

Put the flour, sugar and salt in a bowl. Make a well in the center, add the egg yolks and whisk, adding the milk and butter, until the batter is smooth. Fold in the egg whites.

Heat a little oil in a crepe pan. Pour in enough batter to cover the base of the pan. When the edges start to brown, turn the crepe to cook the other side. Continue to make crepes until the batter is used up.

To make the filling, beat the egg yolks with the sugar until pale and creamy, then add the heavy cream and beat well together. Add the vanilla extract or lemon peel or, better still, both. Butter a 1-quart [1-liter] charlotte mold and sprinkle it with dry bread crumbs. Layer the crepes in the mold, separating each layer with some of the cream filling. Top with a crepe.

Cook in an oven, preheated to 375° F. [190° C.], for about 20 minutes to set the cream. Unmold and sprinkle with sugar. Serve cold.

H. WITWICKA ET S. SOSKINE
LA CUISINE RUSSE CLASSIQUE

# Layered Crepe Cake with Cheese Filling

*Gâteau Livonien*

*To serve 8*

| | | |
|---|---|---|
| 10 to 12 | crepes (recipe, page 166) | 10 to 12 |
| 2 lb. | pot cheese or ricotta | 1 kg. |
| 12 tbsp. | butter, softened | 180 ml. |
| 1 cup | superfine sugar | ¼ liter |
| | salt | |
| 8 | egg yolks | 8 |
| ½ cup | raisins, soaked in warm water for 15 minutes and drained | 125 ml. |
| ½ cup | dried currants, soaked in warm water for 15 minutes and drained | 125 ml. |
| ½ cup | candied citron, chopped | 125 ml. |
| ½ cup | angelica, chopped | 125 ml. |
| 4 | egg whites, stiffly beaten | 4 |
| 1 cup | heavy cream, whipped | ¼ liter |

First prepare the crepes. Then, in a bowl, mix together thoroughly the cheese, butter, sugar, a pinch of salt and the egg yolks. Put the mixture through a strainer into a bowl and add the raisins, currants, citron and angelica. Fold in the stiffly beaten egg whites.

Generously butter a 2-quart [2-liter] charlotte mold or soufflé dish, and line the bottom and sides of the mold with crepes. Pour in a quarter of the cheese mixture, cover with a crepe and continue layering in this way, finishing with a crepe. Bake in a preheated 375° F. [190° C.] oven for about 45 minutes, or until golden.

Turn onto a napkin-covered serving platter and serve a sauceboat of whipped cream at the same time.

A. PETIT
LA GASTRONOMIE EN RUSSIE

## Slid Pancakes

### Csúsztatott Palacsinta

*The unusual English title of this recipe is a literal translation of its Hungarian name, and refers to the way the pancakes slide from the pan.*

|  | To serve 8 to 12 |  |
|---|---|---|
| 4 tbsp. | butter, softened | 60 ml. |
| 1 tbsp. | sugar | 15 ml. |
| 4 | eggs, the yolks separated from the whites | 4 |
|  | salt |  |
| ½ cup | milk | 125 ml. |
| 3 tbsp. | flour | 45 ml. |
| ¼ cup | heavy cream | 50 ml. |
|  | clarified butter |  |
|  | **Pancake filling** |  |
| ¼ cup | vanilla sugar | 50 ml. |
| 4 oz. | semisweet baking chocolate, grated (optional) | 125 g. |
| 1 cup | thick jam (optional) | ¼ liter |

In a bowl, beat together the butter, sugar, egg yolks and a pinch of salt. Gradually incorporate the milk, then the flour, and beat until the batter is smooth. Finally, add the cream, and let the batter rest for one hour before using it.

Preheat the oven to 350° F. [180° C.]. Beat the egg whites until stiff, and fold them into the batter. Melt a little butter in an 8-inch [20-cm.] crepe pan. With a ladle, dip out about ½ cup [125 ml.] of the batter and pour it onto the hot pan. With a circular motion, swirl the batter to cover the bottom of the pan. Adjust the amount of batter to conform to the size of your pan. Fry the pancake slowly, but only on one side.

Slide the pancake, cooked-side down, into a fairly deep 8-inch ovenproof dish. Sprinkle the pancake with some of the vanilla sugar and grated chocolate and/or spread with jam. The chocolate and jam can be used together or on alternate layers, or one or the other can be used throughout.

When the second pancake is cooked, slide it on top of the first. Sprinkle with more sugar and chocolate, and/or jam. Continue to cook and layer the pancakes in this fashion.

Cook the last pancake on both sides and use it as a cover for the torte of stacked pancakes. Bake the torte in the preheated oven for 10 to 15 minutes. To serve, cut the torte as you would a cake.

GEORGE LANG
THE CUISINE OF HUNGARY

## Charlotte Malakoff

This is a rather extravagant pudding, but luckily it is so rich that no one can eat very much of it. It is particularly delicious served with a rather tart fruit purée, such as raspberry or red currant.

You can make the following variations of this pudding: For a raspberry charlotte malakoff, add 1¾ cups [400 ml.] of raspberries to the list of ingredients. Pour one third of the malakoff mixture into the prepared mold, cover with a layer of raspberries, repeat the process and finish with a layer of the malakoff mixture. For a walnut charlotte malakoff, substitute ground walnuts for the ground almonds. (This is only for those who love walnuts, as the taste is very strong.)

For a chocolate charlotte malakoff, add 4 ounces [125 g.] of semisweet baking chocolate and 2 tablespoons [30 ml.] of freshly made strong coffee to the basic ingredients, and use Tía María or other coffee liqueur for the Grand Marnier. Dip the ladyfingers in a mixture of the liqueur and 1 tablespoon [15 ml.] of the coffee. Melt the chocolate with the other tablespoon of coffee over gentle heat or in a double boiler, and add it to the well-beaten butter-and-sugar mixture.

|  | To serve 12 |  |
|---|---|---|
| 2 tbsp. | Grand Marnier or other orange-flavored liqueur | 30 ml. |
| 1 tbsp. | water | 15 ml. |
| about 24 | ladyfingers *(recipe, page 167)* | about 24 |
| 16 tbsp. | unsalted butter (½ lb. [¼ kg.]) | 240 ml. |
| 1 cup | superfine sugar | ¼ liter |
| 2 cups | ground blanched almonds | ½ liter |
| 1¼ cups | heavy cream | 300 ml. |

Mix 1 tablespoon [15 ml.] of the Grand Marnier with the water and briefly dip the smooth sides of the ladyfingers into the liquid. Line the bottom and sides of a 5-cup [1¼-liter] charlotte mold or pudding basin with the ladyfingers, standing them around the sides and trimming them to size.

Cream the butter and the sugar until they are white and fluffy and add the rest of the Grand Marnier and the ground almonds. Whip the cream lightly and fold it in. Pour this mixture into the lined mold and tap it sharply on the table two or three times to get rid of any air bubbles.

Chill in the refrigerator for three to four hours, turn out of the mold and serve.

HELGE RUBINSTEIN AND SHEILA BUSH
A PENGUIN FREEZER COOKBOOK

# Malakoff Pudding

### Pouding à la Malakoff

*The ladyfingers may be soaked in any orange-flavored liqueur or in rum. The technique of making sugar syrup is explained on pages 8-9. To prepare the apple and pear purées called for in this recipe, peel, core and slice about 1½ pounds [¾ kg.] of each fruit; simmer the fruits in separate saucepans with enough water to prevent scorching; when tender, purée the fruits through a food mill.*

To serve 4 to 6

| | | |
|---|---|---|
| 2 cups | pouring custard *(recipe, page 165),* mixed with 2 tbsp. [30 ml.] unflavored powdered gelatin softened in 4 tbsp. [60 ml.] warm water | ½ liter |
| 12 | ladyfingers *(recipe, page 167),* soaked in ½ cup [125 ml.] liqueur | 12 |
| 1 cup | apple purée | ¼ liter |
| ½ cup | finely sliced blanched almonds | 125 ml. |
| 1 tbsp. | finely diced orange peel | 15 ml. |
| ¼ cup | raisins, soaked in ⅓ cup [75 ml.] medium-light sugar syrup | 50 ml. |
| 1 cup | pear purée | ¼ liter |
| 2 cups | sabayon sauce *(recipe, page 165),* chilled | ½ liter |

Lightly oil a 6-cup [1½-liter] charlotte mold. Put in a layer of custard about ½ inch [1 cm.] thick, cover with a layer of ladyfingers, spread with a layer of apple purée and sprinkle with the almonds, orange peel and raisins. Add another layer of custard, more ladyfingers, pear purée and more almonds, orange peel and raisins. Continue layering, alternating layers of apple and pear purée, until the mold is full, finishing with the ladyfingers. Refrigerate until firm—at least four hours. Unmold and serve with cold sabayon sauce.

COUNTESS MORPHY
SWEETS AND PUDDINGS

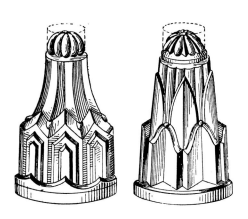

# Vanilla Charlotte Russe

### Charlotte à la Russe

*The technique of making charlotte russe is demonstrated on pages 80-81. To make a raspberry charlotte russe, add ½ cup [125 ml.] of puréed raspberries to the custard before adding the whipped cream. Surround the unmolded pudding with raspberries macerated in kirsch and heavily sugared.*

To serve 6

| | | |
|---|---|---|
| 20 | ladyfingers *(recipe, page 167),* sides and ends neatly cut | 20 |
| ½ cup | superfine sugar | 125 ml. |
| 4 | egg yolks | 4 |
| 1 cup | milk or half-and-half cream | ¼ liter |
| 1 | vanilla bean | 1 |
| 1 tbsp. | unflavored powdered gelatin, softened in ½ tbsp. [7 ml.] cold water | 15 ml. |
| ⅔ cup | heavy cream, whipped and flavored with 2 tbsp. sugar [30 ml.] and ½ tsp. [2 ml.] vanilla sugar | 150 ml. |

Cover the bottom and sides of a 1½-quart [1½-liter] charlotte mold with white paper, a round piece for the bottom and a long strip for the sides. Cover the paper in the bottom of the mold with ladyfingers cut into triangles to form a rosette. (Save the crumbs when you cut the ladyfingers.) Line the sides of the mold with ladyfingers cut ½ to ¾ inch [1 to 2 cm.] higher than the mold and all the same length, so that the charlotte balances when unmolded. The ladyfingers should be placed side by side, very close together, with the curved sides against the mold where they will show when the dessert is unmolded.

Prepare a *crème anglaise:* Bring the milk or milk and cream to a boil, remove the saucepan from the heat, add the vanilla bean and leave to steep, covered. In a bowl mix the sugar and the egg yolks; beat this mixture with a wooden spoon until it is frothy, thick and nearly white. Then remove the vanilla bean from the milk and slowly add the milk to the egg mixture. Pour the egg-and-milk mixture into the saucepan, and cook over low heat; stir continuously with the wooden spoon, moving it all around the bottom of the pan to prevent the egg yolks from coagulating into tiny lumps. As the sauce heats, the egg yolks will thicken the mixture. As soon as the mixture starts to coat the spoon, remove the pan from the heat and add the softened gelatin. Stir until dissolved. Strain the mixture through a fine sieve into a bowl.

Stirring often, cool the custard on ice or in the refrigerator. As soon as it starts to set, carefully fold in the whipped cream. Pour the mixture into the lined mold, filling it to the top. Smooth the surface with a knife blade and sprinkle with ladyfinger crumbs; refrigerate for at least two hours.

To serve, unmold the charlotte onto a round platter covered with a doily.

PAUL BOCUSE
PAUL BOCUSE'S FRENCH COOKING

## Strawberry and Raspberry Charlotte

*Fraisalia*

| | To serve 6 | |
|---|---|---|
| 1½ cups | strawberries, hulled | 375 ml. |
| 1½ cups | raspberries | 375 ml. |
| about 30 | ladyfingers *(recipe, page 167)* | about 30 |
| ½ cup | sugar | 125 ml. |
| ¼ cup | rum | 50 ml. |
| | vanilla pouring custard *(recipe, page 165)* | |

Place a layer of ladyfingers in the bottom of a lightly oiled 1-quart [1-liter] charlotte mold, then add a layer of strawberries followed by a layer of raspberries. Sprinkle the berries with sugar and rum. Continue to layer the ladyfingers and fruit in the same order until the mold is full, pressing each layer down well and sprinkling it with sugar and rum. Finish with a layer of ladyfingers.

Cover the contents of the mold with a round of cardboard wrapped in foil; put a 2- to 3-pound [1- to 1½-kg.] weight on top to press the pudding down lightly. Refrigerate the charlotte for five to six hours, or overnight.

To serve, unmold the charlotte onto a serving dish and pour the custard over it.

MME. JEANNE SAVARIN (EDITOR)
LA CUISINE DES FAMILLES (MAGAZINE)

## Charlotte Russe

*A fruit-flavored liqueur such as kirsch may be substituted for the bitter-almond-flavored noyau suggested by the author.*

Almost any cream mixture stiffened with gelatin may be used as a filling for this dessert *(recipes, pages 97-103)*.

| | To serve 5 or 6 | |
|---|---|---|
| 16 to 20 | ladyfingers *(recipe, page 167)*, sides and ends trimmed straight, or finger-length strips of spongecake | 16 to 20 |
| 1 | egg white (optional) | 1 |
| 1¾ cups | heavy cream | 400 ml. |
| about 2 tsp. | superfine sugar | about 10 ml. |
| about ½ tsp. | vanilla extract or about 1 tbsp. [15 ml.] noyau or other liqueur | about 2 ml. |
| 2 tbsp. | unflavored powdered gelatin, softened in 5 tbsp. [75 ml.] water, warmed for 5 minutes until dissolved, then cooled | 30 ml. |

A plain 1-quart [1-liter] mold is required, with straight sides and a flat bottom like a soufflé dish. First place at the bottom of the mold, oiled side down, a round of oiled wax paper cut to fit it exactly. Then arrange ladyfingers or strips of cake evenly around the sides of the mold; they should be long enough to reach to the top of the mold and must be packed very closely together. The joints between the ladyfingers may be brushed over with a little white of egg to seal them. The bottom of the mold may also be lined with ladyfingers, cut into triangular-shaped pieces and fitted in evenly.

Whip the cream to a stiff froth and add sugar to taste. Flavor to taste with vanilla extract or liqueur. Strain the dissolved gelatin slowly into the cream, stirring all the time. Chill just until the cream mixture begins to stiffen, then spoon it into the prepared mold. Chill again.

When the cream is set, turn out the charlotte russe on a glass or silver dish covered with a lace-edged paper.

FLORENCE B. JACK
COOKERY FOR EVERY HOUSEHOLD

## Prune Charlotte with Wine Custard Sauce

*Charlotte aux Pruneaux, Crème Sabayon*

| | To serve 6 | |
|---|---|---|
| 1 lb. | dried pitted prunes (about 3½ cups [875 ml.]), soaked in warm water for 2 to 3 hours | ½ kg. |
| | strip lemon peel | |
| 1 cup | heavy cream | ¼ liter |
| ⅓ cup | sugar | 75 ml. |
| about 25 | ladyfingers *(recipe, page 167)*, dipped in sherry | about 25 |
| | wine custard *(recipe, page 165)*, flavored with sherry or port, cooled | |

Drain the prunes and simmer them with the lemon peel in fresh water for 15 minutes. Remove and discard the lemon peel, drain the prunes and mash them. Whip the cream and add the sugar. Fold the prunes into the whipped cream.

Line the sides of a 2-quart [2-liter] charlotte mold with ladyfingers. Half-fill the mold with the prune-and-cream mixture. Add a layer of ladyfingers, then the rest of the prune-and-cream mixture and another layer of ladyfingers.

Cover the mold with a plate and refrigerate for three hours. To serve, unmold the prune charlotte. Pour the wine custard over the charlotte.

ELIZABETH W. ESTERLING (EDITOR)
LE COOKBOOK

# Apple Charlotte

*To clarify the butter called for in this recipe, melt about 12 tablespoons [180 ml.] of butter over low heat, remove the pan from the heat and let the butter stand until the milk solids settle to the bottom. Spoon off the clear yellow surface liquid and strain it. Discard the milk solids.*

To serve 8 to 10

| | | |
|---|---|---|
| 24 | medium-sized apples, peeled, cored and sliced | 24 |
| 2 cups | sugar | ½ liter |
| 4 tbsp. | butter | 60 ml. |
| 1 | strip fresh lemon peel | 1 |
| 3-inch | stick cinnamon | 8-cm. |
| 1¼ cups | water | 300 ml. |
| 1 lb. | loaf 2-day-old finely grained white bread, crusts removed | ½ kg. |
| about 8 tbsp. | clarified butter, melted | about 120 ml. |
| about ¼ cup | sifted confectioners' sugar | about 50 ml. |
| 1 cup | apricot jam, diluted with 2 to 3 tbsp. [30 to 45 ml.] boiling water | ¼ liter |

First of all, some apple marmalade, or thick purée, must be prepared as follows: Let the apples be placed in a stewpan with the sugar, butter, and some lemon peel and cinnamon tied together; moisten with the water, place the lid on the stewpan, and then set the apples to boil over brisk heat until they are softened. You then remove the lid and, with a wooden spoon, continue stirring the marmalade until it is reduced to a rather stiff, porridge-like consistency.

A plain, round, 2-quart [2-liter] charlotte mold must now be lined at the bottom with small, thin, circular pieces of bread that are dipped in the clarified butter and placed so as to overlap one another until the bottom of the mold is well covered. Next, cut some thin, oblong squares of bread, dip them in clarified butter and set these up the sides of the mold, overlapping each other to hold to the sides. Fill the cavity with the apple marmalade, cover the top with a thin circular piece of bread dipped in clarified butter, place the charlotte on a baking sheet and bake in a preheated 375° F. [190° C.] oven for 30 to 50 minutes, or until the bread is lightly colored.

Remove the charlotte, let it cool for a few minutes and carefully turn it onto a heatproof serving dish. Sprinkle the top with sifted confectioners' sugar and glaze under a hot broiler for a few minutes. Pour the diluted apricot jam around the base of the charlotte and serve.

CHARLES ELMÉ FRANCATELLI
THE MODERN COOK

# Chilled Dessert Belvedere

*Dolce Freddo Belvedere*

To serve 8 to 12

| | | |
|---|---|---|
| 8 tbsp. | butter, at room temperature | 120 ml. |
| 6 | hard-boiled egg yolks | 6 |
| ½ cup | sugar | 125 ml. |
| ⅛ tsp. | salt | ½ ml. |
| 6 tbsp. | rum | 90 ml. |
| 36 | ladyfingers *(recipe, page 167)* | 36 |
| 1½ cups | white port wine | 375 ml. |

In an electric blender combine the butter, egg yolks, sugar, salt and rum. Blend at medium speed for three to four minutes, until this butter cream is smooth and fluffy.

Quickly dip ladyfingers, one at a time, into the wine and arrange them in a layer on a serving platter. Carefully spread a portion of the butter cream over them. Repeat for three or four layers, ending with a top layer of butter cream. Cover and refrigerate for 24 hours before serving.

TERESA GILARDI CANDLER
THE NORTHERN ITALIAN COOKBOOK

# Chocolate Rum Soufflé

To serve 8

| | | |
|---|---|---|
| 16 oz. | semisweet baking chocolate | ½ kg. |
| ½ cup | rum | 125 ml. |
| 12 | macaroons *(recipe, page 167)* | 12 |
| 6 tbsp. | water | 90 ml. |
| 7 tbsp. | sugar | 105 ml. |
| 6 | eggs, the yolks separated from the whites | 6 |
| 24 | ladyfingers *(recipe, page 167)* | 24 |
| 1 cup | heavy cream, whipped | ¼ liter |
| | grated chocolate (optional) | |

Soak the macaroons in the rum. In a double boiler, melt the chocolate with the water and 6 tablespoons [90 ml.] of the sugar. Mix well, remove the chocolate mixture from the heat and add the egg yolks, one at a time. Let the mixture cool.

Beat the egg whites, adding the remaining 1 tablespoon [15 ml.] of sugar to make them more dense. Carefully fold the egg whites into the chocolate mixture. Line the bottom and sides of an oiled 8-inch [20-cm.] spring-form pan with split ladyfingers. Add half of the chocolate mixture and then a layer of soaked macaroons. Add the remaining chocolate mixture, top with the remaining ladyfingers and refrigerate for at least six hours, or overnight.

To serve, unmold the soufflé, top it with whipped cream and, if desired, sprinkle on grated chocolate.

THE JUNIOR LEAGUE OF NEW ORLEANS
THE PLANTATION COOKBOOK

# Macaroon Mold

## Le Délicieux

*The techniques of preparing caramel and coating a mold are shown on page 24.*

| | To serve 8 | |
|---|---|---|
| 1¼ lb. | macaroons, about 30 (recipe, page 167), dried out in the oven, finely pounded in a mortar and sieved | 600 g. |
| ½ cup | hot caramel, made from 1 cup [¼ liter] sugar and 2 tbsp. [30 ml.] water | 125 ml. |
| 8 | egg whites | 8 |
| about ¼ cup | confectioners' sugar | about 50 ml. |
| 4 oz. | semisweet baking chocolate, melted with 1 or 2 tbsp. [15 or 30 ml.] water over low heat | 125 g. |
| 2 cups | cold wine custard (recipe, page 165), flavored with kirsch or other white cherry-flavored liqueur | ½ liter |
| 8-inch | round spongecake | 20-cm. |

Line a 2-quart [2-liter] charlotte mold with the caramel. Beat the egg whites until they are stiff, then gradually whisk in confectioners' sugar to taste, the melted chocolate and the sieved macaroons. Ladle the macaroon mixture into the mold. Bake in a preheated 350° F. [180° C.] oven for 25 minutes until the top puffs up and the macaroon mixture begins pulling away from the sides.

Remove the mold from the oven and allow the dessert to cool, then unmold it onto the spongecake. Just before serving, pour the cold wine custard over the top.

ÉDOUARD NIGNON
LES PLAISIRS DE LA TABLE

# Lemon Icebox Cake

This dessert freezes beautifully; I always keep one on hand.

| | To serve 6 | |
|---|---|---|
| 1 | lemon, the peel grated and the juice strained | 1 |
| 1½ | oranges, the peel grated and the juice strained | 1½ |
| 16 tbsp. | butter | 240 ml. |
| 1 cup | sugar | ¼ liter |
| 3 | eggs, the yolks separated from the whites | 3 |
| | spongecake, cut into fingers, or 15 ladyfingers (recipe, page 167) | |

Cream the butter and sugar together and add the egg yolks, grated lemon and orange peel, and the fruit juices. Beat the egg whites until stiff and fold them into the butter mixture. Line the bottom of a 1-quart [1-liter] mold or cake tin with the spongecake fingers and cover them with a layer of the mixture. Repeat for as many layers as you wish, ending with the cake on top. Refrigerate overnight, or freeze for at least two hours. Unmold before serving.

HELEN CORBITT
HELEN CORBITT'S COOKBOOK

# Coffee and Cream Assembly

## Biskuit Fanny

*Toast almonds in a shallow pan in a 350° F. [180° C.] oven for 10 minutes, turning them frequently to brown them evenly. Roll the nuts in a towel to remove their skins (page 13).*

| | To serve 4 to 6 | |
|---|---|---|
| ¼ cup | freshly made strong black coffee, chilled | 50 ml. |
| 1 cup | heavy cream, whipped | ¼ liter |
| 12 tbsp. | butter, softened | 180 ml. |
| 3 | egg yolks | 3 |
| ¼ cup | sifted confectioners' sugar | 50 ml. |
| 20 | ladyfingers (recipe, page 167) | 20 |
| ⅓ cup | toasted blanched almonds | 75 ml. |

Beat the butter until it is creamy. Add the egg yolks and confectioners' sugar alternately. Add the cold coffee, drop by drop, and beat until the mixture is thick and creamy. On a glass platter heap the coffee mixture and the ladyfingers in alternate layers. Cover the whole with the whipped cream and sprinkle with the toasted almonds.

ELIZABETH SCHULER
MEIN KOCHBUCH

## Molded Fruit Pudding
### *Diplomate aux Fruits*

*To serve 6 to 8*

| | | |
|---|---|---|
| 2 cups | fresh strawberries | ½ liter |
| 1 cup | fresh red currants or raspberries | ¼ liter |
| 10 | ladyfingers *(recipe, page 167)*, soaked in ¼ cup [50 ml.] water mixed with ¼ cup kirsch or rum | 10 |
| 2 cups | pouring custard *(recipe, page 165)*, chilled | ½ liter |

In a bowl, mash the strawberries with the red currants or raspberries. Place the soaked ladyfingers in a 1-quart [1-liter] mold in layers, alternating them with mashed berries. Cover the mold with foil and refrigerate it overnight, with a weight of about 2 pounds [1 kg.] over the foil.

Turn the pudding out of the mold and serve it very cold, accompanied by the cold pouring custard.

X. MARCEL BOULESTIN
THE FINER COOKING

---

## Lemon Mousse

*To serve 10*

| | | |
|---|---|---|
| ½ cup | strained fresh lemon juice | 125 ml. |
| 2 tbsp. | finely grated fresh lemon peel | 30 ml. |
| 8 | eggs, the yolks separated from the whites | 8 |
| 1 cup | granulated sugar | ¼ liter |
| 2 tbsp. | unflavored powdered gelatin, softened in ¼ cup [50 ml.] cold water | 30 ml. |
| 24 | ladyfingers | 24 |
| 1 cup | heavy cream | ¼ liter |
| 2 tsp. | confectioners' sugar | 10 ml. |
| ¼ tsp. | vanilla extract | 1 ml. |
| | fresh mint sprigs | |

In the top of a double boiler—off the heat—beat the egg yolks until thick and very pale yellow. Add the granulated sugar gradually while beating constantly. Stir in the lemon juice and 4 teaspoons [20 ml.] of the grated lemon peel. Place over gently boiling water in the bottom of the double boiler,

making sure that the water does not touch the bottom of the pot with the sauce. Cook, stirring constantly, until the sauce forms a thick custard. Add the gelatin to the hot mixture, stirring well until the gelatin is dissolved. Pour the mixture into a bowl and let it cool thoroughly, stirring occasionally.

Line the sides and bottom of a 9-inch [23-cm.] spring-form pan with the ladyfingers. Beat the egg whites until stiff and fold them into the cooled mixture. Pour into the lined mold and refrigerate until the mousse sets firmly.

To serve, remove the sides of the pan and, using a large metal spatula, slide the mousse from the pan bottom onto a serving plate. Whip the cream, adding the confectioners' sugar and vanilla. Top the mousse with whipped cream. Decorate with the remaining grated lemon peel and with the sprigs of mint.

THE JUNIOR LEAGUE OF NEW ORLEANS
THE PLANTATION COOKBOOK

---

# Sauces

---

## Honey Cream

*To make about 1 cup [¼ liter] sauce*

| | | |
|---|---|---|
| ½ cup | honey | 125 ml. |
| ¾ cup | heavy cream | 175 ml. |
| 2 tbsp. | butter | 30 ml. |

Heat the honey and butter in a small enameled saucepan, stirring until the butter melts. Stir in the heavy cream. Cool before using as a sauce for ice-cream parfaits. Refrigerated in a glass jar, this sauce will keep for about one week.

DIANA COLLIER AND NANCY GOFF
FROZEN DELIGHTS

---

## Marshmallow Sundae Sauce

*To make about 1 ½ cups [375 ml.] sauce*

| | | |
|---|---|---|
| ½ cup | sugar | 125 ml. |
| ¼ cup | water | 50 ml. |
| 12 | marshmallows, cut into pieces | 12 |
| 1 | egg white, beaten until stiff | 1 |

Boil the sugar and water for about five minutes to make a syrup. Remove the pan from the heat and add the marshmallows. Let the mixture stand for two minutes without stirring. Then pour it gradually onto the beaten egg white, beating constantly until the sauce is smooth and cool.

THE SETTLEMENT COOK BOOK

## Hot Fudge Sauce

This is the grand kind of sauce that, when cooked for the longer period and served hot, grows hard on ice cream and enraptures children.

*To make about 1 cup [¼ liter] sauce*

| | | |
|---|---|---|
| 2 oz. | unsweetened baking chocolate | 75 g. |
| 1 tbsp. | butter | 15 ml. |
| ⅓ cup | boiling water | 75 ml. |
| 1 cup | sugar | ¼ liter |
| 2 tbsp. | corn syrup | 30 ml. |
| 1 tsp. | vanilla extract or 2 tsp. [10 ml.] rum | 5 ml. |

Melt in a double boiler, over—not in—boiling water, the chocolate and butter. Stir and blend well, then add the boiling water. Stir well and add the sugar and corn syrup. Let the sauce boil readily, but not too furiously, over direct heat. Do not stir. If you wish an ordinary sauce, boil it, covered, for about three minutes to wash down any crystals which may have formed on the sides of the pan. Uncover, reduce the heat, and cook two minutes more without stirring. If you wish a hot sauce that will harden over ice cream, boil it, uncovered, about three minutes more. Add the vanilla or rum just before serving.

When cold, this sauce is very thick; it may be reheated over—not in—boiling water.

IRMA S. ROMBAUER AND MARION ROMBAUER BECKER
JOY OF COOKING

---

## Old Faithful Chocolate Sauce

This sauce looks thin while warm but it keeps well in the refrigerator, thickening as it chills.

*To make about 1 ½ cups [375 ml.] sauce*

| | | |
|---|---|---|
| 2 oz. | unsweetened baking chocolate | 75 g. |
| ¾ cup | water | 175 ml. |
| 1 cup | sugar | ¼ liter |
| | salt | |
| 1 tbsp. | butter | 15 ml. |

Put the chocolate and water in the top of a double boiler over boiling water, stirring until the chocolate melts. Then stir in the sugar, a pinch of salt and the butter. Continue cooking slowly, stirring occasionally, for about 15 minutes until the sauce is smooth.

JOYCE AND CHRISTOPHER W. DUEKER
THE OLD FASHIONED HOMEMADE ICE CREAM COOKBOOK

---

## Basic Hard Sauce

For Brandy Hard Sauce, beat in 2 or more tablespoons [30 ml.] of brandy and omit the vanilla.

*To make about 1 cup [¼ liter] sauce*

| | | |
|---|---|---|
| 8 tbsp. | butter | 120 ml. |
| 2 cups | sifted confectioners' sugar | ½ liter |
| | salt | |
| 1 tsp. | vanilla extract | 5 ml. |

Cream the butter, sugar, salt and vanilla extract together until the sauce becomes light and fluffy. Chill for two hours before serving.

THE JUNIOR LEAGUE OF PINE BLUFF
SOUTHERN ACCENT

## Hot Spiced Blueberry Sauce

This sauce is delicious on ice cream.

*To make about ⅔ cup [150 ml.] sauce*

| | | |
|---|---|---|
| 1 cup | fresh blueberries | ¼ liter |
| ½ tsp. | ground cinnamon | 2 ml. |
| ¼ tsp. | grated nutmeg | 1 ml. |
| ¼ cup | sugar | 50 ml. |

Combine the blueberries, sugar, cinnamon and nutmeg in an enameled pan. Stirring occasionally, bring the blueberry mixture to the boiling point over medium heat and boil for five minutes. Serve the sauce hot.

PETER HUNT
PETER HUNT'S CAPE COD COOKBOOK

---

## Strawberry Sauce

*To make about 2 cups [½ liter] sauce*

| | | |
|---|---|---|
| 2 cups | crushed fresh strawberries | ½ liter |
| 1 cup | sugar | ¼ liter |
| ½ cup | water | 125 ml. |

In an enameled saucepan, boil the sugar and water over medium heat until the syrup reaches the soft-ball stage—234° F. [112° C.]—after about 12 minutes. Add the strawberries and cook for one minute more.

Chill the sauce before serving.

RUTH BEROLZHEIMER (EDITOR)
THE UNITED STATES REGIONAL COOK BOOK

## Butterscotch Ice Cream Sauce

*The soft-ball stage specified here is described on page 9.*

*To make about 1 cup [¼ liter] sauce*

| | | |
|---|---|---|
| 1 cup | firmly packed, dark brown sugar | ¼ liter |
| ⅓ cup | dark corn syrup | 75 ml. |
| ¼ cup | water | 50 ml. |
| 4 tbsp. | butter | 60 ml. |
| ⅓ cup | light cream | 75 ml. |
| | salt | |
| ½ tsp. | vanilla extract | 2 ml. |

In a saucepan combine the brown sugar, corn syrup, water and butter. Bring to a boil and cook, stirring from time to time, until the mixture reaches the soft-ball stage (236° F. [117° C.]) on a candy thermometer; this takes about four minutes. Remove the pan immediately from the heat and let the mixture cool slightly.

Add the light cream, a pinch of salt and the vanilla. Beat the sauce well. Serve it warm or cold.

ELISE W. MANNING (EDITOR)
HOMEMADE ICE CREAM AND CAKE

## Walnut Topping

*To make 1 cup [¼ liter] sauce*

| | | |
|---|---|---|
| ⅔ cup | chopped or whole walnuts | 150 ml. |
| ⅔ cup | sugar | 150 ml. |
| | water | |
| ¼ cup | maple syrup | 50 ml. |

In a small enameled saucepan, combine the sugar and 2 tablespoons [30 ml.] of water. Over high heat, swirl the pan until the sugar caramelizes and turns a light amber color. Do not stir the mixture with a spoon.

Remove the pan from the heat and pour in ½ cup [125 ml.] of water. Stir the sauce over medium heat until the caramel sugar is totally dissolved in the water. Let this syrup cool. When cooled, combine the caramel syrup with the maple syrup and the chopped or whole nuts. If the sauce is being used to decorate a mold, the nuts should be left whole. If the sauce is to be used as a topping for ice cream, the nuts should be chopped.

DIANA COLLIER AND NANCY GOFF
FROZEN DELIGHTS

## Praline Parfait Sauce

To make a praline parfait, spoon alternate layers of vanilla ice cream and praline parfait sauce into a tall parfait glass, ending with a layer of sauce. Top with whipped cream and garnish with pecan halves.

*To make about 3 cups [¾ liter] sauce*

| | | |
|---|---|---|
| 1 cup | chopped pecans (or small halves) | ¼ liter |
| 2 cups | dark corn syrup | ½ liter |
| ⅓ cup | sugar | 75 ml. |
| ⅓ cup | boiling water | 75 ml. |

Combine the corn syrup, sugar, boiling water and pecans in a saucepan and bring to a boil over medium heat. As soon as the mixture reaches the boiling stage, remove the pan from the heat. Cool before serving.

HERMANN B. DEUTSCH
BRENNAN'S NEW ORLEANS COOKBOOK

# Standard Preparations

## Calf's-Foot Jelly

This basic jelly will jell as much as 2 cups [½ liter] of wine or fruit juice. Start preparing the jelly the day before you need it. The technique of splitting calf's feet is shown on page 16.

*To make about 2½ cups [625 ml.] jelly*

| | | |
|---|---|---|
| 2 | calf's feet, split | 2 |
| 5 cups | water | 1¼ liters |
| ¾ cup | sugar | 175 ml. |
| | ground cinnamon | |
| | thin strips orange or lemon peel | |
| 6 tbsp. | strained fresh orange juice | 90 ml. |
| 3 tbsp. | strained fresh lemon juice | 45 ml. |
| 2 | egg whites | 2 |
| ⅓ cup | dry white wine | 75 ml. |
| 2 | egg shells, crushed | 2 |

Soak the calf's feet in cold water for several hours to draw out any remaining traces of blood. Drain the calf's feet, place them in a pan and cover them generously with cold water. Bring to a boil and simmer for eight to 10 minutes.

Drain the calf's feet, rinse them well and place them in a clean, deep saucepan. Add the 5 cups [1¼ liters] of water, which should amply cover the pieces, bring to a boil and skim. Cover the pan, setting the lid slightly ajar, and cook the calf's feet at a bare simmer for about seven hours. The calf's feet should remain immersed throughout the cooking: if necessary, add a little boiling water from time to time. Pour the liquid jelly through a strainer into a bowl and discard the calf's feet. Refrigerate the jelly overnight.

The next day, cleanse all traces of fat from the surface of the jelly by scraping it with a spoon. Then wipe the surface with a cloth that has been dipped in hot water and wrung out. In a large saucepan, warm the jelly over low heat to melt it. Add the sugar, a pinch of ground cinnamon, several strips of orange and lemon peel and the orange and lemon juice.

Beat the egg whites and the white wine together in a large bowl, then add the mixture to the liquid jelly. Whisking all the while, add the crushed egg shells. Bring the jelly to a boil. When a thick layer of froth forms on the surface, reduce the heat to very low and simmer the jelly gently for two or three minutes. Strain the liquid jelly into a bowl through a jelly bag, or a strainer lined with tightly woven dampened cheesecloth or a tea towel. The liquid should be quite clear: if necessary, strain it again. Covered and refrigerated, the jelly will keep for up to five days.

## Wine Custard

### Sabayon

*To make about 6 cups [1 ½ liters] sabayon*

| 6 | egg yolks | 6 |
|---|---|---|
| 1 cup | superfine sugar | ¼ liter |
| 1¼ cups | dry white wine, Sauternes, Champagne, Marsala or sherry | 300 ml. |
| 6 | strips lemon peel, cut into tiny julienne (optional) | 6 |

In a sabayon pan or a broad 2-quart [2-liter] saucepan, beat together the egg yolks and sugar until the mixture is thick and creamy and forms a slowly dissolving ribbon when it is dribbled back into the pan from the lifted whisk. This will take about seven to 10 minutes. Set the pan over a larger pan partly filled with water heated to just below the boiling point. Whisking constantly, slowly pour in the wine of your choice and, if desired, add the lemon peel julienne. Continue to whisk until the mixture froths to almost triple its original volume and is pale yellow in color. Remove the pan of custard from the heat and continue whisking for a minute or so.

As a dessert, sabayon is usually eaten hot; pour it into individual glasses and serve it immediately. As a sauce, sabayon may be used hot or cold. For a cold sauce, set the pan in a bowl of ice cubes and whisk the sabayon until sufficiently chilled. Whipped cream may be added if desired.

## Basic Pouring Custard

### Crème Anglaise

*To make about 2 ½ cups [625 ml.] custard*

| 6 | egg yolks | 6 |
|---|---|---|
| ¼ to ½ cup | superfine sugar | 50 to 125 ml. |
| 2½ cups | milk, scalded and slightly cooled | 625 ml. |

In a mixing bowl, beat the eggs and sugar together with a wire whisk until the mixture is thick and pale, and forms a slowly dissolving ribbon when dribbled from the whisk. Whisking gently all the time, slowly add the scalded milk.

Transfer this custard mixture to a heavy saucepan and set over very low heat, or put the pan on a trivet in a larger pan partly filled with simmering water. Cook the custard, stirring it constantly in a figure-8 pattern with a wooden spoon. Do not let it boil. When the custard coats the spoon, immediately remove the pan from the heat; in order to arrest the cooking and prevent the custard from curdling, stand the pan in a bowl filled with ice cubes and a little water. To ensure a smooth texture, continue to stir the custard for five minutes until it cools a little. To remove any lumps, strain the custard into a bowl.

For a warm custard, set the bowl in a pan partly filled with hot water and stir the custard occasionally. For a cold custard, set the bowl over ice cubes and stir until the custard is sufficiently chilled.

*Vanilla custard.* Place a vanilla bean in the pan of scalded milk, cover the pan and let the milk infuse for 20 minutes before removing the bean. (The bean can be rinsed and used one more time.)

*Coffee custard.* Place ⅓ cup [75 ml.] of fresh coffee beans in the pan of scalding hot milk; cover the pan and let the milk infuse for 20 minutes; strain the milk through a fine sieve before using it.

*Caramel custard.* In a heavy pan, caramelize ⅓ cup [75 ml.] of sugar with 1 tablespoon [15 ml.] of water. Remove the pan from the heat and immediately pour the scalded milk onto the caramel. Return the pan to low heat and stir until the caramel dissolves into the milk.

*Rum custard.* Stir about 1 tablespoon of rum into the prepared custard.

## Basic Custard Ice Cream

All of the flavorings for basic ice cream *(recipe, below)* can be added in the same way to this custard-based mixture. To ensure an especially smooth ice cream, the heavy cream called for can be whipped before it is added to the custard; in this case the custard should be chilled alone and the cream added just before the mixture is frozen.

*To make about 1 gallon [4 liters] ice cream*

| | | |
|---|---|---|
| 4 cups | milk | 1 liter |
| 1 | vanilla bean | 1 |
| 12 | egg yolks | 12 |
| 2 cups | sugar | ½ liter |
| 4 cups | heavy cream | 1 liter |

In a large, heavy saucepan, warm the milk over medium heat until bubbles appear around the rim of the pan. Remove the pan from the heat, add the vanilla bean, cover the pan and let the milk infuse for 20 minutes. Remove the bean.

Meanwhile, with a whisk, beat the egg yolks and sugar together in a bowl until the mixture is thick and pale and forms a slowly dissolving ribbon when it is dribbled from the whisk. Gradually add the warm milk, stirring constantly. Pour the mixture into the saucepan and set over very low heat—or place the pan on a trivet in a larger pan partly filled with hot water. Stir and cook the custard mixture without allowing it to boil, until it coats the spoon. Strain the custard into a bowl and stir occasionally as it cools. Stir in the cream, cover the bowl and refrigerate for about one hour. Then freeze the mixture, preferably in an ice-cream maker.

## Basic Ice Cream

The technique of using an ice-cream maker is demonstrated on pages 56-57.

*To make about 1 gallon [4 liters] ice cream*

| | | |
|---|---|---|
| 2½ quarts | heavy cream | 2½ liters |
| 2 cups | sugar | ½ liter |
| 1 | vanilla bean | 1 |
| ¼ tsp. | salt | 1 ml. |

In a heavy saucepan, mix 1 quart [1 liter] of the cream with the sugar, vanilla bean and salt. Stir over medium heat until the sugar dissolves and the mixture is scalded, but not boiling. Remove the pan from the heat, cover it and let the cream cool to room temperature. Take out the vanilla bean, and wash and dry it to reserve it for another use. Stir the remaining 1½ quarts [1½ liters] of cream into the mixture. Cover the pan and refrigerate the mixture for one hour, or until

well chilled. Pour the mixture into the canister of an ice-cream maker and freeze it.

*Philadelphia vanilla ice cream.* As soon as the cream mixture is removed from the heat, take out the vanilla bean and split it lengthwise. Scrape the vanilla-bean seeds into the pan and discard the pod.

*Chocolate ice cream.* Melt 4 ounces [125 g.] semisweet baking chocolate in 1 cup [¼ liter] of the cream and stir it into the sweetened mixture after removing the vanilla bean.

*Chocolate chip ice cream.* Grate 14 ounces [420 g.] semisweet baking chocolate and stir it into the frozen ice cream while it is still soft.

*Fruit ice cream.* While the frozen ice cream is still soft, stir in 3 cups [¾ liter] crushed or sliced, peeled and pitted peaches; 3 cups crushed or sliced strawberries; 3 cups crushed raspberries; or 12 mashed and sieved bananas.

*Nut ice cream.* Stir 1 cup [¼ liter] chopped or coarsely ground pecans or walnuts plus 1½ tablespoons [22 ml.] vanilla extract into the mixture while or after churning.

## Crepes

*To make about fifteen 6- to 7-inch [15- to 18-cm.] crepes*

| | | |
|---|---|---|
| 1 cup | flour | ¼ liter |
| | salt | |
| 2 | eggs | 2 |
| 1 to 1¼ cups | milk | 250 to 300 ml. |
| 2 tbsp. | melted butter | 30 ml. |
| 1 tbsp. | brandy or Grand Marnier (optional) | 15 ml. |

Sift the flour with a pinch of salt into a mixing bowl. Make a well in the center of the flour and break the eggs into the well. Gradually whisk the eggs into the flour, working from the center outward and adding 1 cup [¼ liter] of milk at the same time. Whisk only until smooth, then stir in the melted butter and the brandy or Grand Marnier if desired. The crepe batter should have the consistency of light cream; if necessary, add more milk to achieve the right consistency.

Heat a lightly greased 6- to 7-inch [15- to 18-cm.] crepe pan. Pour in about 3 tablespoons [45 ml.] of crepe batter and quickly spread it by tilting the pan back and forth until the base is covered with a film of batter; pour the excess batter back into the bowl. Cook the crepe for about 10 seconds until it slides easily back and forth when you shake the pan. Slide a round-tipped knife or spatula under the crepe and turn it, then cook the other side for eight to 10 seconds until it is pale gold. Slide the crepe onto a warmed dish. Cook the rest of the crepe batter similarly, but do not grease the pan again unless the crepes stick: the butter in the batter should keep the pan greased.

## Ladyfingers

Ladyfingers will keep for two to three weeks in an airtight container. To flavor the ladyfingers with chocolate, sift ½ to 1 tablespoon [7 to 15 ml.] of cocoa with the flour. To flavor them with orange, add 1 tablespoon of finely grated orange peel to the egg-yolk-and-sugar mixture, along with the flour. To give them an almond flavor, add ¼ teaspoon [1 ml.] of almond extract.

| | To make about 30 ladyfingers | |
|---|---|---|
| 3 | large eggs, the yolks separated from the whites | 3 |
| | superfine sugar | |
| ½ cup | flour, sifted with a pinch of salt | 125 ml. |

Butter three baking sheets, line them with buttered wax paper and dust the paper with flour. Preheat the oven to 350° F. [180° C.].

Put the egg yolks and ⅓ cup [75 ml.] of superfine sugar into a heatproof bowl or a pan, and place in a large pan partly filled with hot water and set over low heat. Beat the egg yolks and sugar together until they are very thick and very pale: This should take about five minutes if you use an electric mixer, about 15 minutes with a hand whisk. Remove from the heat and transfer the mixture to a large bowl. Carefully fold in the sifted flour. In a separate bowl, beat the egg whites until they stand in stiff peaks. Fold a quarter of the egg whites into the egg-yolk mixture to lighten it, then very carefully fold in the remaining egg whites.

Fit a large pastry bag with a ½-inch [1-cm.] plain tube. Fill the bag with the ladyfinger mixture and pipe strips 4 inches [10 cm.] long onto the prepared baking sheets, leaving about 2 inches [5 cm.] between the strips. Dust the piped strips with superfine sugar and bake in the oven for about 20 minutes, or until the ladyfingers are lightly browned. With a wide spatula carefully remove the ladyfingers from the paper and place them on wire cake racks to cool.

## Almond Macaroons

*The technique of making almond paste is shown on page 12.*

| | To make about 30 macaroons | |
|---|---|---|
| 1 cup | almond paste | ¼ liter |
| 1 cup | granulated sugar | ¼ liter |
| 3 | egg whites | 3 |
| ⅓ cup | confectioners' sugar | 75 ml. |
| 2 tbsp. | cake flour | 30 ml. |
| | salt | |

In a bowl, work the almond paste with your hands until it is soft and smooth. Gradually mix in the granulated sugar, then use a wooden spoon to beat in the egg whites, one by one. Combine in a sifter the confectioners' sugar, cake flour and a pinch of salt, then sift them—a little at a time—over the almond mixture, beating vigorously after each addition.

Line baking sheets with parchment paper (not wax paper). Drop teaspoonfuls of the macaroon mixture onto the lined sheets, spacing the macaroons an inch [2½ cm.] or so apart; then dip your fingers in cold water and flatten the macaroons slightly. Or use a pastry bag fitted with a plain or fancy tube to pipe macaroons onto the lined sheets. Cover the macaroons with plastic wrap and let them stand at room temperature for at least two hours.

Preheat the oven to 300° F. [150° C.]. Bake the macaroons for 30 minutes, or until they are firm and delicately browned. Remove the baking sheets from the oven, carefully pick up the macaroon-covered paper linings and place them on damp towels to soften the bottoms of the macaroons enough so that they can be easily lifted off the paper. After about 30 minutes, use a metal spatula to transfer the macaroons to wire racks to cool.

## Ratafias

Ratafias—or ratafia biscuits, as they are often called in England—are small almond macaroons, no more than an inch [2½ cm.] in diameter, made with bitter-almond paste. Bitter almonds are not obtainable in America, but you can simulate their flavor by adding a few drops of almond extract to the macaroon mixture before baking it.

# Recipe Index

All recipes in the index that follows are listed by their English titles except in cases where a dessert of foreign origin, such as crêpes suzette, is universally recognized by its source name. Entries are organized by the types of desserts and also by the major ingredients specified in the recipe titles. Sauces and fillings are listed separately. Foreign recipes are listed by country or region of origin. Recipe credits appear on pages 173-175.

**ouffl é pudding:** and egg whites, ; made with semolina, 36-37; nut f made with almonds and stachios, 36-37; cooking in water ath, 36, 37

**oufflé ed crepes,** 46; served with hampagne sabayon sauce, 21, 46

**oufflé ed omelet:** branding with a ewer, 49; cooking method, 48-49; nd eggs, 48; equipment, 48; fillings, ; flavoring, 48

**eaming:** Christmas plum pudding, )-41

**rawberries:** in dessert omelet, 49

**et:** beef fat from around the imal's kidneys. Available at butcher ops; 40

**gar:** beating with egg whites, 28, ?; caramelized, 8-9; coating soufflé sh with, 32; combining with hipped cream, 15; in custard, 20;

dusting an omelet with, 48; history of use, 5-6

**Sugar syrup:** in butterscotch sauce, 60; candy syrups, 8, 9; caramel, 8, 9; coating fruits with, 10; cooking times, 8-9; crystallization, 8; equipment, 8; forming balls, 8, 9, 61; glazing citrus peel, 10, 11; glazing nuts, 12; hard-crack stage, 9; simple syrups, 8, 9; small-thread stage, 9; stages, testing, *chart* 9; testing with candy thermometer, 8, 9; testing without candy thermometer, 8, 9, 60, 61; in water ices, 54

**Summer pudding,** 66, 67, 74-75; choosing bread, 74; choosing fruit, 75

**Sundae, ice-cream:** assembling, 60-61; butterscotch sauce for, 60-61; chocolate sauce for, 60; coffee sauce for, 60; cooking sauces for, 60, 61; fruit purée for, 60; liqueur sauce for,

60; parfait, 60

**Syrup.** *See* Sugar syrup

**Tangerine:** juice in crepes suzette, 47

**Thermometer:** candy, 8, 9; deep-frying, 50

**Threads of caramel:** decoration, 10

**Toasting nuts:** to remove skins, 12

**Tokay:** Hungarian dessert wine, serving with desserts, 7

**Vanilla bean:** infusion, 22; flavoring, 22, 51, 86

**Vanilla-flavored sugar:** *sugar made by placing a whole vanilla bean in a closed container of sugar for about a week;* 64

**Water bath.** *See* Bain-marie

**Water ice,** 54-55; adding brandy, 55; and egg whites, 54; freezing process, 53, 54; fruit, 54; melon-and-

Champagne ice, 54-55; serving in hollowed-out fruit shells, 55; sugar syrup, 54; texture of, 54

**Whip (huff),** 67; gooseberry, 67, 68, 69; served with wine, 7

**Whipped cream:** adding sugar to, 15; in Bavarian cream, 26; butterfat content, 15; in fool, 67; Mont Blanc, 68-69; whipping, 15

**Wine:** as ingredient, 7; in semolina *flamri,* 36; serving with desserts, 7

**Wine custard (sabayon):** cooking method, 20, 21; and egg yolks, 20; as a sauce, 21, 46; served with soufflé ed crepes, 46

**Zabaglione (wine custard),** 19. *See also* Sabayon

**Zest:** *the colored outer peel of oranges, lemons and other citrus fruits when scraped, sliced or grated off for use in cooking.*

# ecipe Credits

e sources for the recipes in this volume are shown below. ge references in parentheses indicate where the recipes pear in the anthology.

**ston, Elizabeth,** *The Best of Natural Eating Around the rld.* Copyright © 1973 by Elizabeth Alston. Published by vid McKay Company, Inc., New York. Reprinted by per-ssion of David McKay Company, Inc.(121).

*e Art of Cookery Made Plain and Easy.* By a dy. The Sixth Edition, 1758(102).

**dot, L. E.,** *La Cuisinière de la Campagne et de la Ville la Nouvelle Cuisine Economique.* Published by Librairie dot, 1881 edition(95, 96).

**rton, Elisabeth,** *The Cookery of England.* Copyright Elisabeth Ayrton, 1974. Published by Penguin Books Ltd., ndon. By permission of Penguin Books Ltd.(100, 135, 4).

**rberousse, Michel,** *Cuisine Normande.* Published by itions Barberousse, Paris. Translated by permission of chel Barberousse(113).

**Bayley, Monica,** *Black Africa Cook Book.* Copyright © 1977 by Determined Productions, Inc., San Francisco. Pub-lished by Determined Productions, Inc. Reprinted by per-mission of Determined Productions, Inc.(92).

**Beard, James,** *James Beard's American Cookery.* Copy-right © 1972 by James A. Beard. Published by Little, Brown and Company, Boston. By permission of Little, Brown and Company(150).

**Beard, James and Sam Aaron,** *How to Eat Better for Less Money.* Copyright © 1954, 1970 by James A. Beard and Sam Aaron. Published by Simon & Schuster, New York. Reprinted by permission of Simon & Schuster, a Divi-sion of Gulf & Western Corporation(136).

**Beck, Simone,** *Simca's Cuisine,* in collaboration with Pa-tricia Simon. Copyright © 1972 by Simone Beck and Patri-cia Simon. Reprinted by permission of Alfred A. Knopf, Inc.(130).

**Beeton, Mrs. Isabella,** *The Book of Household Man-agement* (1861). Reproduced in facsimile by Jonathan Cape Ltd., London(107, 154).

**Berolzheimer, Ruth,** *The United States Regional Cook Book.* Copyright © 1947 by Processing & Books, Inc. Copyright © 1940, 1939 by Consolidated Book Publishers, Inc., New York. Published by Culinary Arts Institute, Chica-go. Reprinted by permission of Consolidated Book Publishers(163).

**Besson, Joséphine,** *La Mère Besson "Ma Cuisine Pro-vençale."* © Éditions Albin Michel, 1977. Published by Édi-tions Albin Michel, Paris. Translated by permission of Édi-tions Albin Michel(131).

**Bobinet, Adrien-Jean,** *Gastronomie.* Copyright by Adrien-Jean Bobinet, Lyon, 1949. Published by Éditions Adrien-Jean Bobinet, Lyon(120).

**Bocuse, Paul,** *Paul Bocuse's French Cooking.* Copyright © 1977 by Random House, Inc. Published by Pantheon Books. Reprinted by permission of Pantheon Books, a Divi-sion of Random House, Inc.(152, 158).

**Bouillard, Paul,** *La Cuisine au Coin du Feu.* Copyright 1928 by Albin Michel. Published by Éditions Albin Michel, Paris. Translated by permission of Éditions Albin Michel(127).

**Boulestin, X. Marcel,** *The Finer Cooking.* Published by Cassell & Company Limited, London, 1937. By permission of A. D. Peters and Co., Ltd.(162).

**Brazier, Eugénie,** *Les Secrets de la Mère Brazier.* © So-lar 1977. Published by Solar, Paris. Translated by permis-sion of Solar(104, 111).

**Breteuil, Jules,** *Le Cuisinier Européen.* Published by Garnier Frères Libraires-Éditeurs c. 1860(93).

**Brown, Helen,** *Helen Brown's West Coast Cook Book.* Copyright 1952, by Helen Evans Brown. Published by Little, Brown and Company, Boston. By permission of Little,

Brown and Company(116).

**Bugialli, Giuliano,** *The Fine Art of Italian Cooking.* Copyright © 1977 by Giuliano Bugialli. Published by Times Books, a Division of Quadrangle/The New York Times Book Co. Inc., New York. Reprinted by permission of Times Books, a Division of Quadrangle/The New York Times Book Co. Inc.(94, 132).

**Byron, May,** *May Byron's Puddings, Pastries and Sweet Dishes.* Published by Hodder and Stoughton Limited, London, 1929. By permission of Hodder and Stoughton Limited(124, 142).

**Campbell, Susan,** *The Times of London,* July 5, 1978. By permission of Susan Campbell(139).

**Camrass, Zoë,** *The Only Cookbook You'll Ever Need.* Copyright © 1977 by Mitchell Beazley Publishers Ltd. Published in the U.S. by Rand McNally & Company. Reprinted by permission of Rand McNally & Company(104).

**Candler, Teresa Gilardi,** *The Northern Italian Cookbook.* Copyright © 1977 by Teresa Gilardi Candler. Published by McGraw-Hill Book Company. Reprinted by permission of McGraw-Hill Book Company(160).

**Carrier, Robert,** *The Robert Carrier Cookery Course.* © Robert Carrier, 1974. Published by W. H. Allen and Co. Ltd. By permission of W. H. Allen and Co. Ltd.(103, 144).

**Collier, Diana and Nancy Goff,** *Frozen Delights.* Copyright © 1976 by Diana Collier and Nancy Goff. Published by Thomas Y. Crowell Company, New York. Reprinted by permission of Harper & Row, Publishers, Inc.(162, 164).

**Corbitt, Helen,** *Helen Corbitt's Cookbook.* Copyright © 1957 by Helen Corbitt. Published by Houghton Mifflin Company, Boston. Reprinted by permission of Houghton Mifflin Company(161).

**Costa, Margaret,** *Margaret Costa's Four Seasons Cookery Book.* Copyright © Margaret Costa. First published in Great Britain by Thomas Nelson & Sons Ltd., 1970, also by Sphere Books Ltd., London, 1976. By permission of Margaret Costa(114, ·134).

**Cox, J. Stevens** (Editor), *Dorset Dishes of the 17th Century.* © J. Stevens Cox, 1967. Published by The Toucan Press, Guernsey. Reprinted by permission of J. Stevens Cox, The Toucan Press(99).

*Le Cuisinier Gascon — 1740.* Reprinted in 1976 by Éditions Daniel Morcrette, B.P.26, 95270, Luzarches, France. Translated by permission of Éditions Daniel Morcrette(96).

**Cutler, Carol,** *The Six-Minute Soufflé and Other Culinary Delights.* Copyright © 1976 by Carol Cutler. Published by Clarkson N. Potter, Inc. Used by permission of Clarkson N. Potter, Inc.(93).

**D'Agostino, Giovanna,** *Mama D's Homestyle Italian Cookbook.* Copyright © 1975, 1972 by Western Publishing Company, Inc. Published by Western Publishing Company, Inc., Wisconsin. Reprinted by permission of Western Publishing Company, Inc.(126).

**Dannenbaum, Julie,** *Julie Dannenbaum's Creative Cooking School.* Copyright © 1971 by Julie Dannenbaum. Published by E. P. Dutton & Co. Inc., New York. By permission of Edward J. Acton Inc. (Author's Agent)(139).

**David, Elizabeth,** *Summer Cooking.* Copyright © Elizabeth David, 1955, 1965. Published by Penguin Books Ltd., London. By permission of Penguin Books Ltd.(134).

**David, Elizabeth,** *Syllabubs and Fruit Fools.* Copyright © Elizabeth David, 1969. By permission of Elizabeth David(98, 100).

**de Croze, Austin,** *Les Plats Régionaux de France.* Published by Éditions Daniel Morcrette, B.P.26, 95270 Luzarches, France. Translated by permission of Éditions Daniel Morcrette(122, 150).

**de Gouy, Jean,** *La Cuisine et la Pâtisserie Bourgeoises à la Portée de Tous.* Published by J. Lebègue & Cie. Libraires-Éditeurs, Paris, 1896(105, 110).

**De Gouy, Louis P.,** *Ice Cream and Ice Cream Desserts.* Copyright © 1938 by L. P. De Gouy. Copyright © 1966 by Mrs. Louis P. De Gouy. Published by Dover Publications, Inc., New York. Reprinted by permission of Dover Publications, Inc.(139).

**de Pomiane, Edouard,** *Le Code de la Bonne Chere.* Published by Éditions Albin Michel, Paris. Translated by permission of Éditions Albin Michel(118).

**Deutsch, Herman B.,** *Brennan's New Orleans Cookbook.* Copyright © 1961 Brennan's Restaurant and Herman B. Deutsch. Published by Robert L. Crager & Co., New Orleans. Used by permission of Robert L. Crager & Co.(164).

**Douglas, Joyce,** *Old Pendle Recipes.* Copyright © Joyce Douglas, 1976. Published by Hendon Publishing Co. Ltd., Nelson, Lancaster. By permission of Hendon Publishing Co., Ltd.(100).

**Dueker, Joyce and Christopher W.,** *The Old Fashioned Homemade Ice Cream Cookbook.* Copyright © 1974 by Joyce and Christopher Dueker. Published by The Bobbs-Merrill Company, Inc. Reprinted by permission of The Bobbs-Merrill Company, Inc.(163).

**Dumont, Emile,** *La Bonne Cuisine.* Published by Degorce-Cadot, Paris, 1873(147, 148).

**Esterling, Elizabeth W.** (Editor), *Le Cookbook.* © The American Hospital of Paris, 1976. Published by The American Hospital of Paris. Translated by permission of The American Hospital of Paris(159).

**Favre, Joseph,** *Dictionnaire Universel de Cuisine Pratique.* Published by Laffitte Reprints, Marseilles, 1978. Translated by permission of Laffitte Reprints(144).

**Field, Michael,** *All Manner of Food.* Copyright © 1965, 1966, 1967, 1968, 1970 by Michael Field. Published by Alfred A. Knopf, New York. Reprinted by permission of Jonathan Rude-Field(131).

*The Fine Arts Cookbook.* Copyright © by the Museum of Fine Arts, Boston. Published by the Museum of Fine Arts. Reprinted by permission of the Musuem of Fine Arts(116 — Mrs. Frank G. Allen).

**Flower, Barbara and Elisabeth Rosenbaum,** *The Roman Cookery Book.* A critical translation of "The Art of Cooking by Apicius." © E. Rosenbaum, 1958. Published by George G. Harrap and Co. Ltd., London. By permission of George G. Harrap and Co. Ltd.(96).

*Foods of the World,* African Cooking; American Cooking: The Melting Pot; American Cooking: New England; Classic French Cooking; The Cooking of India; The Cooking of Vienna's Empire; Latin American Cooking. Copyright © 1970 Time Inc.; Copyright © 1975 Time Inc.; Copyright © 1976 Time Inc.; Copyright © 1978 Time-Life Books Inc.; Copyright © 1975 Time Inc.; Copyright © 1974 Time-Life Books Inc.; Copyright © 1976 Time Inc. Published by Time-Life Books, Alexandria(95, 116, 118, 120, 123, 126, 128, 138, 153).

**Francatelli, Charles Elmé,** *The Modern Cook: A Practical Guide to the Culinary Art in All Its Branches.* Published by Richard Bentley, London, 1862(160).

**Gilbert, Philéas,** *La Cuisine de Tous les Mois.* Published by Abel Goubaud, Éditeur, Paris, 1893(152).

**Gins, Patricia** (Editor), *Great South West Cooking Classic.* Copyright © 1977 The Albuquerque Tribune. Published by The Albuquerque Tribune. Reprinted by permission of The Albuquerque Tribune(136 — Nancy Weaver).

**Graves, Eleanor,** *Great Dinners from Life.* Copyright © 1969 Time Inc. Published by Time-Life Books, Alexandria(91, 135).

*The Great Cook's Guide to Crêpes & Soufflés.* Copyright © by Arthur Cowen Jr. Published by Random House and Bernard Glaser Wolf Ltd. Used by permission of Carol Cutler(126 — Carol Cutler).

*The Great Cook's Guide to Ice Cream & Other Frozen Desserts.* Copyright © by Edward Scheerin. Published by Random House and Bernard Glaser Wolf Ltd. Used by permission of Elizabeth Schneider Colchie(137 — Elizabeth Schneider Colchie).

**Grigson, Jane,** *English Food.* Copyright © Jane Grigson, 1974. First published by Macmillan 1974. Published by Penguin Books Ltd., London, 1977. By permission of David Higham Associates Ltd. (Author's Agent)(91, 140).

**Guérard, Michel,** *Michel Guérard's Cuisine Gourmande.* Originally published in French as "La Cuisine Gourmande." © Éditions Robert Laffont S.A., Paris, 1978. Published by William Morrow and Company, New York. By permission of William Morrow and Company(135, 136).

**Hazelton, Nika Standen,** *The Regional Italian Kitchen.* Copyright © 1978 by Nika Standen Hazelton. Published by M. Evans and Company, Inc., New York. Translated by

permission of M. Evans and Company, Inc.(109).

**Hellermann, Dorothee V.,** *Das Kochbuch aus Hamburg.* © Copyright 1975 by Verlagsteam Wolfgang Hö Published by Wolfgang Hölker. Translated by permissic of Wolfgang Hölker(113).

**Herbert, Col. A. F. Kenny (Wyvern),** *Fifty Dinners.* Published by Edward Arnold, London, 1895(100).

**Herbert, Col. A. F. Kenny (Wyvern),** *Sweet Dishes.* Published by Higginbotham & Co., Madras, 1900(115)

**Hewitt, Jean.** *The New York Times Weekend Cookbook.* Copyright © 1975 by Jean Hewitt. Published by Times Books, a Division of Quadrangle/The New York Times Book Co. By permission of Times Books, a Division of Quadrangle/The New York Times Book Co., Inc., and Jean Hewitt(98).

**Editors of House & Garden,** *House & Garden's New Cook Book.* Copyright © 1967 by House & Garden's N Cook Book. Published by Simon & Schuster, New York. permission of Condé Nast Publications Inc.(112, 142).

**Hunt, Peter,** *Peter Hunt's Cape Cod Cookbook.* Copyright © 1954 by Hawthorn Books, Inc. Copyright © 196 the Stephen Greene Press. Published by Gramercy Publishing Company, New York. Reprinted by permission o Stephen Greene Press(163).

**Isnard, Léon,** *La Cuisine Française et Africaine.* Copyright 1949 by Éditions Albin Michel. Published by Éditio Albin Michel, Paris. Translated by permission of Éditions Albin Michel(141).

**Jack, Florence B.,** *Cookery for Every Household.* Published by Thomas Nelson and Sons, Ltd., London, 1934. permission of Thomas Nelson and Sons, Ltd.(94, 159).

**Jarrin, G. A.,** *The Italian Confectioner.* Published by E. S Ebers and Co., London, 1841(117).

**Jeanes, William,** *Gunter's Modern Confectioner.* Published by Dean & Son, Publishers and Factors, London, 1861(141).

**Jewry, Mary** (Editor), *Warne's Model Cookery and Housekeeping Book.* © Copyright F. Warne (Publishers) Published by Frederick Warne & Co. Ltd., London. By p mission of Frederick Warne & Co. Ltd.(102, 104, 156).

**Johns, Yohanni,** *Dishes from Indonesia.* Copyright © 1971 by Yohanni Johns. Published by Chilton Book Cor pany, Radnor, Pennsylvania. Reprinted by permission o Chilton Book Company(142).

**Junior League of Baton Rouge, The,** *River Road Recipes.* Copyright © 1959 by The Junior League of Bat Rouge, Inc. Published by The Junior League of Baton Rouge. Reprinted by permission of The Junior League o Baton Rouge(122).

**Junior League of New Orleans, The,** *The Plantation Cookbook.* Copyright © 1972 by The Junior League of New Orleans, Inc. Published by Doubleday & Compan Inc., New York. Reprinted by permission of Doubleday Company, Inc.(108, 160, 162).

**Junior League of Pine Bluff, The,** *Southern Accent.* Copyright © 1976 by The Junior League of Pine Bluff, I Published by The Junior League of Pine Bluff, Inc. By pe mission of The Junior League of Pine Bluff, Arkansas, Inc.(163).

**Kiehnle, Hermine and Maria Hädecke,** *Das Neue Kiehnle Kochbuch.* © Walter Hädecke Verlag. (Vorm. Sü deutsches Verlagshaus). Published by Walter Hädecke Verlag. Translated by permission of Walter Hädecke Verlag(110).

**King, Susan,** *Susan King's Cook Book.* © Copyright Woman's Realm 1967. Published by Paul Hamlyn Limite London. By permission of Woman's Realm(117).

**King, Susan,** *Woman's Realm* (magazine). Translated by permission of Woman's Realm, London(125).

**Lang, George,** *The Cuisine of Hungary.* Copyright © 1971 by George Lang. Published by Atheneum Publishe New York. By permission of Atheneum Publishers(157).

**Lecourt, H.,** *La Cuisine Chinoise.* Copyright Éditions Rob ert Laffont S.A. 1968. Published by Éditions Robert Laffc Paris. Translated by permission of Éditions Robert Laffont(131).

**Leone, Gene,** *Leone's Italian Cookbook.* Copyright © 1967 by Gene Leone. Published by Harper & Row, Pub ers, Inc., New York. Reprinted by permission of Harper

...w, Publishers, Inc.(155).

...**n, Florence,** *Florence Lin's Chinese Vegetarian Cook-ok.* Copyright © 1976 Florence S. Lin. Published by ...awthorn Books, Inc., New York. By permission of Haw-...orn Books, Inc.(104, 132).

...**owinsky, Ruth,** *More Lovely Food.* Published by the ...onesuch Press, London, 1935(140, 149).

...**cas, Dione, and Marion Gorman,** *The Dione Lu-*...s *Book of French Cooking.* Copyright 1947 by Dione Lu-...as. Copyright © 1973 by Mark Lucas and Marion F. Gor-...an. Published by Little, Brown and Company, Boston. By ...ermission of Little, Brown and Company(111, 129).

...**ine, Pierre de,** *Le Nouveau Cuisinier,* 1656(91, 130).

...**acnicol, Fred,** *Hungarian Cookery.* Copyright © Fred ...acnicol, 1978. Published by Penguin Books Ltd., London. ... permission of Penguin Books Ltd.(109).

...**anning, Elise W.** (Editor), *Homemade Ice Cream and* ...ake. Copyright © 1972 by Farm Journal, Inc. Published by ...oubleday & Company, Inc. Reprinted by permission of ...e Farm Journal, Inc.(140, 164).

...**arshall, Mrs. A. B.,** *Fancy Ices.* Published by Simpkin, ...arshall, Hamilton, Kent and Co. Ltd. c. 1890(145).

...**cNeill, F. Marian,** *The Scots Kitchen.* Published by ...ackie and Son Limited, London. By permission of Blackie ...nd Son Limited(125, 141).

...**) Médecins de France.** *Le Trésor de la Cuisine du* ...assin Méditerranéen(115).

...**enon,** *Les Soupers de la Cour,* 1746(94, 132).

...**iller, Amy Bess Williams and Persis Wellington** ...**uller** (Editors), *The Best of Shaker Cooking.* Copyright © ...970 by Shaker Community, Inc. Published by the Macmil-...n Publishing Company, Inc. Reprinted by permission of ...e Macmillan Publishing Company, Inc.(95, 111, ...49].

...**olchanova, O. P., et al.,** *Kniga O Vkusnoĭ I Zdorovoĭ* ...shche. Published by Pishchepromizdat Publishing House, ...loscow, 1952(127).

...**olokhovets, Elena,** *Podarok Molodým Khozyaĭkam.* ...ublished in St. Petersburg, 1892(121, 151).

...**ontagné, Prosper,** *The New Larousse Gastronomique.* ...nglish translation © 1977 by The Hamlyn Publishing ...roup Limited. Published by Crown Publishers, Inc. By per-...ssion of Crown Publishers, Inc.(101, 122, 132).

...**ontagné, Prosper and A. Gottschalk,** *Mon* ...enu —Guide d'Hygiène Alimentaire. Published by Société ...'Applications Scientifiques, Paris(106, 108).

...**orphy, Countess,** *Sweets and Puddings.* Published by ...erbert Joseph Limited, London, 1936. By permission of ...erbert Joseph(158).

...**ignon, Edouard,** *Les Plaisirs de la Table.* Published by ...e Éditions Daniel Morcrette, c. 1920. Reprinted by ...P.26, 95270 Luzarches, France, 1979. Translated by per-...iission of Éditions Daniel Morcrette(90, 101, 161).

...**orberg, Inga,** *Good Food from Sweden.* Published by ...hatto & Windus, London, 1935. By permission of Curtis ...rown Ltd.(98, 106).

...**Ohio Housewives,** *Ohio Housewives Companion,* ...876(146).

...**)liver, Raymond,** *La Cuisine — Sa Technique, Ses Se-*...rets. Published by Éditions Bordas, Paris. Translated by ...ermission of Leon Amiel Publishers, New York(96).

...**)lney, Judith,** *Summer Food.* Copyright © 1978 by Ju-...ith Olney. Published by Atheneum Publishers, New York. ...y permission of Atheneum Publishers(134, 148).

...**)lney, Richard,** *The French Menu Cookbook.* Copyright ...© 1970 by Richard Olney. Published by Simon & Schuster, ...New York. By permission of John Schaffner, Literary ...Agent(112).

...**)lney, Richard,** *Simple French Food.* Copyright © 1974 ...y Richard Olney. Published by Atheneum Publishers, New ...ork. By permission of Atheneum Publishers, New ...ork(119, 136).

...**)rga, Irfan,** *Cooking the Middle East Way.* © Paul Ham-...yn Limited, 1962. Published by The Hamlyn Publishing ...roup Limited, London. By permission of The Hamlyn Pub-...shing Group Limited(120, 132).

...**he Original Picayune Creole Cook Book.** Copy-...ght © 1901, 1906, 1916, 1922, 1928 and 1936 by the ...imes-Picayune Publishing Company, New Orleans. Pub-lished by the Times-Picayune Publishing Company. Re-printed by permission of the Times-Picayune Publishing Company(114, 119).

**Orosa del Rosario, Helen** (Editor), *Maria Y. Orosa: Her Life and Work.* Copyright 1970 by Helen Orosa del Rosario. Published by Helen Orosa del Rosario, Philippines 1970. By permission of Helen Orosa del Rosario(92).

**Pappas, Lou Seibert,** *Egg Cookery.* Copyright © 1976 Lou Seibert Pappas. Published by 101 Productions, California. By permission of 101 Productions(138).

**Pasternak, Joseph,** *Cooking with Love and Paprika.* Copyright © 1966 by Joseph Pasternak. Published by Bernard Geis Associates, Inc. Reprinted by permission of Bernard Geis Associates, Inc.(107).

**Peck, Paula,** *Paula Peck's Art of Good Cooking.* Copyright © 1961, 1966 by Paula Peck. Published by Simon & Schuster, a Division of Gulf & Western Corporation, New York. By permission of Simon & Schuster, a Division of Gulf & Western Corporation, New York(98).

**Petit, A.,** *La Gastronomie en Russie.* Published by Emile Mellier, Libraire-Éditeur, Paris, 1860(156).

**Les Petits Plats et Les Grands.** © 1977, by Éditions Denoël, Paris. Published by Éditions Denoël Sarl, Paris. Translated by permission of Éditions Denoël Sarl(112, 129).

**Petrov, Dr. L., Dr. N. Djelepov, Dr. E. Iordanov and S. Uzunova,** *Bulgarska Nazionalna Kuchniya.* Copyright © by the four authors. Published by Zemizdat, Sofia, 1978. Translated by permission of Jusautor (Bulgarian Copyright Agency)(116).

**Philpot, Rosl,** *Viennese Cookery.* © 1965 by Rosl Philpot. Published by Hodder and Stoughton Limited, London. By permission of Hodder and Stoughton Limited(125).

**Les Princes de la Gastronomie.** © 1.2.1975 — Les Éditions Mondiales. Published by Modes de Paris. Translated by permission of Les Éditions Mondiales(128, 146).

**Ray, Elizabeth** (Editor), *The Best of Eliza Acton.* Copyright © Longmans, Green & Co. Ltd., 1968. Introduction Copyright © Elizabeth David 1968. Published by Penguin Books Ltd., London. By permission of Penguin Books Ltd.(155).

**Reboul, J. B.,** *La Cuisinière Provençale.* Published by Tacussel, Marseilles. Translated by permission of Tacussel, Éditeur(99).

**Rombauer, Irma S. and Marion Rombauer Becker,** *Joy of Cooking.* Copyright © 1931, 1936, 1941, 1942, 1943, 1946, 1951, 1952, 1953, 1962, 1963, 1964, 1975 by The Bobbs-Merrill Company, Inc., New York. Reprinted by permission of The Bobbs-Merrill Company(105, 163).

**Rubinstein, Helge and Sheila Bush,** *Ices Galore.* Copyright © 1977 by Helge Rubinstein & Sheila Bush. Published by André Deutsch Limited, London. By permission of A. P. Watt Ltd., Literary Agents, London(143).

**Rubinstein, Helge and Sheila Bush,** *A Penguin Freezer Cookbook.* © Helge Rubinstein and Sheila Bush, 1973. Published by Penguin Books, Ltd., London. By permission of Penguin Books, Ltd.(147, 157).

**Rundell, Mrs.,** *Modern Domestic Cookery.* Published by Milner and Company, Limited, London(108).

**Saint-Ange, Madame,** *La Cuisine de Madame Saint-Ange.* © Éditions Chaix. Published by Éditions Chaix, Grenoble. Translated by permission of Éditions Chaix(90).

**Salta, Romeo,** *The Pleasures of Italian Cooking.* Copyright © 1962 by Romeo Salta. Published by the Macmillan Publishing Company, Inc. Reprinted by permission of the Macmillan Publishing Company(110).

**Savarin, Mme. Jeanne** (Editor), *La Cuisine des Familles,* (magazine). No. 107, July 7, 1907(159).

**Schuler, Elizabeth,** *Mein Kochbuch.* © Copyright 1948 by Schuler-Verlag, Stuttgart-N, Lenzholde 28. Published by Schuler Verlagsgesellschaft, Stuttgart. Translated by permission of Schuler-Verlag(161).

**Seranne, Ann,** *Delectable Desserts.* Copyright © 1952 by Ann Seranne. Published by Little, Brown and Company, Boston. Reprinted by permission of The Harold Matson Company, Inc.(117).

**The Settlement Cook Book.** Copyright © 1965, 1976 by the Settlement Book Book Co. Published by Simon & Schuster, New York. Reprinted by permission of Simon &

Schuster, a Division of Gulf & Western Corporation(162).

**Skipwith, Sofka,** *Eat Russian.* © Sofka Skipwith 1973. Published by David & Charles (Holdings) Ltd., Newton Abbot. By permission of David & Charles (Holdings) Ltd.(151).

**Smith, Michael,** *Fine English Cookery.* © Michael Smith 1973. Published by Faber and Faber, London. By permission of David Higham Associates Limited, London (Author's Agent)(103).

**Spagnol, Elena,** *I Gelati Fatti in Casa con o senza Macchina.* © 1975 Rizzoli Editore, Milano. Published by Rizzoli Editore, Milano. Translated by permission of Rizzoli Editore(145).

**Stamm, Sara B. B. and the Lady Editors of** *Yankee Magazine, Favorite New England Recipes.* Copyright © 1972 Sara B. B. Stamm and Yankee, Inc. Published by Yankee, Inc., Dublin, New Hampshire. Reprinted by permission of Yankee, Inc.(115).

**Taglienti, Maria Luisa,** *The Italian Cookbook.* Copyright © 1955 by Maria Luisa Taglienti. Published by Random House, New York. Reprinted by permission of Random House(97).

**Tibbott, S. Minwel,** *Welsh Fare.* © National Museum of Wales (Welsh Folk Museum). Published by the National Museum of Wales (Welsh Folk Museum) 1976. By permission of the National Museum of Wales (Welsh Folk Museum)(124).

**Toklas, Alice B.,** *The Alice B. Toklas Cook Book.* Copyright 1954 by Alice B. Toklas. Published by Harper & Row, Publishers, Inc., New York. By permission of Harper & Row, Publishers, Inc.(97, 102, 134, 140).

**Troisgros, Jean and Pierre,** *The Nouvelle Cuisine of Jean & Pierre Troisgros.* Copyright © 1978 in the English translation by William Morrow and Company, Inc. Originally published under the title *Cuisiniers à Roanne.* Copyright © 1977 by Éditions Robert Laffont, S.A. Used by permission of William Morrow and Company, Inc.(123).

**Tschirky, Oscar,** *The Cook Book by "Oscar" of the Waldorf.* Published by The Werner Company, New York(99).

**Turgeon, Charlotte,** *Tante Marie's French Kitchen.* Copyright 1950 by Cartes Taride, Éditeurs Libraires, Paris. Published by S.A.R.L. Cartes Taride, Paris. By permission of S.A.R.L. Cartes Taride & Kaye and Ward Ltd.(93, 118).

**Uvezian, Sonia,** *The Book of Yogurt.* Copyright © 1978 by Sonia Uvezian. Published by 101 Productions. Reprinted by permission of 101 Productions(137, 138).

**Vence, Céline and Robert Courtine,** *The Grand Masters of French Cuisine.* Copyright © 1978 by G. P. Putnam's Sons. Published by G. P. Putnam's Sons, New York. Reprinted by permission of G. P. Putnam's Sons(149).

**Viard and Fouret,** *Le Cuisinier Royal,* 1828(92, 105, 107).

**Waldo, Myra,** *The Complete Round-the-World Cookbook.* Copyright 1954 by Myra Waldo. Published by Doubleday & Company, Inc., New York. By permission of Doubleday & Company, Inc.(119).

**Wason, Betty,** *The Art of German Cooking.* © Elizabeth Wason Hall 1967. First published in Great Britain by Allen & Unwin 1971. By permission of Doubleday & Company, Inc., New York(121).

**Weber, J. M. Erich,** *Theory and Practice of the Confectioner.* Published by Internationaler Fachverlag, Dresden c. 1927(148).

**Willan, Anne,** *Great Cooks and their Recipes from Taillevent to Escoffier.* Copyright © 1977 by McGraw-Hill Book Company (U.K.) Limited, Maidenhead. First published in Great Britain in 1977 by Elm Tree Books/Hamish Hamilton Ltd., London. By permission of McGraw-Hill Book Company, New York(106).

**Willinsky, Grete,** *Kochbuch der Büchergilde.* © Büchergilde Gutenberg, Frankfurt am Main 1958. Published by Büchergilde Gutenberg, Frankfurt. Translated by permission of Büchergilde Gutenberg(97).

**Witwicka, H. and S. Soskine,** *La Cuisine Russe Classique.* © Éditions Albin Michel, 1968 et 1978. Published by Éditions Albin Michel, Paris. Translated by permission of Éditions Albin Michel(133, 156).

**Wren, Jenny,** *Modern Domestic Cookery.* Published by Alexander Gardner, Paisley 1880(114).

## Acknowledgments

The indexes for this book were prepared by Louise W. Hedberg. The editors are particularly indebted to Pat Alburey, Hertfordshire, England; Karen Bates-Logan, San Francisco, California; and A. R. Huelin, Westminster College, London.

The editors also wish to thank: Dr. Wendell S. Arbuckle, Department of Dairy Science, University of Maryland, College Park; Skeffington Ardron, London; Dr. G. Norris Bollenback, The Sugar Association, Inc., Washington, D.C.; Robert Bruce, London; Sarah Bunney, London; The Chelmer Institute of Higher Education, Essex, England; R. C. Coates, London; Thomas C. Cone, Mildred Francis, Rice Council, Houston, Texas; Jennifer Davidson, London; Pamela Davidson, London; Dr. Arthur B. Davis, American Baking Institute, Manhattan, Kansas; Fiona Duncan, London; Mary Gotschall, Falls Church, Virginia; Diana Grant, London; Fayal Greene, London; Noreen Griffee, California Raisin Advisory Board, Fresno, California; Gretchen Heid, Thomas J. Lipton, Inc., Englewood Cliffs, New Jersey; Maggie Heinz, London; Harold Horn, CPC International, Englewood Cliffs, New Jersey; Marion Hunter, Surrey, England; Brenda Jayes, London; Lorraine Kealiher, McCormick Co., Baltimore, Maryland; Shirley King, London; Debra Kraft, Kellogg Company, Battle Creek, Michigan; John Leslie, London; Dr. Pericles Markakis, Department of Food Science and Human Nutrition, Michigan State University, East Lansing; William W. Menz, American Dairy Association, Rosemont, Illinois; Robert R. Mickus, Rice Grower's Association of California, Sacramento, California; Elizabeth Moreau, Langley Park, England; Maria Mosby, London; Dilys Naylor, Surrey, England; John P. Orcino, Avignone Frères, Washington, D.C.; Jo Oxley, Surrey, England; Lynne M. Paino, Nestlé Enterprises, White Plains, New York; Christopolous Poulc, J. F. Braun & Sons, Inc., Lake Success, New York; Joanne Roberts, London; Noreen Sanders, General Foods, White Plains, New York; Henri-Philippe Sandifer, Worldwide Wines, Meriden, Connecticut; Robert Shoffner, *The Washingtonian* magazine, Washington, D.C.; David Simpson, London; Anne Stephenson, London; Stephanie Thompson, Surrey, England; J. M. Turnell & Co., London; Eileen Turner, Sussex, England; Dr. John H. Woychik, Da Lab, Eastern Regional Research Center, U.S. Department of Agriculture, Philadelphia, Pennsylvania; Marsha Zelik, *Food & Wine* magazine, New York City.

## Picture Credits

*The sources for the pictures in this book are listed below. Credits for the photographers and illustrators are listed by page number with successive pages indicated by hyphens; where necessary, the locations of pictures within pages also are indicated—separated from page numbers by dashes.*

Photographs by Tom Belshaw: cover, 4, 8, 10—top, 11—bottom, 12—bottom right, 13—top right and bottom, 14-15—bottom, 16—bottom, 21—bottom, 22-23, 26-27—bottom, 28-29, 33—top, 34, 35—bottom 40-41, 44-45—bottom, 46—bottom, 52, 54, 55—bottom, 58-59, 62-65, 74, 80-83, 85—center and bottom right, 88.

Photographs by Alan Duns: 9, 10—bottom, 18, 20, 21—top, 24-25, 38-39, 42, 44-45—top, 46—top, 55—top, 68-73, 75-77, 84, 85—top and bottom left.

Other photographs (alphabetically): Gina Harris, 16-17—top, 26-27—top, 30, 32, 33—bottom, 35—top. Louis Klein, 2. David Levin, 12—bottom left and center, 13—top left and center, 36-37. Aldo Tutino, 11—top, 15—top, 17—bottom, 47-51, 56-57, 60-61, 66, 78, 86-87.

Illustrations: Mary Evans Picture Library and private sources, 6-7, 90-167.

*Library of Congress Cataloguing in Publication Data*
Main entry under title:
Classic desserts.
    (The Good cook, techniques and recipes)
    Includes index.
    1.Desserts.    I.Time-Life Books.    II.Series:
Good cook, techniques and recipes.
TX773.C57        641.8'6        79-20805
ISBN 0-8094-2872-5
ISBN 0-8094-2871-7 lib. bdg.
ISBN 0-8094-2870-9 retail ed.